# DO IT RIGHT
# THE FIRST TIME

# DO IT RIGHT THE FIRST TIME

## A SHORT GUIDE TO LEARNING FROM YOUR MOST MEMORABLE ERRORS, MISTAKES, AND BLUNDERS

GERARD I. NIERENBERG

John Wiley & Sons, Inc.

New York • Chichester • Brisbane • Toronto • Singapore

Copyright © 1996 by Gerard I. Nierenberg
Published by John Wiley & Sons, Inc.

*Library of Congress Cataloging-in-Publication Data:*

Nierenberg, Gerard I.
    Do it right the first time : A short guide to learning from your most
    memorable errors, mistakes, and blunders / Gerard I. Nierenberg.
        p.    cm.
    Includes bibliographical references and index.
    ISBN 0-471-14889-X (paper : alk. paper)
    1. Thought and thinking.   2. Decision-making.   3. Errors-
-Psychological aspects.   I. Title.
BF441.N53     1996
153.4'2—dc20                                                96-2172

Printed in the United States of America

10 9 8 7 6 5 4 3 2 1

*To my sons, Roy, Roger, and George*

# ACKNOWLEDGMENTS

The subject of errors was first brought to my attention many years ago by the late William Exton Jr., who had already gathered some research on this topic with reference to insurance companies. At the time, I suggested to Exton that he had hit upon an extremely important concept that could be expanded. Although he died in a tragic auto accident before we had the opportunity to work together, I know that he would have wanted me to continue developing and expanding work on the subject despite his death.

I am also grateful to Mike Hamilton at John Wiley & Sons, Inc., who recognized the necessity and timeliness of a book on error awareness. And, I am indebted to my astute and sensitive editor, Susan K. Golant, who helped me organize and clarify my thoughts in record time.

# CONTENTS

PART V
# STRATEGIES TO REDUCE YOUR ERRORS

# PART I

# THE
# ERRORS
# OF OUR
# WAYS

# 1

## NO SHAME, NO BLAME

THE MAN WHO ADMITS HIS MISTAKES IS BETTER
THAN A SAGE; HE HAS BOTH WISDOM AND COURAGE.
—ANONYMOUS

Have you ever made a mistake? Maybe just a simple error? Of course you have. I know I certainly have. The critical question in building error awareness is not whether you have made errors, but rather, what have you learned from them? And how can you keep learning from them?

Far too many of us bury our mistakes in a shroud of blame and shame. Instead of accepting responsibility for our gaffes and trying to learn as much as we can from them, we feel ashamed of them and look for ways to blame others or circumstances, thereby avoiding accountability for our own decisions and actions.

On May 26, 1991, a Boeing 767 crashed shortly after takeoff from Bangkok, Thailand, killing 223 passenger and crew members. Within four days, Pratt & Whitney, the manufacturer of the plane's engines, had issued a statement claiming that reports attributing the crash to engine failure were "totally unfounded." And this while the investigation was still going on!

Blame—and its close cousin shame (self-blame)—never lead to greater awareness. The investigation of a mistake to gain error awareness requires open eyes and an open mind. Blame and shame, however, shut eyes and close minds, preventing people from learning as much as they can from their errors (as well as the errors of those around them). In issuing such a statement, Pratt & Whitney demonstrated their emphasis on damage control at the expense of quality control. They wanted to redirect the investigation of the accident. Rather than admit even the possibility of error, they released a categorical denial—introducing a further obstacle to error awareness.

Sadly, blame and shame have become the predominant means of dealing with errors in our culture. Pratt & Whitney is not alone in its reluctance to accept responsibility for its errors (if indeed it made any). The managers of most Western corporations all too often attempt to shift blame for their companies' mistakes and inadequacies to suppliers, the labor force, the educational system, or the government. And individuals follow this corporate lead. Within an organization, managers blame other departments, the bureaucracy, or the unions for their own errors. In this culture, making excuses for errors too often takes precedence over making sense of them.

Some manufacturers or service providers go so far as to blame their own failings on consumers or customers. Developers of computer software, for example, know how costly and difficult it can be to correct errors in their programs. The intricacies and interdependency of software mean that in trying to change an error-filled program, chances are good that they will end up introducing different errors. Because trying to correct or replace software is so costly, computer salespeople often end up blaming the victim if a particular program has rampant errors: They tell customers that they have "outgrown their old system" and need to buy a new one!

A 1989 study of 114 interns and residents further illustrates the bankruptcy of shame and blame. Researchers found that almost half of the physicians-in-training (46%) neither informed nor discussed their most serious errors with their supervising doctors. As a result, according to one official of the American Medical Association, many of these doctors probably blamed themselves for problems that might have occurred anyway. Those doctors who did accept responsibility for their mistakes, the study found, were much more likely to make constructive changes in the way they practiced medicine. No blame, no shame. My goal in writing this book is to help restore the practice of learning from our mistakes.

## HOW THIS BOOK CAN HELP

Many people have inquired how a book on error awareness can help them. "After all," these healthy skeptics ask, "what can you tell me about my errors that I don't already know?" The simplest, most honest answer is, "I can't tell you about your specific errors, but by applying the methods in *Do It Right the First Time*, you *will* gain new insight into your own errors and the patterns you follow in making them."

Throughout the industrial age, the computer age, and the age of information, we have come up with a great many proven techniques that can locate, diagnose, and fix *machine* errors. In focusing our efforts in this direction, however, we have overlooked a critical fact: Most errors do not arise from machine failure, but rather from *human* shortcomings. This book will redirect your focus to correct and prevent human errors.

For the young, errors provide experience and the opportunity to learn from their mistakes—the most important tools they have to help them mature. Discovering she has erred, a young person will remark, "That's the first time I've ever goofed like that." As we grow older, too many of us fall out of the habit of pinpointing just where we "goofed." The methods described in *Do It Right the First Time* will help you regain the ability to learn from your errors. By using these methods to acknowledge and analyze your mistakes, you will recapture their essential value: They are a tool for learning about yourself, your abilities, and the world around you.

Through the error-awareness system, you will begin to look at your errors in an entirely new way:

1.  You will first recognize and own up to the existence of your errors, free of blame or shame. You will see your actual and potential errors more clearly, and more easily identify the *kinds* of errors you make.

2.  You will understand how to evaluate the cost of your errors. You will see more clearly their consequences and *effects*.

3.  You will be encouraged and guided to analyze your errors in detail and improve your ability to think about their *causes*.

4.  You will develop *strategies* to reduce future errors.

You will gain insight into how to correct your errors as quickly and responsibly as possible. In fact, I have organized this book to correspond to these stages.

Your enhanced understanding of the error-making process will also allow you to become a better customer, client, and/or patient by anticipating and thereby protecting yourself from others' errors that might affect you. Most people today fail to deal with errors in this way—ignoring any value they might otherwise draw from them.

## PUTTING ERRORS TO WORK

The world's most creative thinkers—fueled by an insatiable curiosity about everything, including their errors—never lose the ability to learn from their own mistakes. The road to creativity is strewn with errors that were put to good use before being discarded. Alexander Fleming, a zealous advocate of maintaining sterile conditions in the laboratory, once made the mistake of leaving a culture dish coated with staphylococcus germs unsterilized and out in the open for several weeks. When he returned, he discovered that due to his error, penicillin mold had begun to grow on the dish. But rather than throw the mistake away, Fleming examined it and discovered that microbes did not grow in the neighborhood of the mold. Fleming had discovered a drug that would save millions of lives over the next several decades.

In 1853, Sir William Henry Perkin attempted to synthesize quinine from coal tar chemicals, including aniline. Treating aniline with potassium dichromate, Perkin failed to achieve his express goal. He was about to discard the mess when his eye caught the purplish glint of the chemicals. Instead of burying it as "just an error," Perkin took advantage of his mistake. When he added alcohol to the mixture, the "mess" turned a beautiful purple. This substance, which had excellent dyeing properties, became known as "aniline purple," and later as "mauve." As so many creative thinkers have done, Perkin thus transformed his error into a fortune.

Like Fleming and Perkin, most creative thinkers do not ignore, hide, or feel ashamed of their errors. To these geniuses, mistakes represent treasured opportunities to discover something unexpected about themselves or their work. They take the time to analyze their errors—applying to their own mistakes the tools of common observations, self-inquiry, reflection, the acquisition of additional knowledge, scientific verification, and philosophizing. Through this process, creative thinkers invariably gain a heightened understanding of themselves, the errors they have made, and the reasons that contributed to their errors. And, they never merely disregard their errors and move on to something else.

As poet and satirist Samuel Butler wrote over 300 years ago:

> All the inventions that the world contains,
> Were not by reason first found out, nor brains;
> But pass for theirs that had the luck to light
> Upon them by mistake or oversight.

When you reach the end of this book, through checklists, guidelines, and insight that you develop, you will have gained a powerful new understanding of your own errors and what you must guard against to prevent or minimize them. In addition, you will have a new insight into errors in general, especially those made by others that might have a dangerous or damaging impact on you. You will learn how to limit and control the effects of the errors you make and even make productive, constructive use of them, turning them to your own benefit. And you will become better able to protect yourself from the often dangerous errors of others.

The specific errors used as illustrations in this book are derived primarily from a business context. Given my strong personal background as an attorney and author in this field, this emphasis is inevitable. I sincerely believe, however, that you can apply the insights and methods I suggest to all errors. Whether your errors occur in your personal life, in the context of business or professional affairs, or in a supervisory or management role, this book will teach you how to learn from them—and how to avoid repeating many of them.

## WHY INCREASE YOUR ERROR AWARENESS?

You may still wonder whether it's worth the effort to identify and analyze your errors. After all, what's done is done, and no amount of analysis will transform an error into the right action. True. Yet thinking about the error, making an effort to understand and limit the damage it causes, and analyzing why you made the error in the first place can radically alter its effect. Your increased awareness may provide the immediate benefit of insight into the most appropriate action to correct or mitigate your error.

But error awareness has far-reaching benefits as well. First of all, this heightened sensitivity to the errors you make will allow you to catch *actual* errors soon after they have occurred, and certainly sooner than if you had had no training in error awareness whatsoever. Second, it will allow you to catch certain *potential* errors even *before* they occur—and prevent them from happening.

*You will therefore find it well worth your while to put in the time and effort to identify and analyze the errors you (and others) make!*

Tony Gwynn of the San Diego Padres, perhaps the most error-aware hitter in baseball, constantly analyzes his at bats to detect flaws in his "mechanics": his preparation, approach, stance, and swing. Gwynn's wife videotapes his every at bat—over 600 a year—and Gwynn studies them carefully after each game. In a field in which the best performers *fail* two out of three times, Gwynn carefully compares his successes and his failures, painstakingly differentiating between the ingredients of a good at bat and a bad one. If he discovers an error in his approach, stance, or swing, he moves quickly to correct it. Gwynn recognizes that what's done is done, but that doesn't mean he can't learn from it. Although he cannot turn back the clock and transform the bad at bat into a good one, he can make changes that will minimize his chances of error and heighten his opportunities for success in subsequent at bats.

Gwynn's error-awareness methods have paid off. He seldom suffers through a prolonged hitting slump, has won four National League batting titles, and has established a level of consistently high performance that other players envy.

Like Gwynn's methodical approach, the application of the error-awareness system will help you acquire the insight and ability to foresee the likelihood of future errors. And this new foresight, heightened awareness of errors, and understanding of how to prevent them will give you much greater confidence in your day-to-day decisions and actions. You will no longer fear making errors, because you will know that the procedure you follow or the action you choose is much *less* likely to be the wrong one.

Improved performance and confidence are not the only benefits you will derive from the pursuit and application of error awareness. In addition, you will:

- Eliminate the need to scrap error-filled work and/or redo the same work.

- Eventually reduce the number of inspections and tests required to uncover errors in work that has already been completed.

- Reduce the costs and wasted time and energy associated with the prevalence of errors.

- Improve your own morale as well as the morale of those who work with or under you.

- Develop a more positive and resilient outlook on life in general.

- Demonstrate mastery of tasks that currently pose a challenge, thereby freeing you up to accept greater responsibilities and new challenges—and the rewards that come from accepting them.

## THE ERRORS YOU CAN REDUCE OR ELIMINATE THROUGH ERROR AWARENESS

The techniques and methods that lead to error awareness can be usefully applied to mistakes of any kind. Although the list that follows does not pretend to be comprehensive, it covers some of the most common errors made today. Error awareness can help eliminate:

- *Misreadings.* Errors in reading or comprehending written information or instructions.

- *Mishearings.* Errors in listening or understanding verbal information or instructions.

- *Mistranscription.* Errors in transferring written or verbal material from one format to another.

- *Errors with Numbers.* Errors in reading, listening, writing, keyboarding, or transcribing numbers, or in making calculations using those numbers.

- *Routine Errors.* Errors in the performance of simple, familiar, and repetitive tasks such as typing, dialing a telephone, and filing.

- *Memory Lapses.* Errors that involve forgetting to communicate some information or skipping one or more essential stages involved in a complex (or group) task.

- *Juggling Errors.* Errors from trying to complete two or more tasks at the same time, activities that interfere with or distract from one another.

- *Differentiation Errors.* Errors in trying to distinguish between symbols, characters, or words—often due to illegibility, too much similarity between the symbols, or both.

- *Detection Errors.* Failure to catch errors made earlier (by oneself or others) or failure to notice that something has gone wrong.

- *Judgment Errors.* Mistakes in forming an intention or choosing an action, often due to overlooking relevant information or pertinent conditions, giving too much weight to irrelevant or relatively unimportant data, or failing to distinguish between fact and opinion.

This list of common errors is not all-inclusive because humans are extremely inventive creatures and can apply this quality to the making of errors as well as more useful pursuits. The rapidly expanding use of computers (see Chapter 6 ) provides just one illustration. Yet the techniques and methods I recommend will work on every kind of error, even those not yet devised. By making error awareness part of your life, you will be better able to deal not only with the errors you already make, but also with those that you will invent in the future.

## SLIP, ERROR, MISTAKE, OR BLUNDER?

In my study of the subject, I have distinguished four different categories of error:

1. *Slips*. Accidents that result from a failure to carry out your otherwise correct intentions. Although slips, such as a slip of the tongue or pen, generally involve only minor deeds and actions (such as calling your younger child by your older child's name), they can have major consequences. They are often controlled by the subconscious, which chooses the wrong automatic action in response to a particular situation. Slips occur only after you have developed the specific skill involved (such as writing or speaking), because when you are first learning the skill, you proceed slowly, cautiously, and *attentively*.

2. *Errors*. Any results that involve a deviation from a standard in a situation in which you have a certain degree of control. If you fail to achieve something you intended, you have made an error. Whenever you dial a wrong number or suffer a typo, you are making an error.

3. *Mistakes*. Errors in your intentions. You choose the wrong action, and then do precisely what you had intended to do. Your action, based on incorrect or poor planning, decisions, or judgments, brings the wrong results. A plane crash in December 1995 near Cali, Colombia, that took the lives of more than 150 people resulted from the pilot's mistake. Failing to realize that he had passed a checkpoint, he miscalculated his position and set his computer to slam the plane right into the side of a mountain.

4. *Blunders*. Blatant, ongoing, snowballing cases of mistakes and bad judgment. Any error is a blunder when it results in the loss of huge sums of money or the great loss of human life including the blunderer's. A blunder can involve a natural catastrophe worsened through human actions (or failure to act). Or it may result in its entirety from acts of human beings, rather than from a force of nature or act of God. In short, a blunder is a disaster that might have been avoided, were it not for human error.

As I will explain in the following section, mistakes and blunders are hazardous. Nevertheless, in this book we will focus primarily on slips and errors because you can achieve the most satisfactory results in these areas. By discovering what causes your errors and learning how to minimize them, you will acquire the tools to help you avoid costly mistakes and blunders.

## THE DESTRUCTIVENESS OF BLUNDERS

Blunders invariably begin as simple slips, errors, or mistakes that either go uncaught or build on one another. Errors and mistakes can quickly escalate into full-scale blunders. In July 1940, for example, the state of Washington erected the Tacoma Narrows Bridge over Puget Sound. The bridge's violent up-and-down motion, caused by strong winds that blew over the Sound, soon gained it the nickname, "Galloping Gertie." Within months, the design proved itself woefully defective.

On November 7, 1940, the winds above the Sound ripped a 600-foot section from the bridge, causing its complete collapse. This blunder, which the engineers attributed to the designer, is well known throughout the Northwest. But the state had magnified it by adding one of its own: the failure to maintain insurance on the bridge. The municipality that owned and operated the bridge had paid the insurance premium to its insurance broker about a week before the collapse—rather than directly to the insurance company the proper way. The broker had pocketed the money rather than paying it to the insurance company. He no doubt felt that this theft would never be discovered. After all, how often does a bridge collapse? This illustration shows how one blunder can compound another, greatly magnifying the cost in time, money, and lives.

Another more recent debacle is the crisis in the savings and loan industry. A brief overview of its history can provide additional insight into the high cost of blunders. The difficulties in this industry date back through several presidencies. During the Carter administration, high interest rates and inflation had seriously weakened savings and loan institutions. Since the law restricted them to writing mortgages only for residential property, all their money was tied up in fixed low-interest loans. This placed them in great financial difficulty.

The Reagan administration, in cooperation with the Congress, decided that the best way to assist these troubled institutions was to permit them to become more competitive. They eased restrictions on savings and loans, allowing them to pay higher interest on savings accounts and—for the first time—to begin dealing in the commercial properties that had formerly been off limits. At the same time, the Reagan administration raised the insured limit from $40,000 to $100,000 per deposit. All these strategies only served to compound this tragic blunder:

In 1987, Congress was assured that the problem could be solved for about $10 billion. By last year, the estimated cost had reached $159 billion. And now, as troubled savings institutions that have not been closed continue to lose money, private analysts say the total is likely to exceed $200 billion. — *New York Times*, March 18, 1990

That was in 1990. Only two months later, Alan Greenspan, chairman of the Federal Reserve, raised the possibility that the eventual cost of the bailout could exceed a *half-trillion* dollars. Latest reports estimate the cost of this fiasco to be *one trillion dollars!*

Who pays for this colossal blunder? Why, we all do. And we're feeling it now with budgetary reductions across the board. Moreover, according to Keith Bradsher's report in the *New York Times* (October 23, 1995), the interest we must pay on government bonds issued in the late 1980s to pay for part of the bailout may now be tacked onto new home mortgages as additional fees.

This book will focus primarily on slips and errors, especially the most common, universal kind—the goofs we make on computer screens or paper—and offer many ways to deal with them. Catching slips and errors requires careful attention and feedback. However, developing a more refined understanding of even these minor, absent-minded slips and errors can give us great insight into our mistakes, which will eventually allow us to avoid future catastrophic blunders. For even the worst blunders can be avoided or minimized through error awareness.

## ERROR AWARENESS EXERCISES

An aspiring pianist can learn many aspects of the skill of piano playing from a good teacher. The musician can also learn by imitating experienced players. But real skill only develops through the pianist's experimentation and practice. A musician learns to play jazz by playing jazz, to improvise by improvising. The same combination of skills and improvisational practice goes into learning to use language, play tennis, solve business problems, or recognize and examine errors.

This book will serve as your teacher. Throughout, you will become familiar with a number of helpful learning tools that will further your understanding, appreciation, and practice of error awareness. The examples will demonstrate how you can use error awareness to your advantage—or how failing to pursue error awareness can retard learning and personal growth, as well as contribute to future errors. I will be posing questions that should prompt you to think about certain issues. All in all, the "Heightening Your Error Awareness" sections will encourage you to explore certain questions on your own, applying your own experience to particular problems or questions.

These exercises at the end of each chapter will help stimulate your understanding of the error-awareness concepts and techniques. Occasionally, I will pose a problem related to the text at hand, and generally I will suggest at least one possible solution to each problem. I will also recommend various applications, methods, and techniques that will help you apply the lessons of error awareness to your current situation. Finally, this book will offer a variety of tips and do's and don'ts—guidelines that not only will help you expand your error awareness and cut down on errors, but also will improve your overall task performance.

For those seeking personal, in-depth self-examination, the Negotiation Institute in New York City offers seminars in error awareness to business, government, and the general public.

Taken together, these learning tools will expand your understanding of errors and illustrate the techniques and fundamental skills involved in analyzing them. And, once you have learned the methods and techniques of error awareness, just as you did when learning how to play tennis or piano, it will be up to you to master them through practice—and improvisation—on your own.

## HEIGHTENING YOUR ERROR AWARENESS

### PRACTICE MAKES PERFECT

Think back to your childhood. Do you remember taking lessons to learn a particular art or skill? Perhaps it was formal dancing: the waltz, the box step, the lindy, the tango. Or maybe it was karate, judo, tae kwan do, or another of the martial arts disciplines. Perhaps it was tennis: lobs, overheads, backhands, ground strokes. Or maybe it was piano: scales, simple pieces, chord progressions, sonatas.

Whatever it was, ask yourself exactly what aspects of that art the teacher pointed out to you. Did you learn anything more through other means? Perhaps from watching others? Or through practicing on your own?

*(continued)*

*(continued)*

## ANALYZE YOUR MOST RECENT ERRORS

Make a list of several of your recent errors or what you consider may be potential errors. Briefly describe at least three of your errors or mistakes.

1. Can you identify any similarity among them (though not necessarily all of them)?

2. What was the immediate effect of each error? What was its larger or long-term impact on you? Was anyone else affected by the error? In what way?

3. Next to each error on your list, write down any factor(s) whether immediate or remote, that you believe might have caused or contributed to the error.

## HOW DID YOU DEAL WITH YOUR ERRORS?

Review the list of errors you made in response to the preceding activity and ask yourself the following questions about each error: Did you acknowledge making this error as soon as you (or someone else) discovered it? Did you admit it to anyone else? Did you take responsibility for correcting it or mitigating its effects? Before completing this exercise, had you ever stopped to analyze the error according to its kind, effects, or cause? If not, did you even wonder why you might have made the error? If you answered "no" to any of these questions, you will benefit from the error-awareness system.

# 2

---

# REAPING THE
# REWARDS OF
# TRIAL AND ERROR

THE ONLY WAY HUMANITY HAS EVER GOT
ANYWHERE IS BY MAKING MISTAKES, BY *LEARNING
WHAT IS A MISTAKE.*

—R. BUCKMINSTER FULLER

How do humans learn? Most of us learn, or at least have the potential to learn, through our experience. That's why experience—everything we have perceived, thought, or done and everything that has happened to us from birth until the very instant in which we read these words—is generally acknowledged as the best teacher.

All of us have many different kinds of experiences. Some center on the simple elements of our senses: seeing, hearing, feeling, tasting, and smelling. Others are more complex. Reading and listening to others, for example, involve the interpretation of verbal symbols. Still another type of experience—education—is expressly designed to build on these simpler elements to foster learning.

Yet since infancy, you have learned through all your experiences, whether they were labeled "educational" or not. As an infant, you first mastered simple instinctive actions such as sucking to obtain milk and crying to gain comfort, attention, and nourishment. Later, you started to crawl and then to walk. Though you may have fallen several times while learning, you continued to try until you had achieved what you had set out to do. You learned then—as you do now—by trying, by doing. And we refer to this process of learning with a name that explicitly recognizes making mistakes as an essential part of the process: "trial and error."

In recent years, this most powerful of all learning experiences has acquired a new name: "hands-on training." Though the name may be new, the idea behind it remains what it has always been. You learn today just as you did yesterday by making mistakes and correcting them, by succeeding and seeing what works best, by progressively increasing your awareness.

> If you put a mouse into a maze, and it gets it right the first time, it has not learned to run the maze. It does not learn until it makes some mistakes and learns to avoid them.—J. Bronowski, *The Common Sense of Science*, 1977, Cambridge Publishers M.I.T. Press.

Think back to your childhood, recalling a skill or task that you got right the very first time you tried it. Maybe you sank a jumpshot from the top of the key in your first basketball game. Or perhaps you beat your older sister the first time you played gin rummy. If it was a sport or a game, do you remember how your opponent reacted? The odds are overwhelming that he or she dismissed your triumph saying, "Beginner's luck!" And why not? In all likelihood, that's what it was. In all honesty, did you really learn anything from your basketball triumph? Did your understanding of the strategies involved in gin rummy improve markedly with your victory? Probably not.

Now think back to the first time you failed in attempting to exercise the same skill. The same questions might now begin to yield different answers. By comparing the successful jumpshot and the failed one, you might have gained some insight into what works and what doesn't. And when you put down the king of spades and your opponent picked it up and went out, just two cards after picking up your discarded king of hearts, you probably learned a lesson in the effective strategies of winning gin rummy. In many aspects of your life, you can learn as much—or more—from your defeats as from your victories.

Small children, much like Bronowski's mice, learn from their errors: They learn what to do and what not to do to accomplish certain ends. By trying, failing, trying again, and succeeding, they master the behavior that most effectively realizes their goals and ambitions. Left to their own curiosity, children do not fear making errors. And they shouldn't. For where errors are concerned, the sooner one makes them and learns from them, the better. Most children instinctively understand what adults too often forget: An error is not the *end* of anything. In fact, an error is a *beginning*: It should, at the very least, prompt you to think about it, and often it can teach you an important lesson. We humans learn by amassing experience, both successful and disappointing: defeats as well as victories.

Trial-and-error learning follows this natural and productive course throughout our lives. Jonas Salk once echoed this sentiment, writing, "Life is an error-making and error-correcting process." You should not fear making errors. Indeed, since they have the potential to teach so much, you should rather embrace them. Where errors are concerned, however, the sooner one makes them and learns from them, the better. The wisdom of making errors early in life is expressed in the old proverb, "Little children, little mistakes; big children, big mistakes." Children need to learn while they are still young, when their mistakes carry less severe repercussions.

As we grew older, too many of us became less willing to risk error and are therefore unable to reap its rewards. Even with the best intentions, some parents unwittingly contribute to the development of this timidity. Fearing that any mistake might deliver a severe blow to their children's egos, these well-meaning parents attempt to shield their youngsters from this kind of discomfort. Some, for example, "clean up" after their kids' mistakes instead of bringing them out into the open and discussing them. This strategy of keeping their children "happy" at any cost ends up *costing* kids dearly. They recognize their parents' attempts to cover up and conclude that that's the way to deal with errors. This strategy not only instills in children the unwillingness to risk or acknowledge error, but actually denies them error's greatest benefit: learning to distinguish between actions that work to their advantage and behaviors that end up thwarting their aims.

## LEARNING FROM ERRORS

The ability to learn from error is the hallmark of intelligent behavior. Scientists, for example, regard chimpanzees as intelligent because they are proficient at mastering certain tasks through trial and error—they have the ability to *learn*. Like chimpanzees, humans can teach themselves how to avoid repeating mistakes. But you can do even more with your intelligence. You can also learn simply by exploring the *causes* of error, by not meekly accepting them as an inevitable matter of course, and by recognizing that the results of error are not always adverse. If you remain open to them, errors can lead to unexpected insight or discoveries. Indeed, many scientific breakthroughs including Goodyear's accidental discovery of the process for vulcanizing rubber have resulted from error. Yet scientists do not reap the rewards of error by ignoring their mistakes, but rather by evaluating them and trying to find out what led to them.

Most formal teaching does not mirror the trial-and-error method. Teachers fail to teach students what an error is. Instead, most organized attempts at teaching skills focus on successes: established techniques of arithmetic, playing the piano, spelling, ice skating, and brain surgery. As students, we watch as experts demonstrate flawless technique with ease. But far too few teachers demonstrate errors, the dangers to watch out for. In fact, in *The End of Education*, Neil Postman (Alfred A. Knopf, New York, 1995) suggests that teachers ought to instruct students (for at least one semester) on subjects with which they are unfamiliar: "The teacher would be forced to see the situation the way most students do . . . ," he writes. "Perhaps he or she . . . would learn how nerve-racking the fear of making a mistake is."

Yet because you cannot hope to match the teacher's perfection, at least without practice (which forces you to learn the errors and dangers on your own), you can become frustrated with trying to perform the task in question. In fact, you may feel so overwhelmed that you quit trying.

An article by Dr. Samuel Rosen in the *American Journal of Surgery* (November 1950) that explains how otologists were taught a complicated surgical procedure (called fenestration) points out the damaging impact of blaming ourselves for our errors. The surgical students (no doubt abetted by their teachers) apparently expected to perform the surgery flawlessly at the conclusion of the six-week course. Those who made errors therefore blamed themselves. As Dr. Rosen noted, "Since the performance of these surgeons was not up to their expectations, they believed the entire reason for their failure lay within themselves—that unless they could perform the operation with absolute success they were 'absolute' failures. They therefore ceased doing the operation."

Human intelligence grows through scrutinizing, evaluating, and integrating errors. At birth, each of us has an innate *potential* for intelligent behavior. But unless you allow yourself to learn, intelligence will never come close to reaching that potential. Freedom from error is by no means inborn. You do, however, have the ability to train yourself to recognize and admit errors, and then to analyze and correct them. Making mistakes can thus be an integral part of the learning experience, an essential stepping-stone that adds to our growing intelligence.

## HOW ERRORS RECUR

Most of us make the same or similar errors over and over again through-out our lifetimes. Why? Because the failure to recognize, admit, analyze, or correct errors makes it impossible to learn as much as you can, and should, from them. Some people fail to recognize (or to admit) their errors. Yet unless you realize that you have erred, you will never stop to evaluate the experience. Alcoholics Anonymous and similar 12-step programs that help people overcome addictions (correct the "errors" of their ways) recognize the critical nature of this acknowledgment. The first step toward recovery in any of these programs is the person's recognition and admission that a problem exists. Similarly, unless you first acknowledge that you have made an error, you will probably continue repeating it. Only by stopping and analyzing what happened can you learn what you did wrong, and how to avoid doing the same thing in the future.

Once again, it will prove instructive to look at how infants learn. Babies do not bother trying to hide their mistakes from themselves or others. They don't attempt to place the blame for their errors on others or on circumstances. (These strategies don't come until later in early childhood.) Instead, they learn from their mistakes, working to understand them and minimize their recurrence. They learn how to adapt their own behavior to produce fewer errors and increase their own efficiency.

As children grow older though, others—parents, teachers, siblings, friends—may either help or hinder their learning by the way they react to the children's errors. Parents can help advance their children's language skills, for example, by gently pointing out errors as they occur, and then suggesting or exploring why the child might have made the mistake. In this way, the child not only learns those skills but also discovers that errors are neither shameful nor frightening. Sometimes, however, others react to children's mistakes with severe punishments, discipline, or other harsh signs of disapproval. A teacher might intentionally or unintentionally humiliate a child for offering a wrong answer in class. Parents may take away one of their child's privileges or sources of enjoyment as punishment for accidentally breaking a vase. Siblings may withhold affection, or status may drop among friends and classmates in response to a youthful error. Such harsh rebukes or unwanted consequences of error have a powerful impact on children and on the way they will handle future errors throughout their lives. Even in adulthood, most people still carry vivid negative memories of certain early errors and the punishments that followed. Yet often it seems the punishment sticks in the mind while the original error has faded or remains somewhat unclear.

Think back to some of the most memorable errors you made as a child. How did your parents or teachers respond when they found out about them? What did you learn from these adults about how to deal with your errors?

In an attempt to avoid secondary consequences such as punishment, you probably learned different ways of softening, diminishing, or even eliminating errors. In some cases, this strategy can produce a positive result. When you direct attempts to avoid the adverse effects of error toward *preventing* their repetition (and in that way to avoid suffering the *future* consequences), you have mastered the fundamental method of trial-and-error learning.

Many people, however, learn not how to avoid error, but simply *how to evade responsibility for it.* Instead of analyzing the cause of the error, children — and later adults — search for ways to blunt, derail, or entirely escape their adverse secondary effects. Children may try to shift blame and avoid responsibility by claiming, "He did it!" or "The wind knocked it over!" If their attempts to escape the consequences succeed, then consciously or unconsciously they feel free to continue making these same errors. Even if their escape attempts are only partially successful, they may regard the blunted consequences as an acceptable price for continuing their wayward behavior. And the excuses and evasions to avoid responsible acknowledgment and analysis of errors only become more adept, elaborate, and practiced as children grow into adulthood.

No matter how illogical or unreasonable it may seem to persist in errors, all of us are more or less guilty of just such attitudes. By adopting these evasive strategies, you impede your ability to learn from your mistakes. If you become conscious of having recently made an error, you may react defensively: seeking and finding excuses, attributing much of or all the blame to others, or to circumstances or contributing factors out of your control. In *Think of This,* Gunter Eich offered a wry comment on the strength and universality of this tendency: "After a great destruction, everyone will prove that he was innocent." But in denying responsibility for your errors, you destroy the only possible value you might derive from them. You throw away the opportunity to learn everything possible about *how* and *why* you erred, and about how you can avoid or prevent making the same or a similar error in the future.

A recent illustration from the airline industry frighteningly demonstrates how spurious attempts to blame others for errors prevents one from learning from them. On January 25, 1990, Avianca Airlines Flight 52 crashed on Long Island after running out of fuel, killing 73 people. Five months later, at a National Transportation Safety Board hearing investigating the crash, the airline and air traffic controllers were still trying to blame each other for it, rather than analyzing the breakdown of communications that had helped cause it. The controllers claimed they had not given Flight 52 priority treatment because its crew had not used the specific words, "minimum fuel" or "fuel emergency." Representatives of Avianca countered by saying they did not train their flight crews to use specific words, but that the crew of the crashed plane had used the terms "priority" and "running out of fuel." They accused the controllers of ignoring common sense in demanding specific phrases to express an emergency. Instead of assessing their own part in the tragedy—and thus perhaps learning how to avoid repeating the mistake in the future—each side blamed the other.

A month after the hearing, on July 31, the captain of another incoming Avianca flight told air traffic controllers at Kennedy Airport he had "only 15 minutes of fuel left." Controllers, confused as to whether the pilot meant 15 minutes of fuel period or 15 minutes before he would have to tap into the plane's fuel reserves, declared a fuel emergency and gave the flight immediate clearance to land. In doing so, the controllers bypassed the captain's authority to declare a fuel emergency. "We would rather have them [the controllers] declare a fuel emergency and err on the side of safety," an FAA spokesman commented after the incident. Though the controllers were right to err on the side of safety, both they and the Avianca flight crew still erred in precisely the same way the earlier crew and controllers had. Both had expended so much effort in trying to blame the other that neither had done anything to gain greater error awareness and correct the primary cause of the earlier crash. Communications procedures between Avianca crews and air traffic controllers had not improved at all.

## TAKING RESPONSIBILITY

Instead of burying yourself in a vain attempt to avoid responsibility for errors and/or blaming them on others or on circumstances beyond your control, you need to train yourself to recognize errors as soon as possible. Stop and analyze the error, and the ongoing situation or process that surrounded it. To remove the burden of blame and shame from error, give up defensiveness and look at yourself and the situation objectively. Any efforts directed solely toward self-justification, as the Avianca example shows, can only obscure the lessons to be gained from errors. The goal of objectivity is difficult to attain in any case—but even more so when you feel embarrassed or ashamed. Perhaps the error damaged yourself or others; or perhaps it led directly to an economic loss or the loss of status.

For authors of scientific and medical articles, acknowledging their mistakes seems to be a supreme embarrassment. In 1984, the news media widely reported that a woman had contracted AIDS through kissing alone, a finding that had been published in a respected medical journal. The media concluded that the virus could be transmitted through saliva and that kissing was now tantamount to playing Russian roulette. Although additional tests proved that the woman had never actually contracted the AIDS virus, this later discovery did not receive nearly the same degree of publicity as the earlier, more sensational, yet erroneous finding. Indeed, the correction was buried in a 1988 article by entirely different authors, who cited the author of the original article as their source. As Lawrence K. Altman, MD, reviewing this questionable course of events in the *New York Times* (May 31, 1988), concluded:

> The obscure way in which the original report was corrected is one example of a serious flaw in the way researchers follow up the reports in scientific journals. Corrections, if they appear at all, are often expressed in indirect language or in forums that do not reach a wide audience. Crucial backup or amplifying information may appear in inaccessible places or not at all.
>
> Such shortcomings are critically important because the thousands of journals that cover a range of specialties are the central reservoir of scientific knowledge. . . .

Similar conclusions could easily be applied to the acknowledgment of errors in many fields. Look at how the news media handle criminal suspects or rumors of scandal. No matter how unfounded the allegations, the media will trumpet them. Yet if the accusations later turn out to be false, the story dies with hardly a word of apology. Even a newspaper as respected as the *New York Times* usually buries its corrections on page 3.

## THREE APPROACHES TO DEALING WITH ERROR

The repetition of errors typified by the Avianca case is not at all uncommon. In virtually every field, certain errors of a similar kind tend to proliferate and recur. As a result, actual performance—whether in golf, typing, or assembly-line production—usually falls short of the performer's potential.

Sadly, we are doomed to repeat our errors because far too few of us stop to analyze them in any meaningful way. In the mid-1970s, British comic actors Peter Cook and Dudley Moore performed a Broadway show entitled *Good Evening*. One of the skits featured a journalist (Moore) interviewing an unsuccessful and rather dense restaurateur (Cook), who showed extraordinarily bad judgment in opening a restaurant (The Frog and Peach) that served only two dishes: Frog a la Peche and Peche a la Frog. Near the end of the interview, Moore's character asks the restaurateur, "Do you feel you've learned from your mistakes?" Cook replies, "Oh, certainly. Certainly. I have learned from my mistakes, and I'm sure that I could repeat them exactly."

Far too many of us deal with our errors in this tragicomic way. We either pay little or no attention to our errors or we seize on the easiest available explanation for them. In either case, because we fail to learn from them, we "could repeat them exactly."

After making an error, people can choose one of three different approaches:

1. The *Error Ignorers* are reluctant to admit the existence of an error or acknowledge their responsibility for it. These ostriches hope that by ignoring the error, it—and its consequences—will disappear. If they do admit their responsibility, the Error Ignorers try to gloss over it as quickly as possible. They tend to accept errors as inevitable. Claiming that they want to put the mistake behind them and move on, the Error Ignorers refuse to subject their errors to any kind of rigorous analysis.

2. The *Error Excusers* want to explain away the error or the cause of the error. Many react to their mistakes in a manner that mirrors alcoholics who blame their drinking on their spouses, their jobs (or the lack thereof), or any other handy alibi. They tend to seize on the easiest and most readily available explanations, often resorting to blaming others or outside circumstances. Alternatively, they may rely heavily on past explanations, citing previously (perhaps erroneously) identified factors, whether or not they have relevance to the error in question. Although the Error Excusers do attempt some analysis, it never goes deeper than the surface.

3. The *Error Aware* want to discover, as fully as they can, the real cause(s) of the error. The Error Aware agree with Aristotle, "The unexamined life is not worth living." They hope to develop a systematic approach to eliminate or minimize future errors. But they recognize

that to develop the right plan, they must first subject their errors to complete analysis according to kinds, effects, and causes.

The first two approaches to error are inadequate at best. The Error Ignorers learn little or nothing from their errors, and may even ignore the consequences of error. The Error Excusers may correct the consequences of error but do little to address the causes. As a result of their surface analysis, the Error Excusers adopt false beliefs or at best learn half-truths about their errors. For example, they may identify a single cause that contributed to the error, but fail to recognize other contributory factors.

Only the Error Aware recognize that errors seldom spring from a single, easily identifiable cause. The Error Aware recognize that attempting to fix a problem without first fully analyzing its cause merely treats the consequences (if it even accomplishes that). By developing a complete analysis, the Error Aware learn not only the most appropriate way to correct the consequences of their errors, but also how to prevent future errors of the same kind.

If errors were a disease (and they certainly are a plague!), the Error Ignorers would ignore the symptoms, hoping they would just go away of their own accord. The Error Excusers might treat the symptoms, but would devote little effort to uncovering the underlying disease. With this approach, the operation might be a success, but the patient would die anyway. The Error Aware, however, would do their best to discover the underlying disease causing the symptoms, so that they could develop the most complete and appropriate treatment. Granted, sometimes the best the Error Aware can do is treat the symptoms—the consequences— of error. Yet only the Error Aware will *know* that this is the right course. And they alone will know when they can do more than just treat the symptoms.

## LEARNING A NEW RESPONSE

As you use this book to train yourself to become more aware of errors, you will also need to change the way you react to your own mistakes and those of others. When you notice such errors, don't waste the opportunity to learn something. Attempts to make excuses, place blame, sweep it under the carpet, bury it in a footnote or an obscure journal, or otherwise evade responsibility destroy the value of errors. Soon, no matter how grave the consequences that sprang from it, the error itself will be forgotten; it will no longer exist in our minds.

Russell L. Ackoff, in his groundbreaking book *The Art of Problem Solving*,[1] described a test that will shed some light on this discussion. A number of executives were asked, just prior to the initiation of a new program, to write down their projections of how the experimental program would affect parts inventory. A little over a year later, the executives were told that these sealed projections had been lost, and asked again to write down what they had originally projected. These projections were then compared with the original projections, which had not been misplaced at all. Curiously, the average of the recalled projections estimated a 300 percent increase in the parts inventory—almost exactly what had resulted—while the actual projections had estimated a 50 percent *decrease*.

Ackoff correctly concluded, "Memory erases mistakes and thus prevents our learning from them." If we refuse to acknowledge them, errors soon cease to "exist." We believe ourselves when we claim, "That's exactly what I said (or did or guessed)!" We need to put aside such defensive posturing, along with our attempts to excuse errors by blaming them on others or on vague sets of conditions or circumstances.

Instead, try to look on each error as an opportunity to learn something new about yourself or the other person and about the mistake itself. Acknowledge that you have made an error and then take the time to analyze it. As fairly and accurately as possible, examine the error, the conditions that led up to it, and the consequences that sprang from it.

Analysis of a recent error taught me the value of redundancy and/or alternatives in certain office procedures. On January 4, 1991, my office suddenly lost all long-distance phone service. Though we could receive some incoming calls, we could not place any outgoing calls. We later learned that an AT&T repair crew had cut a cable the size of my wrist, thereby knocking out AT&T's long-distance service for most of Manhattan. Always having used only AT&T, I had never thought about the possibility of alternatives. Many of the largest corporations in Manhattan did not suffer from the loss of AT&T because they regularly employ more than one long-distance carrier. Finding AT&T shut down, the corporations' computerized phone systems automatically switched to alternative carriers.

As I found out in the next day's *New York Times*, however, I also could have temporarily switched to other long-distance carriers like MCI or Sprint simply by dialing their access codes. Then all I would have had to do was make my call in the usual way. Although the error itself caused my office great inconvenience, I learned some valuable lessons from it.

If you truly want to "learn from your experience," arriving at a deeper understanding that will really help you (and others who depend on you) in the future, you need to avoid the temptation merely to salve your ego. Swallow your embarrassment and own up to your errors. This is the critical first step toward diminishing their number and severity.

## THE ROLE OF SELF-BLAME

No matter what task you are performing, you want to do well in your own eyes as well as in the eyes of others. When you make a mistake, you therefore want to justify it, to explain and excuse it in a way that fixes fault elsewhere. But shame or self-blame can damage the development of error awareness just as severely as attempts to blame others or circumstances. Like blaming others, self-blame discourages any examination of the error and the circumstances surrounding it. It encourages you to conceal your errors rather than investigate them. To make matters worse, shame leaves you feeling like a failure, helpless to avoid error. Indeed, a tendency toward self-blame can lead to a debilitating syndrome known as "learned helplessness." As described by Donald A. Norman in *The Design of Everyday Things*,[2] when people experience failure at a particular task several times (or even just once), ". . . they decide that the task cannot be done, at least not by them: they are helpless. They stop trying." This attitude amounts to a concession that error awareness is impossible, that no matter how much effort people put into learning from their errors, they will never succeed.

Shame does not acknowledge the human tendency to make errors. Because it holds up an unattainable standard of perfection, it cannot help but condemn as a failure any performance that falls short of realizing that impossible ideal. What's worse, self-blame does not recognize the potential to improve performance. Those who succumb to the burden of shame and self-blame, like the medical students learning a difficult new surgery, may quit trying to accomplish tasks at which they have erred in the past.

Acknowledging responsibility for errors you have made is actually quite different from blaming yourself for those errors. Where shame encourages concealment, accepting responsibility prompts investigation aimed at preventing a recurrence. And where self-blame often leads to helplessness, accepting responsibility truly empowers us. A responsible and thorough investigation of the causes and consequences of your errors leaves you feeling more powerful and *better* able to avoid similar errors in the future.

As adults, we need to work on regaining the fearlessness small children have regarding their errors—and on nurturing and encouraging that same fearlessness in those around us. Making an error is not a crime; ignoring or excusing it is. Errors should not be regarded as either shameful or frightening. For this reason, you should not react to errors with quick accusations or assignations of blame. Nor should you fear making or acknowledging errors. Indeed, since they have the potential to teach so much, you should embrace errors.

The ability to learn from error is the hallmark of intelligent behavior. The Error Aware can teach themselves how to avoid repeating mistakes of a similar kind. But the Error Aware can do even more with their intelligence. They can also learn simply by exploring the *causes* of error, by not meekly accepting error as an inevitable matter of course, and by recognizing that the results of error can sometimes be positive.

## DOS AND DON'TS WHEN YOU HAVE MADE AN ERROR

| *Do* | *Don't* |
| --- | --- |
| Acknowledge the error as soon as you recognize it. | Feel ashamed of having made an error. |
| Admit the error to yourself as well as to others. | Cover up your error in the hope that no one else will discover it. |
| Openly and honestly accept responsibility for your error. | Hide behind self-justification, lies, and other attempts to escape or blunt the consequences of your error. |
| Make the most of your opportunity to learn something from the error. | Waste time trying to blame others or circumstances for your own errors. |
| Increase your error awareness by analyzing the error fairly and objectively and asking yourself what you might learn from it. | Allow defensive posturing to inhibit your ability to augment your error awareness and your intelligence. |
| Seek and accept advice, criticism, and suggestions from others. | Keep the error to yourself in order to maintain an illusory image of perfection. |
| Ask yourself what you might do differently to avoid making the same error next time. | Feel afraid of making the same error the next time you attempt the same task. |

# HEIGHTENING YOUR ERROR AWARENESS

### LEARNING BY TRIAL AND ERROR

What are some of the myriad skills, tasks, and responsibilities entailed in your job? How did you learn to perform all these functions? How did you gain the knowledge required for the job and how did you learn the best ways to apply this knowledge?

Did you go to a trade or professional school? If so, did your schooling teach you everything you needed to know? Did you get on-the-job training from a wise and helpful mentor or supervisor? Did you observe the job performance of colleagues or superiors to see how they handled certain problems or tasks? Did you read books or subscribe to professional journals or magazines related to the performance of your job? Did schooling, training, coworkers, and reading teach you everything you needed to know? Did you learn how to perform certain tasks simply by jumping in and doing them? Did you learn to improvise simply by improvising? Did you learn from your failures as well as your successes?

### PAYING FOR YOUR MISTAKES

Think back to your childhood. Do you remember any occasions when you received harsh punishment for something you did wrong? Which do you recall more vividly: the punishment or what you did wrong in the first place?

### EVADING RESPONSIBILITY

Again, think of your childhood. Did you ever attempt to justify or explain away one of your mistakes by detailing "extenuating circumstances" to a parent or teacher (or police officer or other authority figure)? Did you ever lie in an attempt to escape the consequences of error? Were you successful in your attempts to avoid responsibility? Whether or not you escaped the consequences, what did that experience teach you?

(*continued*)

## TURNING POINTS

If you had to pinpoint just one event in your entire life, from what one experience have you learned the most? Would you characterize that experience as an error or a mistake? Was it a success or failure?

## HOW GOOD IS YOUR MEMORY?

If you hold a supervisory or management position, try this experiment with those who work under you. Ask everyone to write down their six-month (or one-year) projections of a particular quantitative business function (such as incoming orders, production errors, or the impact of a new design modification on efficiency). At the end of the designated period, tell everyone that you lost the original projections, and ask them to write down again the figures they had originally projected. Then reveal the original projections (which you did not actually lose), and allow everyone to compare them with the "remembered" projections to see if—and how—they diverge. Has "memory" improved "accuracy"?

## HOW DO YOU RESPOND TO OTHERS' ERRORS?

Although employees are certainly not children, similar approaches to errors can produce similar effects. If you hold a supervisory position, have you ever simply cleaned up after an employee's error rather than bring it to his or her attention? Did you ever fire an employee or publicly lambaste or humiliate someone for making an error? What do you suppose that person learned about the mistake from the way you reacted?

## SHIFTING THE BLAME

Consider some of the tricks or strategies that you or others use to avoid—or attempt to avoid—responsibility for errors. Do they (or you) ever try to shift the blame to coworkers? Do they (or you) blame circumstances or situations beyond their (or your) control? Are any other strategies utilized to escape the consequences of error? What do they (or you) learn about the error by employing these strategies?

(*continued*)

*(continued)*

### YOUR RESPONSE TO BEING AT FAULT

How do you most often react when someone else points out an error that you have made? Does your desire for perfection ever prevent you from recognizing the possibility that you might have made an error? Do you accept constructive criticism when it is offered? Do you react defensively to any hint that you might have done something poorly, unthinkingly, or mistakenly?

### LEARNING FROM YOUR ERRORS

Reconsider some of the errors you listed in the preceding exercises as well as in the previous chapter. Have you learned anything about these errors? If so, when did you learn it—before or after working through the applications and exercises in this book? If not, what do you think you might learn by subjecting these errors to further analysis?

### THE VALUE OF ERRORS

Ask yourself the following questions:

1. Up to this reading, what importance, if any, have I given the errors made by myself or others?
2. Did I ever approach these errors as opportunities to learn?
3. Did I ever view errors as any opportunity to become more creative?

## NOTES

1. Russell L. Ackoff, *The Art of Problem Solving* (New York: John Wiley & Sons, Inc., 1987).
2. Donald A. Norman, *Design of Everyday Things* (New York: Doubleday & Co., 1987).

# 3

## THE ERROR-AWARENESS SYSTEM

**THE PROPER WAY FOR HASTENING THE DECAY OF ERROR IS . . . BY TEACHING EVERY MAN TO THINK FOR HIMSELF.**

**—WILLIAM GODWIN**

E veryone makes errors. If you think you know someone who never does, check the condition of his or her pencils. Erasers offer great clues!

But even though everyone makes errors, you can still learn to make fewer.

Nevertheless, as imperfect beings, we're bound to foul up from time to time. And though mistakes certainly bring about serious costs and consequences, you may believe that, in general, we might be willing to accept, say, a 1 percent rate of error. If this is an acceptable figure to you, consider just some of what would happen if everyone settled for getting things right only 99 percent of the time:

- One out of every 100 prescriptions would be filled incorrectly.
- Every page of this text would have two misspelled words.

- Your water would be unfit to drink four days a year.
- Your telephone would be out of service for 15 minutes every day.

Even becoming 99 percent error-free is not good enough! An error rate of one-tenth of one percent would be significantly better. Nonetheless, even this should not necessarily be "acceptable." Defining an acceptable level of errors, although a fundamental tenet of quality control methods, sometimes fosters an unconscious sense of complacency. For this reason, you should always strive toward the *ideal* of perfection, no matter how unrealizable it may be. As the poet Robert Browning wrote in "Andrea del Sarto": "A man's reach should exceed his grasp, Or what's a heaven for?"

Economic constraints, time pressure, or other considerations may certainly cause you to tolerate a certain rate of errors in specific instances. But tolerating that rate does not mean you should accept it as inevitable or the best you can do. You should still learn from the errors that persist and strive toward perfection. Even in such cases, the question is not how many errors are acceptable, but rather how many you are willing to tolerate. When taking economic considerations into account, the more appropriate question therefore centers on a comparison between the costs of the current rate of error and the costs of trying to lower the rate or eliminate the errors altogether.

## THE BAD HABIT OF MAKING ERRORS

Do most errors result from nothing more than bad habits? Indeed, is the making of errors itself really nothing more than a bad habit? Most of us expend a good deal of conscious effort trying to control our thinking and actions so as *not* to make errors. Wouldn't you agree that many of the errors that occur despite such conscious effort must occur on a subconscious — or at least a less than fully conscious — level? After all, no one consciously wants to make them.

Consider the situation in which New York Mets catcher Mackey Sasser found himself in the spring of 1991. Suddenly he was unable to throw the ball back to the pitcher after a pitch — an action performed almost 150 times in the course of an average game. Sasser developed a double-clutch every time he threw to his teammate, pumping his arm twice before releasing the ball. The throws that resulted had no force and sailed upward like pop-ups around the pitcher's mound. Every throw became an adventure, and Met pitchers were forced to perform acrobatics to field the "simple" return throws. Certainly Sasser did not *consciously* want to make these errors. Indeed, as Sasser's coach Doc Edwards attested, "In his heart he wants to do it so badly. And the man has worked hard at it in practice, where he can do it perfectly. But in games, it doesn't work."

Mackey Sasser's throwing problem could rightly be called either an error or a bad habit. Like him, and despite our vigilance, all of us make such errors. Let's assume, then, that many occur outside your consciousness—perhaps somewhere between the conscious and subconscious. Looked on in this way, errors may seem out of our control. Yet, through examination and analysis, you can bring the process of making errors into consciousness and therefore do something about it. Although errors may be bad habits (or their result) these habits can be reformed.

Consider Los Angeles Dodger second baseman Steve Sax's situation. Five years before Mackey Sasser lost the ability to return the ball accurately to the pitcher, Sax developed a similar problem. After fielding a ground ball, he had trouble throwing the ball to first—the shortest throw in baseball. For almost half a season, Sax himself never knew where the ball would end up. But Sax and the Dodger coaches worked on the problem, trying to discover the reason behind the hitch in his throws. This diligent effort paid off, too. Sax conquered his bad habit and has played relatively error-free baseball ever since.

With similar persistence, Met coach Doc Edwards noted, "Maybe there is a key [to Sasser's throwing problem]. Maybe we'll find that key. I won't quit trying." Edwards hints at one of the fundamental tenets of error awareness: you will have much more success in attacking a problem, be it bad habits or making errors, if you first know the key cause(s) of that problem.

Think of some bad habit you developed as a child. Whatever it may have been, most likely you knew it wasn't good for you, yet you did it habitually, almost without thinking. Think of how you broke the habit. Although you may have come up with a number of equally appropriate plans and methods on your own, one strategy that has proved its effectiveness in breaking habits is to increase your overall awareness of them. Smokers, for example, may find it helpful to analyze the situations in which they smoke most often and most unthinkingly, in this way bringing the less than fully conscious habit to a more conscious level. In addition, some smokers trying to quit find that increasing their understanding of the destructive consequences of smoking heightens their motivation to change. These are two of the fundamental techniques of error awareness: assessing the costs of error and examining the context in which they most often occur.

## THE VALUE OF A THOROUGH DIAGNOSIS

The incidence of error in our lives is a lot like the incidence of illness. Because we are all exposed to the germs, viruses, and minor ailments and afflictions that exist in and around us, nobody is ever really 100 percent healthy. Similarly, nobody is perfect; everybody makes errors. But different people develop different illnesses, and some people get much sicker than others. Along the same lines, different people make different kinds of errors, and some make many more than others.

What do you do when you feel really sick? Naturally, you visit the doctor. You want the doctor to tell you exactly what's the matter with you. But how would you react if he or she superficially examined you and then said, "Looks like you're sick!" You wouldn't be at all satisfied with this analysis, of course. You'd want to know precisely what kind of illness you had, its extent, where you got it, and what your doctor could do about it.

Now, imagine how difficult it would be for your physician to treat you without first arriving at this diagnosis: "Okay, first we'll try some surgery. That might take care of things. But if it doesn't work, we'll try drug therapy—maybe morphine first, then perhaps AZT. Wait, that might not work either. Oh well, if it doesn't, we can always amputate your leg. That should fix things up. Unless of course the problem is really in your arm. Or was it your chest?"

Before even beginning to assess how to treat you, the doctor needs to develop a complete diagnosis of your illness. And this would depend on your description of the symptoms, the results of any laboratory tests or X rays, and a comparison of this information with the doctor's knowledge and experience. In addition to yielding critical insight on treating the condition, this analysis also provides an important collateral benefit. It tells you the best course to take to avoid a recurrence of the illness. It may also inform others how best to avoid contracting the disease in the first place. Virtually all advances in preventive medicine have come through this sort of thorough analysis of the type, extent, and cause of various conditions.

In treating an illness, a doctor will follow five basic steps. First, he or she will seek the answers to three critical questions:

**Diagnostic Step 1.** What exactly is wrong? What is the problem (illness)? What are the symptoms?

**Diagnostic Step 2.** How extensive is the damage? How bad are the effects of the illness?

**Diagnostic Step 3.** What caused the problem or illness?

Only after determining the answers, can the doctor proceed to the crucial next steps:

**Treatment Step 1.** What's the best way to treat the problem? How can this illness best be cured?

**Treatment Step 2.** How can a recurrence of this problem best be avoided? Can this illness be prevented from afflicting others?

Complete diagnosis therefore also tells you the best course to take to avoid a recurrence of the illness—and tells others willing to listen how they can best avoid contracting the illness in the first place.


## DIAGNOSING YOUR ERRORS

If you have truly decided that you want to break bad habits and cut down on your errors, pursue your goal with these three basic facts in mind:

1.  Some people make more errors than others.

2.  Different people tend to make different kinds of errors.

3.  *Anyone can learn how to make fewer errors!*

These facts lead to the natural conclusion that it's important for you to find out exactly how many and what kinds of errors you most often make. And just as the failure to make a timely diagnosis can worsen the destructive impact of an illness, any *delay* or failure to evaluate your errors has the potential to prolong the error and/or compound the losses suffered. This calls for a complete diagnostic checkup.

Far too many of us use a haphazard approach in dealing with our errors. We will try almost anything that we think *might* be effective in mopping up the damage, patching things up, or cutting our losses. But in treating errors, we need to adopt a systematic approach similar to the physician's. In the pursuit of *preventive* measures, however, I would hope that we would go further than the medical profession—which devotes only about 5 percent of its resources to preventive medicine and 95 percent to treating people who are already ill. We can no more allow ourselves to accept the response, "I made an error!" than we would accept, "You're sick!" from our doctor. We need to utilize the same diagnostic techniques doctors apply to illness.

The error-awareness system described in this book will follow precisely this strategy of detailed diagnosis (Part II), followed by an analysis of the consequences of error (Part III), a discussion of the causes of the problem (Part IV), and strategies to prevent recurrence (Part V). Error awareness involves a three-step analysis of the error(s) you make, followed by the prescriptive action that best suits your analysis of the problem.

### DIAGNOSTIC STEP 1. WHAT KIND (TYPE, CATEGORY, STRUCTURE) OF ERRORS AM I MAKING?

You will learn how to identify the *kinds* of errors that you most often make. Only when you possess this information, can you begin to focus on ways to stop making such errors.

### DIAGNOSTIC STEP 2. WHAT IS THE EFFECT (CONSEQUENCES, RESULTS, POSSIBLE OUTCOMES) OF MY ERRORS?

You will develop a clearer understanding of the potential damage, the *effects* that can result from each kind of error. Only when you fully understand this, will you realize the importance of stopping specific types of errors—their real, total costs. This deeper understanding reinforces that the reduction and prevention of errors is both necessary and worthwhile.

A 1989 study at the University of Illinois, for example, *quantified* the value of seat belts in terms of preventing injuries and reducing medical costs. The study compared the number of injuries suffered and the medical costs incurred among those involved in car accidents who used seat belts and those who didn't. The researchers found that seat belts "reduced the severity of injury by 60.1 percent, hospital admissions by 64.6 percent and hospital charges by 66.3 percent."[1] Armed with this better understanding of the potential damage, wouldn't you be more inclined to put your seat belt on before driving? Of course you would. That's how awareness increases our motivation to reduce errors.

## DIAGNOSTIC STEP 3.  WHAT IS THE CAUSE OF ERROR?

After you know the kinds of errors you make and their effects, you will have a greater awareness of what you should avoid. At this point, you need to determine the cause of each kind of error through analysis and testing. When you eliminate the cause, you eliminate the errors themselves.

A real-life case study illustrates the importance of understanding the causes of error.

> Audi of America says it feels vindicated by a Federal study concluding that drivers' "misapplying" their feet to gas and brake pedals was the principal cause of sudden, uncontrolled acceleration in some Audi 5000's.
>
> Audi has long insisted that the drivers' actions were the cause of the problem. Still, the Federal report released this week offers little immediate comfort for the company . . . .
>
> "We felt that the investigators could not possibly have come to any other conclusion," said Richard L. Mugg, Audi of America's chief executive. "Audi has suffered for three years waiting for this ruling. We paid a terrible price, and so did our dealers and the owners of our cars."—Doron P. Levin, *New York Times*, March 11, 1989

As you can see, knowing the cause of an error is essential before you can take the proper steps to correct it. And any *delay* or failure to evaluate the causes of error can only prolong it and/or compound the losses. Why did it take Federal investigators so long to determine the cause of the Audi acceleration errors? The three-year delay, as Audi's CEO rightly notes, cost the company, their dealers, and their customers dearly.

Taken together, the answers to these three questions will give you your error-making diagnosis. You will know the nature of the errors you make as well as their consequences and causes. Then and only then can you use your new awareness to take the *appropriate* fourth step.

## TREATMENT STEP 1.  HOW CAN I CORRECT MY ERRORS?

Knowing the cause of an error is essential before you can take the proper steps to correct it. Like a lucky doctor (or one blessed with good instincts), you may hit upon the right remedial action on your first try even without analysis. But complete diagnosis eliminates the guesswork. You will *know* the best route to choose to correct the error.

### TREATMENT STEP 2. HOW CAN I PREVENT SIMILAR ERRORS FROM OCCURRING IN THE FUTURE?

Finally, by analyzing and diagnosing our errors, you can come up with the best preventive measures. And, using the awareness you have gained through your analysis, you will train yourself to make fewer such errors. You may even learn how to eliminate some types of errors *entirely* from your life!

Moreover, you can learn from other people's errors as well as your own. In fact, learning how to anticipate and avoid mistakes similar to those others have made is by far the least costly way to gain error awareness.

## DEALING WITH RELAPSES

Your increasing error awareness will help you cut down on the errors you make. As your awareness increases, you will find that even a relapse—a temporary failure to cut down on errors, an increase in their incidence, or a resurgence of those you thought you had conquered long ago—can help you learn to make fewer of them. A temporary relapse does not signal defeat or a failure in willpower, but rather provides you with an opportunity to learn more about your errors and the context in which you make them. If analyzed thoroughly and properly, a relapse can yield new insights into the situations or circumstances that help contribute to the errors you most commonly make. By learning from these relapses, you will ensure that you need not repeat them.

Expert advice on how to respond to relapses of bad habits or addictive behaviors applies equally to error awareness. As reporter Daniel Goleman detailed in a *New York Times* (December 27, 1988) article on breaking destructive habits such as heavy drinking, smoking, or overeating:

> [A] *temporary lapse can be used as an opportunity for learning and need not signal defeat.* . . .
>
> "A slip is an error in learning, not a failure in willpower," Dr. Marlatt said. "The belief that a slip means you have no willpower or are addicted is a self-fulfilling prophecy. If you think so, then you will act that way. But people who recover from habits they want to change treat slips very differently. They see themselves as having made *a mistake that they needn't repeat.* And recovering

from a slip gives them stronger confidence in their ability to resist temptation." (emphasis added)

Whenever you suffer a relapse, try employing all of the following tactics:

1. Treat the slip as an emergency requiring immediate action. Correct the error and take steps to increase your error awareness as soon as possible.
2. Remember that a few slips do not necessarily indicate a total relapse. A few errors do not signal complete failure. Don't punish yourself with self-blame.
3. Renew your commitment to avoid errors. Don't make excuses or blame others in an attempt to justify your errors.
4. Review the actions that led to the lapse so that you won't repeat them. Search for the cause(s) of the error.
5. Make an immediate plan of action to correct the errors you've made and to prevent recurrence.
6. Ask others for help. Don't let feelings of shame prevent you from getting feedback that can help you.
7. Prevent future slips by identifying high-risk situations and preparing ways to handle them.

Since you can break bad habits and you can learn even from your relapses, you probably have more control over your errors than you may be willing to admit.

## WHAT'S YOUR STAKE?

A friend of mine once told me that he didn't find it very exciting to go to the races and see horses run around a track. When I asked him whether he ever bet on the races, he answered, "No."

"Next time," I told him, "try placing a bet. Once you have a personal stake in it, there's no question you'll be more excited."

The prospect of analyzing your errors may not seem exhilarating to you at first. However, once you recognize the enormous stake that you have in it, you'll find it both exciting and rewarding. Analysis is absolutely essential for you to grow in error awareness. And your increasing error awareness will help you improve your performance in any endeavor you choose to pursue.

If you follow the methods of error awareness outlined in this book, you will soon start to save yourself a lot of time, trouble, and money. This will not only be of enormous benefit to you, it will also make you much more helpful to those making errors around you—and those affected by your errors. And like an annuity, the benefits of error awareness will grow larger and larger in the future.

## HEIGHTENING YOUR ERROR AWARENESS

### WHAT IS AN ACCEPTABLE RATE OF ERROR?

In attempting to cut down on the number of errors you make, when do you think you will reach an acceptable level? Will you be satisfied with anything short of perfection (which is unattainable)? If so, then where do you draw the line between acceptable and unacceptable rates of error? How many errors is too many?

How would you be personally affected if everyone regarded 1 percent as an acceptable rate of error.

### RATES OF ERROR IN THE WORKPLACE

Consider the rate of errors in an operation related to your work. At what point would you judge it to become more economical to accept a certain rate of error than attempt to cut down further on the frequency of errors? Try to take into account not only the monetary losses that result directly from the error, but also the more intangible costs such as damage to one's reputation, lost business, diminishing sales, or poor references. Though it is impossible to assign definitive values to these intangibles, they certainly figure in the high cost of errors, and must therefore be included in any consideration of the "savings" that will be realized in curtailing efforts to reduce errors further.

(*continued*)

## BREAKING HABITS

Think back to a bad habit you once had. Perhaps it was smoking cigarettes. Or maybe it was sucking your thumb or biting your fingernails. Perhaps it was mumbling. Or sitting with poor posture. How did you break the habit? Did you use any techniques or strategies that that might also apply to breaking the habit of making errors?

## ANALYZE YOUR OWN ERRORS

Reexamine some of the errors you listed in Chapter 1. If you identified certain errors as similar, think about the context in which you made them. Are there any constants or parallels? Any circumstance or condition that seems to be present in many or most of the situations in which you make these errors? Do you have any control over these circumstances or conditions? What could you do to change them or minimize their influence on your performance?

## DIAGNOSING YOUR ERRORS

Think of a simple error you have made. Can you analyze its:

1. *Kind* (type, category)?
2. *Effect* (consequences, result)?
3. *Cause* (or causes)?

What does such a diagnosis tell you about the best appropriate treatment?

# NOTE

1. Cory Dean, "Seat Belt Study Assesses Savings in Medical Costs and Injuries," *New York Times*, 10 January, 1989.

# PART II

# THE TYPES OF ERRORS WE MAKE

# 4

# ERRORS IN
# TRANSCRIPTION

WHEN T. E. LAWRENCE JOINED THE RANKS AS
PRIVATE SHAW, NOEL COWARD WROTE TO HIM THAT
FAMOUS LETTER BEGINNING "DEAR 338171 (MAY I
CALL YOU 338?)" . . .

In December 1994, J. Gary Burkhead, the president of Fidelity Investments Company, wrote a letter of apology to his investors informing them of a huge error in accounting, all due to a simple clerical inaccuracy. In his words, "The error occurred when the accountant omitted the minus sign on a net capital *loss* of $1.3 billion and incorrectly treated it as a net capital *gain* on this separate spreadsheet. This meant that the dividend estimate spreadsheet was off by $2.6 billion." Ouch!

Burkhead went on to explain how such an error could have happened in this age of technology. "While many of our processes are computerized," he wrote, "the requirements of the tax code are complex and dictate that some steps be handled manually by our tax managers and accountants, *and people can make mistakes* [emphasis added]."

Perhaps some of the simplest and most common errors made today are those involving the use of "units of meaning"—symbols such as letters, punctuation marks, numbers, and mathematical functions. Whether made with pen and ink, pencil, or on a computer, typewriter, or calculator keyboard, such errors plague every one of us. And as we can see, although the errors are "simple," their consequences can be anything but.

How common are errors that involve the transcription of symbolic units of meaning? We have all discovered transcription errors in reading newspapers, novels, and even advertisements and signs. How often do you (or those who work for you) make errors in using symbols—in balancing your checkbook or the company ledger? Surely, these are at the base of many of our blunders.

## SYMBOLS ARE EVERYWHERE!

Almost everything in our lives—whether related to business or our personal endeavors—depends on the accurate communication and use of words and numerals. Every day, each of us records or transmits a multitude of them. All of the interaction—business or personal—in the world depends on billions of people reading, understanding, recording, and conveying the arrangements of quintillions of these symbols daily.

Yet, astonishingly, to form the infinite variety of semantic symbols—numbers and words—and their arrangement into sentences and equations that convey distinct meanings, we use only 60 or 70 basic symbolic tools: in English, an alphabet of just 26 letters and 10 numerals (0 through 9) complemented with two or three dozen other symbols such as punctuation and arithmetical signs. Specific combinations and arrangements of these 60 or 70 basic symbols can represent such a wide diversity of meanings, that for all practical purposes, we must regard the range of possibilities as virtually infinite.

Different languages employ their own alphanumeric systems, which may have more or less than 26 letters and 10 numerals. The Hebrew alphabet has 22 letters, the Arabic 28, the Russian Cyrillic alphabet 32. And computers use a binary language to record, manipulate, and convey all meanings. They actually need only two basic symbols to form the infinite range of meanings in our world.

How important is accuracy in the communication and use of the symbols in our alphanumeric system? To develop your own answer, consider how small errors in basic symbols can significantly affect the overall semantic meaning of a sentence or equation.

Take the very simple sentence: "What an error!" By changing one punctuation mark and adding another, you could easily transform this exclamation of astonishment or horror into a question that professes (or feigns) ignorance: "What? An error?" This simple "error" in the use of basic symbols of punctuation has changed the overall meaning of the group of identical words.

According to Robert Ripley, famed for his "Believe It or Not" columns, the misplacement of a single period once saved a man's life. In Czarist Russia, a functionary was ordered to send a cable reading: "PARDON IMPOSSIBLE. TO BE SENT TO SIBERIA." The actual cable, however, delivered quite a different message: "PARDON. IMPOSSIBLE TO BE SENT TO SIBERIA."

Consider the sentence: "We will seek no new restrictions on imports from Japan." The omission of just two letters leaves the reader with quite a different impression: "We will seek new restrictions on imports from Japan."

As we have seen from the Fidelity Investment Company's fiasco, the impact of minor errors involving numbers is even clearer. Arithmetical signs ($+$, $-$, $\times$, decimal points, etc.) can exercise a great influence on the meaning of an arrangement of numbers. Compare $10 + 10 + 10$ to $10 \times 10 \times 10$. Altering just two arithmetical signs in this equation has transformed the result from 30 to 1,000. Similarly, the reversal of two numerals can transform \$17,259 to \$71,259—a difference of \$54,000!

The 60 or 70 different symbols in our alphanumeric system provide the basis not only for communication in our personal lives, but also for all our business transactions. Accuracy in our use of these symbols is critically important to those dealings. In many fields, blunders of disastrous proportion might result from errors in the performance of apparently simple clerical tasks—the transcription, reading, interpretation, and/or transmission of symbols. Since accuracy in the use of symbolic units of meaning is so important to all of us, let's apply the principles of error awareness to errors made in transcribing these symbols.

What kinds of errors do we make in transcribing symbols? Surprisingly, all clerical errors can be classified into just a few distinct types. As you will see, however, the effects that can result from these clerical errors may vary widely. This section will explore the five basic kinds of clerical errors.

But before going further, read each of the phrases printed in the following triangles:

Read them over again, repeating out loud what they say. Now, without bothering to arrange them in triangular form, write the phrases on a separate piece of paper, each on a new line. Have you read or copied the phrases exactly? We'll return to your responses in a bit.

## THE FIVE TYPES OF CLERICAL OR TRANSCRIPTION ERRORS

To remain accurate, any record—a correspondence, a ledger, a chemical formula, a recipe, a customer order, a medical prescription, a checkbook, a court transcript, a box score, or a memo—demands the appearance of certain symbols in a particular order. If we deviate any from the appropriate and precise pattern of specific symbols that convey exactly the intended meaning, we have made a *clerical or transcription error.*

Most clerical errors fall into one of five categories: transportation, omission, insertion, repetition, or substitution.

### CLERICAL ERROR 1. TRANSPOSITION (ALSO SOMETIMES CALLED "TRANSPORTATION")

A transposition error involves a change in their proper order of two or more otherwise correct symbols.

For example, as a lawyer, I should certainly be able to spell the word "trial." Yet I frequently make the transposition error of writing "trail" instead—prompting numerous jokes among my office staff. Transposition errors involving numbers, generally harder to spot than those involving letters, are even more common. The numbers "196,234" and "916,234" have significantly different meanings—especially if you're referring to dollars!

### CLERICAL ERROR 2. OMISSION

An error of omission results when one or more symbols that appear in the source material have no equivalent in the transcription. We transcribe symbols incompletely, omitting some that belong in the record.

For example, Morgan Guaranty Trust Company made a costly error of omission early in 1991. Eleven readers of the *New York Times* had sent checks ranging from $13 to $100 after reading about the financial struggles of young Chinese students to stay in rural elementary schools, which cost approximately $13 in annual fees. "Morgan Guaranty," the *Times* reported on April 29, 1991, "in preparing a bank draft for Chinese yuan on behalf of one of the donors, neglected the decimal point in the exchange rate and sent $10,000 dollars worth of yuan instead of $100 worth." ($10,000 is more than the amount that 100 Chinese peasants in the region earn in a year.) The omission of a single decimal point cost Morgan Guaranty $9,900, although a spokesperson tried to put a good face on the error by declaring, "Under the circumstances, we're happy to make a donation of the difference."

## CLERICAL ERROR 3. INSERTION

An insertion error results when one or more symbols that appear in the transcription have no equivalent in the source material. The inclusion of any unnecessary or irrelevant symbolic information in the new record produces error.

In the old days, before cash registers became a staple in almost every store, merchants used to add up the bill by writing the price of each item on the outside of the bag. When customers phoned in orders, however, some merchants—whether by accident or design—wrote the address or apartment number at the top of the bag and then added that number into the total as well. The introduction of this irrelevant information is an insertion error. A publisher who accidentally printed Hamlet's soliloquy as, "To be sure, or not to be believed, that is their question . . ." would be charged with a similar error of insertion three times over.

## CLERICAL ERROR 4. REPETITION

Repetition is a special kind of insertion error that resembles a vocal stutter. It results when same symbol or set of symbols is added a second or third (or more) time in a single transcription.

Look at the triangle exercise I asked you to do at the opening of this chapter. These triangles illustrate how difficult it can be to spot an error of repetition. If you wrote down the phrases, did they read as follows?

PARIS IN THE THE SPRINGTIME

ONCE IN A A LIFETIME

BIRD IN THE THE HAND

Each of the phrases in the triangles contained a repetition of an article, either "the" or "a." Yet because the repetitions occur on different lines (and because the familiarity of the phrases causes us to expect a very specific meaning), the errors elude us. Most people read the phrases in the triangles the way they *expect* them to be, glossing over the errors entirely.

Your response to this activity may illustrate another clerical error as well. If you said or wrote PARIS IN THE SPRINGTIME, ONCE IN A LIFETIME, and/or BIRD IN THE HAND, *you* committed one or more errors of *omission*. After all, the instructions asked you to copy the phrases *exactly*.

## CLERICAL ERROR 5. SUBSTITUTION

A substitution error results when one or more of the symbols that appear in the transcription differ from the symbol(s) in the corresponding position(s) in the source material. Whenever we record one symbol when we intended another, we have made an error. Indeed, we may make a substitution error even when we record precisely the symbol we intended—for example, if we are copying a number and *misread* it.

A wrong number most frequently involves a substitution error. The wrong symbol is dialed in place of the correct one. So instead of 555-1212, perhaps you hit 555-1222. Another ironic example of a substitution error appeared on a commemorative cup sold in July 1990 to benefit Baltimore's *literacy* program. The city's mayor, Kurt Schmoke, did his best to take it in stride when presented with a cup that commended "Kurt L. Sch*noke*" for his initiative in combating illiteracy.

Transposition, omission, insertion, repetition, and substitution occur much too frequently in the performance of routine clerical tasks. In fact, what are called "transcriptions" often differ from their source material by extremes. These are instances of gross error that I refer to as *divagation*. Divagation may result from a combination of several types of clerical or transcription errors. In some cases, the results deviate so significantly from the source material that the term "transcription" becomes wholly inappropriate. However, unless the error-filled "transcription" makes little or no sense to the person processing it or anyone who might check or use it, many, if not all the errors will go entirely unnoticed.

## CATCHING TRANSCRIPTION ERRORS IN WORDS

Catching transcription errors requires the recognition of a significant disruption in meaning—a semantic gap. A sign posted at the Banco de Ponce in New York City in 1979 illustrates what I mean. In the midst of a record-setting rash of bank robberies, the bank was forced to post the following sign at all its teller windows to protect the safety of employees:

*ATTENTION WOULD-BE BANK ROBBERS*

THIS IS A SPANISH-SPEAKING BANK. IF YOU INTEND TO ROB US,
PLEASE BE PATIENT FOR WE MIGHT NEED AN INTERPRETER.

THANK YOU
THE MANAGEMENT

This sign represented management's attempt to correct a semantic
gap—a significant difference between the meaning the bank robbers intended to convey (their *semantic intent*) and the meaning the bank tellers
received (*semantic effect*). Because they spoke little English, the latter did
not always understand what the robbers were trying to tell them. The
bank's managers therefore tried to close this gap—and the danger it presented to employees—by posting the sign.

All transcription errors—no matter what kind—result in a *semantic
gap*, a significant discrepancy between the meaning one wants to convey
and the meaning that is received by another. The discovery of a semantic
gap in transcription may spring either from a painstaking comparison
with the original—a protective double-checking measure undertaken by
far too few corporations, government agencies, and individuals—or from
the production of a meaning that contradicts or clashes with the user's expectations or understanding.

Since most words transmit an immediately recognizable semantic effect on the reader, listener, or user, errors in transcribing them are by far
easier to notice—and therefore to catch—than errors in transcribing
numbers. Computerized spell checkers can, in a purely mechanical way,
catch many transcription errors involving words. (Similarly, computerized sum checkers, though they cannot recognize an incorrectly entered
number, can mechanically check arithmetical errors.) In fact, both humans and computers can usually infer the intended word (and the meaning) despite the transcription error.

Every word has a certain "structure." The letters in the word should
have and are indeed expected to have a certain relationship to one another. This structure makes transcription errors in words easily detected.
In most instances, the incorrect rearrangement of letters often—though
not always—strikes us as meaningless. "Symbel, "smyblo," "symol," and
"symbboll," for instance, do not convey the same sense that "symbol"
does. So when you see the letters of one word jubmled or exxtra letters in
another word, you will usually recognize it. As long as you know the correct way to spell the intended word, you will probably notice the reversed,
missing, wrong, or extraneous letters. Clerical errors violate the structure
of the word, the expected relationship between the letters.

Our expectations can also *cause* clerical errors. In the South, for example, people tend to call me Gerald rather than Gerard. They expect the more familiar name, and err according to those expectations. In general, however, a structural error alters only the relationship of the letters within the word itself. The meaning of the sentence, which can usually be determined by inferring the *intended* meaning of the word that contains the transcription error, remains clearly understood despite it.

In some cases, however, a transcription error *can* change the larger meaning of the sentence. Consider the following sentence: "The ranger pointed his gnu at the bank teller." In reading this sentence, you probably feel fairly certain that the word "gun" has been erroneously transposed. You might also have guessed that the word "stranger" has suffered the effects of an error of omission. Taken at face value, however, the sentence does make a certain whimsical sense—especially if the ranger loves animals! The combination of simple transposition and omission errors has changed its entire meaning.

You may object that these kinds of transcription errors, although they result in other real words that have their own unique structure and integrity, make the sentence nonsensical. Yet these errors commonly slip past even the most experienced copyeditors—and go entirely unnoticed by computerized spell checkers. Nevertheless clerical errors that involve words are relatively easy to catch—and correct. For this reason, transcription errors in the letters of words, however regrettable or even embarrassing, seldom lead to very painful consequences.

The following activity may help you become more aware of transcription errors in words.

## EXERCISE: PIANO ORDERS

Examine the two "identical" lists of order numbers, pianos, original prices, and sale prices. Consider the data in the first list to be entirely accurate. The second list, however, contains some accurate and some inaccurate information, in words and numbers. Find the discrepancies (the semantic gaps) in the two lists on page 53.

You should have found 20 errors in the second list. If you missed any, look for them again. What kind of errors did you miss: transposition, omission, insertion, repetition, or substitution? Were the errors that you missed order numbers, words, or prices? In general, did you find clerical errors easier to spot in the words or in the numbers? In the case of numbers, were the clerical errors easier to find in the "real" amounts or in the identification numbers?

## LIST 1

| Order # | Description | Original | Sale |
|---------|-------------|----------|------|
| DKFHN33 | Mahogany Spinet | $ 1299 | $ 544 |
| GJFG39 | Primavera Console | $ 1350 | $ 589 |
| GMVGF05 | Leatherette Spinet | $ 1425 | $ 688 |
| LKG86 | Walnut Studio | $ 1775 | $ 844 |
| DHHJ45 | Ebony Digital Piano | $ 1899 | $ 989 |
| GFV63 | Country French Console | $ 2775 | $1244 |
| LKCSG60 | Glazed Baby Grand | $ 3895 | $1776 |
| LGJ98 | Hi-Polish Parlor Grand | $ 10,395 | $4114 |
| GTKB85 | Professional Grand | $ 12,495 | $4717 |

## LIST 2

| Order # | Description | Original | Sale |
|---------|-------------|----------|------|
| DKFGN33 | Mahogany Spinet | $ 1299 | $5444 |
| GJFG39 | Primavera Cobsole | $ 13500 | $5289 |
| GVGF05 | Leatherette Sprinet | $ 1425 | $ 688 |
| LLKG86 | Walnut Studio | $ 1775 | $ 484 |
| DHKHJ45 | Ebony Digtial Piano | $ 1099 | $ 989 |
| GFV63 | County French Console | $ 7275 | $1244 |
| LCKSG60 | Glazed Babbby Grand | $ 3895 | $1776 |
| LGJ98 | Hi-Polish Parlor Grand | $130,395 | $ 414 |
| GTKB85 | Professional Grand | $ 1,495 | $2717 |

The words "cobsole," "sprinet," "digtial," and "babbby," do not convey any meaning to us. In fact, precisely because these arrangements strike us as meaningless, we not only notice them, but many of us also close the semantic gap, almost without thinking. Since we want to invest everything with meaning, we interpret the semantic intent from the otherwise meaningless arrangement of letters, understanding the first three words as "console," "digital," and "baby." And knowing the context helps us recognize the last word as a flawed attempt to spell "spinet" rather than "sprint." Of course, there are exceptions to this generality. The fifth misspelled word in List 2 is "county," an arrangement of basic symbols that certainly has semantic meaning. In such cases, we must depend upon context (or careful comparison with the original) to catch the transcription error.

## THE PROBLEM OF TRANSCRIPTION ERRORS IN NUMBERS

Rearrangements of numerals do not become inherently meaningless. Transcription errors change the meaning conveyed by the arrangement of numerical symbols, but unlike "symbel" and "babbby," they do not result in a nonsensical arrangement. Transposition of the numerals in a multidigit number or the omission of one or more of the numerals almost always yields a *real* and viable number—but one with an entirely different meaning from the one intended. Both "741" and "71" make sense to us, though they convey dramatically different meanings.

This subtlety of distinction makes transcription errors involving numerals not only the most common type of transposition error, but also the most difficult to discover. If you write or type $930.18 instead of $390.18, it may cost somebody—you, your company, your customer, or your client perhaps—$540. Even if it does not ultimately cost anyone $540, it will at the very least take time and trouble to pinpoint the error, correct it, and try to overcome any ill effects that have resulted from it. And these ill effects—in terms of good will, professional reputation, your own confidence, and the confidence others have in you—may cost much more than $540.

When numerals are used to identify rather than quantify, these errors occur even more frequently—and are much more difficult to catch. In the piano order exercise, errors made in recording the item numbers were probably much more difficult for you to spot than the errors made in the price. That's because price conveys a sense of meaning that we just don't get from an order number.

A cartoon that appeared in the September 1991 issue of *Successful Meetings*, provides a humorous illustration of how meaningless identifying numbers can be. The cartoon shows a manager with a stunned expression on his face standing at the desk of a blase computer operator. The caption reads: "What do you mean you ordered 7613457 of them? That's the phone number!"

Just consider how many times you dial a wrong number on the telephone—and how often people call you by mistake. Recognizing how easy it is to make these kinds of errors when dealing with numbers that have no inherent meaning, you may be more considerate to the next person who calls you early in the morning by mistake (instead of responding to callers who ask what city they have reached by answering sarcastically, "Bangkok").

In our increasingly complicated business and personal lives, an ever-wider array of arbitrary combinations of numerals and letters has become commonplace. Every day, numerals and letters are being recombined in novel ways to convey fresh meanings. Yet these new arrangements make sense only in reference to the special system within which they exist. By far the most common of these new combinations provide distinctive identifying references. Assigning a unique array of numerals and/or letters can help us identify precisely one particular person or thing. At one time or another, all of us have used our Social Security numbers, payroll numbers, student identification numbers, customer ID numbers, driver's license numbers, or other numbers to identify ourselves. Similarly, we use specific arrangements of numerals and/or letters to identify particular zip codes, telephone numbers, home or business addresses, automobile licenses, credit card accounts, bank accounts, bank checks, catalog items, and filing or other reference numbers.

These identifying numbers are much more vulnerable to transcription errors than either words or quantifying numbers. Since each code number represents a different item and each identification number a distinct person, these new arrangements definitely have semantic content. Yet, to most of the people on whom we rely to transcribe and use them accurately, such numbers are virtually meaningless, utterly routine, and entirely devoid of interest or content. No wonder clerical tasks involving these identifying numbers result in a plague of transcription errors!

Arrangements of letters specially coded by the government or private corporations for reasons of secrecy in the transmission of information suffer from a similar lack of meaning, and therefore an increased vulnerability to error. Computer services employ coded passwords to provide security to their clients and customers. Many services, however, ran into such a high incidence of customer errors in logging on to their lines that they have eliminated the coded password procedure entirely. Instead, they use a command relayed through just one or two keystrokes. Yet this solution is far from satisfactory. For in eliminating error in this way, these services have compromised their clients' and customers' security.

Workers who deal with such numbering systems day in and day out see no value in the symbols with which they need to work. As a result, the process of transcribing them becomes quasi-mechanical. Many individuals involved in information systems or other data-processing operations, therefore, find it difficult to adapt—on a day long, week long, or annual basis—to the performance requirements of the clerical tasks involved in their jobs.

Readiness, adequacy, and ease of adaptation vary with each individual, depending especially on his or her prior experience, education, and training. Yet the process of adaptation to systems that employ such identifying numbers presents inherent difficulties for even the most appropriately trained, and even under the best conditions. After all, human beings do not function with the level of predictability and reliability that we think of as mechanical. And the work performed is not truly mechanical. Though the general procedures may remain the same, clerical work involving symbols is not cookie-cutter work. Because the semantic symbols themselves vary, referring to different items, people, or companies, the content of each unit of work varies, too. And this nonmechanical quality of needing to apply the same essential procedure to each *new* unit of transcription also makes them vulnerable to error. (We will further explore the complexities involved in apparently simple clerical tasks in Chapter 10.)

## DETECTING NUMBER-RELATED ERRORS OF TRANSCRIPTION

In addition to being more common, transcription errors involving numbers become more difficult to detect. Since these groups of letters and numerals do not represent familiar words, users can't tell just by looking at them whether letters or numbers have been transposed, omitted, added, repeated, or substituted. The transcription error yields an entirely new arrangement, but not one that immediately seems ridiculous. The new arrangement of symbols has its own unique structure and integrity; it also has an entirely different meaning. Errors in any of these identifying numbers result in *misidentification* of the intended person or thing. As a result, the recipient of the mail, shipment, or fax gets the wrong message or the wrong product—or the wrong person may receive the right message or product for the wrong price.

Consider the performance of five clerk typists at the Acme Widget Company who attempted to process the following simple order:

| Quantity | Item | Cost Per Item | Total Cost |
|----------|---------|---------------|------------|
| 3 | XYZ1234 | $7.97 | $23.91 |
| 2 | ABC45678 | 3.99 | 7.98 |
| | | | $31.89 |

This was what the order looked like when it came in on a standardized order form. Yet in transferring this information to the computer, each of the employees made one or more errors in processing. The invoices that resulted read as follows. Can you spot the clerical error(s) in each order and identify each one according to its kind?

---

**CLERK 1: JO SCHMO**

| | | | |
|---|---|---|---|
| 3 | XZY1234 | $ 7.94 | $ 23.82 |
| 2 | AB678 | 33.99 | 67.98 |
| | | | $ 91.80 |

**CLERK 2: JOE SCHMO**

| | | | |
|---|---|---|---|
| 3 | XY1234 | $ 7.97 | $ 23.91 |
| 20 | ABCDEF45678 | .99 | 19.80 |
| | | | $ 43.71 |

**CLERK 3: JOSE SCHMO**

| | | | |
|---|---|---|---|
| 3 | XYZ123456 | $ 27.97 | $ 83.91 |
| 9 | ABC45678 | 3.99 | 35.91 |
| | | | $119.82 |

**CLERK 4: JOSIE SCHMO**

| | | | |
|---|---|---|---|
| 3 | XYZ1234 | $ 7.97 | $ 23.91 |
| 3 | XYZ1234 | 7.97 | 23.91 |
| 2 | ABC17568 | 399.99 | 799.98 |
| | | | $847.80 |

**CLERK 5: JOSIAH SCHMO**

| | | | |
|---|---|---|---|
| 5 | XYZ2234 | $ .97 | $ 4.85 |
| 2 | ABC4567878 | 3.99 | 7.98 |
| | | | $ 12.83 |

---

Which errors did you find most difficult to identify? Were the errors easier to catch within identification numbers or within quantifying numbers (like prices or numbers of items ordered)? What measures do you think might be taken or changes instituted to minimize some of the errors made by these order clerks?

Whether they occur in the reading, recording, transcription, transmission, or other manipulation of words, quantifying numbers, or identification numbers, simple transcription errors often have a snowballing effect. When they slip by, as you shall see in Part III, transcription errors can lead to larger and larger errors, and greater and greater costs. If not caught early, simple clerical errors can grow into blunders of epic proportion. A series of errors, or even small slips, each of which in itself may not appear serious, can lead to major tragedies. Understanding the dangerous progression and escalating costs initiated by clerical slips and errors will make the importance of cutting down or eliminating them absolutely clear.

## HEIGHTENING YOUR ERROR AWARENESS

### THE IMPORTANCE OF SYMBOLS

Write down a sentence or a simple equation. Now change, drop, or add one or two basic symbols in that sentence or equation. Have these deliberate errors altered the overall meaning of the sentence or question at all? How significantly?

### YOUR TRANSCRIPTION ERRORS

1. Think of any of the five transcription errors you have made. Note the types of symbolic errors you make most often.

2. Seeing and understanding the many ways symbolic errors can occur, what changes will you now make in your use of symbols to cut down on the errors you make?

3. Make a list of reminders that you can use to help avoid such errors in the future.

### SEMANTIC GAPS

How often do you think transcription errors produce *noticeable* semantic gaps? How often do these semantic gaps become so great, so significant, or so jarring that they call attention to themselves? Do you think the immediate context (such as a word or number) or the overall context (form or type of document) in

*(continued)*

which the error was made will have an impact on whether or how soon the error will be noticed? Why or why not?

## AVOIDING SYMBOLIC ERRORS IN THE FUTURE

Seeing and understanding the many ways symbolic errors can occur, what changes can you make now in your use of symbols to cut down on such errors? List some reminders that can help you avoid these errors in the future.

# 5

## MISTAKES IN MEANING

**A PERSON GETS FROM A SYMBOL THE MEANING HE
PUTS INTO IT, AND WHAT IS ONE MAN'S COMFORT
AND INSPIRATION IS ANOTHER'S JEST AND SCORN.**
**—JUSTICE ROBERT JACKSON,**
***WEST VIRGINIA STATE BOARD V. BARNETTE***

In exploring the kinds and causes of errors that occur in using symbolic units of meaning such as words, sentences, and paragraphs, you may find it helpful to look more closely at the mental processes involved in employing so few symbols to convey so much content. How do we use arbitrary symbols, such as those contained within our alphabet and numerical systems, to represent objects as diverse as clouds, dollars, and quarks, and activities as varied as spelunking, philosophy, and gardening? The ability to use these representations rests on our capacity to associate a distinctive meaning with reading or hearing a word, sentence, or paragraph. This capability develops on three different levels: association, representation, and semantic symbolization.

## USING ARBITRARY SYMBOLS

### ASSOCIATION

Most animals would not survive without the capacity to associate specific sights, sounds, and smells with the presence of food or danger. And the species as a whole would become extinct without the association of particular sights, sounds, and smells with the presence or desirability of a mate! Animals may attain the ability to associate sensory experiences with specific aspects of reality through instinct, learning, or a combination of the two.

In developing the concept of the conditioned reflex, Russian physiologist Ivan Pavlov demonstrated that some animals can "learn" such associations. Pavlov's experiments showed that once an association had been established," a stimulus as novel, arbitrary, and artificial as the sound of a bell could have the same effect on dogs as the smell of food. Pavlov's findings suggested the existence (at least in the more intelligent forms of life) of a basic mechanism in which a distinctive class of sensory experiences (such as the aroma of bacon frying) can evoke an association with an equally distinctive class of reality (breakfast), even when the person or animal does not actually see or hear that reality directly (the meat sizzling in the pan). Though admittedly much less sophisticated than the process used in language, this primitive mechanism presumably parallels the way we associate symbols (like letters, numerals, and words) with the objects or actions that we intend for them to represent.

## REPRESENTATION

Peoples in prehistoric times, children, and even animals with a certain degree of intelligence have demonstrated that one doesn't need to be literate to use artificially contrived symbols to represent objects, actions, quantities, or other aspects of reality. To both primitive and sophisticated peoples, an arrow indicates a particular direction, while a cairn marks a certain location. Holding two fingers up can mean two crayons, two tickets to the movies, or two martinis, very dry. Similarly, on an abacus, each bead represents whatever is being counted or calculated. More abstract symbols require a greater degree of sophistication and intelligence. Yet we recognized and made some primitive use of numerals long before we knew how to perform simple arithmetic. We familiarize ourselves with the basic symbols before we can begin to master the infinite range of possible meanings created by combining them.

## SEMANTIC SYMBOLIZATION

With the combination of these basic symbols, we gradually develop the skill to listen and speak, read and write. This use of language to convey meanings constitutes a quantum leap in our ability to communicate, freeing us from our earlier dependence on grunts, primitive drawings, and finger signals. Similarly, we progress from the limited use of individual numerical symbols to the unrestricted manipulation and application of numbers with multiple digits together with all the sophistication of mathematical procedures that can be performed using them. Likewise, our acquired ability to manipulate multidigit numbers through calculation frees us from being dependent on our fingers and toes and other limited mathematical procedures that require only an understanding of single-digit numbers.

Whether we are reading a book, an interoffice memo, a grocery list, or a shareholder's earnings report, we can immediately see that any material that uses written language affects our consciousness on at least three levels: the *basic symbols* (letters and numerals), the *semantic symbols* (words and numbers), and the *semantic content* (meanings) associated with the words or numbers.

Through the use and interpretation of basic and semantic symbols we can convey (or receive) an infinite range of meaning. The symbolic material may relate a message or piece of news that excites us; or it may be a reminder from a loved one, a colleague, or even ourselves. We may cull information or instruction from written source material—a user's manual, an encyclopedia, a computer database, a cookbook. We may even become absorbed in great literature or poetry, entering worlds created entirely from semantic symbols.

Simply because words convey such a powerful significance, we often react intellectually, physically, or emotionally to them. And our reactions to these symbols alone often parallel what our response to the actual action or object might be. For example, when grandparents read that their granddaughter has spoken her first word, they generally respond with an excitement that almost equals the thrill they might have felt had they witnessed the event themselves. Not entirely unlike Pavlov's dogs, we learn to respond to the symbolic stimulus (in our case, words) almost as we would to the object it represents.

## IT'S AN IMPERFECT SYSTEM

Not all of us react to the same stimuli in the same way, however. Every individual interprets semantic symbols according to his or her own personal associative process, experience, and resources. For this reason, a single written (or spoken) stimulus may produce a different meaning on each individual exposed to it. And all too often, this results in a *semantic gap*—

a significant difference between the meaning the author intended to convey and the meaning that the reader actually received. This semantic gap can produce or contribute to the production of a wide variety of errors in the use of both basic and semantic symbols.

For example, some years ago, Dr. Walter C. Alvarez of the Mayo Clinic wrote about a troubled young man who had misinterpreted a radiologists's communication. "It's all up with me," the worried man had said. "The X-ray man said I have a hopeless cancer of the stomach." Knowing that the radiologist would never say such a thing, Dr. Alvarez asked exactly what he had said. "NP," replied the man.

At the Mayo Clinic NP stands for "no plates." This means, the images of the stomach appeared so normal on the X-ray screen, the radiologist saw no need to make them into film. But the poor patient interpreted NP to mean, "Nothing Possible." He was sure he was dying.

To improve our awareness of the origin of the errors we make in using alphanumeric symbols, we need to probe more deeply into the symbolic systems themselves to develop a better understanding of all the disparate factors involved in our day-to-day use of symbols. The following mental, physiological, and cultural factors affect our use of basic and semantic symbols.

Literacy, as such, is not an "innate" characteristic. Language and the use of artificial visible symbols to convey it developed slowly over the millennia. But it also developed unevenly—different cultures developed language in response to their unique needs and opportunities. As a result, all written language is synthetic, its symbols artificial, arbitrary, and empirically adapted. And a youngster's linguistic development, though it does not take millennia, follows a similar course. Children have to be taught to read; and sadly, many never learn at all. These considerations demonstrate that "reading" and "writing" are highly specialized accomplishments.

Languages differ greatly (and somewhat arbitrarily) in the overall efficiency of their use of symbols, in the richness of their vocabularies, and in the complexity of their syntax. English, for instance, has one word for "snow," while the various languages of the Inuit (Eskimo) have more than a dozen.

The Harvard anthropologist, Clyde Kluckhohn, had written about the cultural differences in language in his book, *Mirror for Man:*[1]

> Every language has a special way of looking at the world and interpreting experience. . . . One sees and hears what the grammatical system of one's language has made one sensitive to, has trained one to look for in experience. This bias is the more insidious because everyone is so unconscious of his

native language as a system. To one brought up to speak a certain language, it is part of the very nature of things.

This results in significant differences in the subtlety and sensitivity of their shadings of meaning and in their literature and traditions. Languages also vary significantly in their openness to additions or changes that reflect and respond to the continuing evolution of society, culture, and technology. For this reason, different languages have contrasting abilities to convey particular aspects of reality. Different languages probably limit the ways we think about reality, perhaps preventing us from having certain thoughts due to the way we construct reality around language.

For example, the Chinese have no words for "yes" or "no." And the Hopis don't divide their verb tenses into present, past, and future. The languages that most of us are familiar with—English, German, and the Romance languages such as French, Italian, and Spanish—have much in common. But once we move out of our own cultural element, to Semitic, Asian, or Native American languages, the internal logic of each is quite unique.

No one language, however, is superior to others in all these respects. English, though it currently dominates international usage, is nevertheless only one of many languages, each with its own peculiar advantages and disadvantages.

The English language employs an alphabet that owes its origins to Latin. Yet it derives its words from a great number of sources in addition to Latin. As a result, English suffers from many disadvantages. For example, in considering the following list of English words, write down the word that accurately describes its opposite gender.

Aunt

Son

Brother

Mother

Uncle

Cousin

Unlike French or Spanish, English does not have gender forms for the term *cousin*.

The most notable disadvantage of English is its rampant inconsistency and irregularity of spelling and pronunciation. Although many efforts have been made to simplify these areas, contradictions continue to abound. All languages have their own similarly unique limitations.

Our numeral system originated with the Phoenicians, coming to us through the Arabic mathematicians of the Middle Ages. It replaced the more awkward and cumbersome Roman numeral system. (Did you ever try to multiply in Roman numerals? It's next to impossible.) Our numeral system is a decimal system, with each of 10 integers from 0 to 9 representing a different value. Movement progresses in a leftward direction, with each successive place increasing the value of the integer by a multiple of ten. The ancient Chaldeans, however, employed a duodecimal system, based on 12 integers. Some say we derived our measurement of time—which divides a single day into two 12-hour periods, with each hour consisting of 60 ($12 \times 5$) minutes and each minute comprising of 60 ($12 \times 5$) seconds—from the Chaldeans. Many believe a duodecimal numeral system would provide many advantages over our decimal system (10 is evenly divisible only by 1, 2, and 5, while 12 is evenly divisible by 1, 2, 3, 4, and 6). Despite those advantages, however, we nonetheless cling to our imperfect decimal system.

Our symbolic systems are thus flawed instruments for considering, constructing, and conveying reality. Our alphabet, numeric system, and the semantic symbols that make up our language and numbers have limitations. And just as the limitations of our tools can lead to problems in the construction of a cabinet, the limitations of our symbolic systems can lead to errors when we attempt to apply these tools to accomplish practical ends.

For example, we may make the mistake of referring to the human body as a machine and then acting as if it actually were such. The obvious fact is that machines are like humans for the simple reason that humans made the machines in their own image. But the moment we say that the human being is a machine, we begin to believe that he or she can function predictably and with a certain regularity. And, as we all know, that can be a big mistake!

## HEIGHTENING YOUR ERROR AWARENESS

### MISTAKES IN MEANING

Think of instances in which you and a colleague or friend interpreted the meaning of written communications in divergent ways. What were the consequences of this miscommunication? How did you resolve your differences?

*(continued)*

*(continued)*

**CULTURAL CONFLICTS**

Have you encountered confusions of meaning or other linguistic difficulties when dealing with those who come from different cultures than yours? How might you approach this problem now?

## NOTE

1. Clyde Kluckhohm, *Mirror for Man: The Relation of Anthropology to Modern Life* (Tucson, AZ: University of Arizona Press, 1987).

# 6

---

# RELYING TOO HEAVILY ON COMPUTERS CAN BE AN ERROR

THERE ARE NO COMPUTER PROBLEMS. THERE ARE
ONLY MANAGEMENT PROBLEMS.
—PAUL STRASSMAN, RETIRED XEROX EXECUTIVE

Where do most computer errors originate? You probably didn't need more than five seconds to answer this question. Programmers or operators, of course! This fact has become so well accepted in our computer culture that it has given rise to one of the most widespread acronyms in the field: GIGO ("Garbage In, Garbage Out!").

Sadly, GIGO—originally merely an observation—has turned into an excuse, a far too facile way to dismiss incorrect computer output. This acronym, by regarding errors as an inevitable part of the process and something we can do little to avoid, sweeps computer inaccuracy under the carpet.

What nonsense! We need to take a more constructive approach to inaccurate computer output by addressing the source of the problem rather than ignoring—or worse—accepting it. To accomplish this, we should develop a more appropriate acronym: ALLGIP (A Lot Less Garbage In, Please!). Until we tackle the problem of inaccurate computer *input*, we will never significantly improve the accuracy of computer output.

The newspapers have been filled with instances in which individuals, companies, and even nations have suffered grave consequences due to inaccurate computer input. Individuals make errors both in the design of computer programs and in their execution. Here's just a sampling:

- On September 27, 1995, the *Los Angeles Times* reported on a computer error that had potentially life-threatening consequences. Millions of personal pagers across the nation were suddenly rendered useless when a computer operator at Space Com, a Tulsa-based satellite transmission service, inadvertently sent out a command that turned off thousands of satellite receivers. "The biggest concern was in the medical field," the article reported, "where doctors are on 24-hour emergency standby." It took the company's 40 technicians to manually reprogram the receivers, and Space Com is now putting backup systems into place to ensure that such a mishap never occurs again.

- On August 8, 1994, Milo Geyelin, a writer for *The Wall Street Journal* reported on how NCR Corporation's highly touted Warehouse Manager computer program which promised to "track the thousands of items in a huge inventory, keep prices current, warn when items were running low, punch up inventories in seconds, and even balance the monthly books—all at the touch of a few keystrokes," turned into a "virtual saboteur." This "doomsday device" altered, corrupted, and otherwise destroyed data; left bookkeeping and orders in shambles; and inflicted records with "silent death."

  One company complained that it hadn't been able to place a purchase order in five weeks, at a cost of $2,000 a day; another protested that the program listed a part for 54 cents that was actually priced at $114. "Operators at different terminals would find that when they tried to get simultaneous access to the central computer, both their terminals would lock up . . . [in a] 'deadly embrace.'" The program's flaws prompted dozens of lawsuits. As one disgruntled customer wrote to NCR, "This software is so unprofessional and is riddled with so many bugs, it may actually put us out of business."

- On April 25, 1994, the *Globe and Mail* reported that a group of Canadian pensioners would get to keep a "gift" of $14 million from the Canadian government. Ottawa decided it would not try to recoup overpayments it had made to about 8,000 people since 1987. Why? Because a government computer was at fault, having miscalculated the pension payments for years.

- In March 1994, Matt Moffett at *The Wall Street Journal*, reported on Juan Pablo Davila, a young Chilean futures trader who secretly lost $207 million of the taxpayers' money due to a simple computer error. Through a foolish "slip of the hand," he recorded several trades as *sells* rather than *buys*.

  "That typing error and Mr. Davila's ill-fated efforts to quietly undo the damage with a speculative trading binge on the London Metals Exchange led Mr. Davila to squander the equivalent of 0.5% of Chile's annual gross national product. Losing so much taxpayers' money has brought the 34-year old trader the kind of notoriety usually reserved for mass murderers."

Computer errors, all, that have evolved into blunders!

## OUR DEPENDENCE ON COMPUTERS

Computers have assumed a pivotal role in all of our lives. But the enormous proliferation of personal and business computers is only the most manifest example of their place in contemporary society. They also have more invisible, yet critical, functions in our everyday lives. Cars employ them to set fuel mixtures, shift gears, and launch airbags. Telephone networks utilize them to route virtually every call we dial. Retailers use them to scan our purchase, ring up the price, and keep inventory. In hospitals, computers administer radiation therapy, intravenous doses of medication, and countless monitoring tasks. Every banking transaction is recorded on computers, while computerized automatic teller machines even dole out cash.

The pervasiveness of these machines in so many aspects of our lives, however, has brought an unsettling side effect. As we have seen, the smallest glitch can cause widespread damage. The expanding networks of computers have not only multiplied the opportunities for malfunctions, but simultaneously magnified their impact. When something goes wrong, it *really* goes wrong.

For example, new call-routing systems have made it possible to use telephone networks more efficiently. But this increased capacity has also made the networks more vulnerable to a widespread collapse. Between June 26 and July 2, 1991, for instance, computer glitches disrupted phone service in Washington, Los Angeles, San Francisco, and twice in Pittsburgh. By November, investigators had discovered the culprit: a single mistyped character in a line of computerized instructions. Ironically, the typo—the substitution of a "6" for a "D"—occurred in a "patch" intended to fix an earlier problem. The error crippled the four phone systems' ability to prioritize and route messages transmitted through the telephone networks.

The crippling of the phone systems in four cities illustrates our everyday dependence on computers—and their potential for disaster. As the *New York Times* (July 7, 1991) warned in its analysis of this problem, "What other undetected bugs are lurking elsewhere in their networks, lying dormant until the right event triggers them?"

Although the increasing complexity of computerized systems makes it unlikely that we can eliminate all bugs, as you will see, we can significantly cut down on the incidence of computer errors through the application of error awareness.

## SOME ACCEPTED HALF-TRUTHS REGARDING COMPUTERS AND ERROR

Before we can critically examine how to reduce computer errors, we need first to reevaluate our assumptions about these machines. They have become so firmly entrenched in our culture that they have become virtually institutionalized. Whether or not we feel comfortable with them, most of us share certain widely held beliefs regarding computers and computerization—just as we do with all institutions. But are our beliefs about computers absolutely true? Or are they merely shared assumptions?

The acceptance of half-truths about computers, errors in general, or any other subject of scrutiny interferes with the process of error awareness. It tends to cloud our ability to evaluate computer technology and applications. In addition, half-truths can sidetrack logical analysis of computer errors and inhibit the invention and/or adoption of appropriate remedial actions. So before applying error-awareness techniques to the question of computer errors, let's examine some of the half-truths regarding computers and errors in more detail.

### HALF-TRUTH 1

*"Mistakes are inevitable."*

This assumption is undoubtedly and deplorably true—but only as an absolute principle. The assumption falls apart when applied to specific errors. For, it is equally true that no particular error is inevitable and that no specific number or proportion of errors is inescapable. Unless you ascribe errors to predetermination, fate, or some other hypothetically controlling but uncontrollable factor, no single mistake is a certainty. And since you *can* avoid any particular error, this means that you also have the power to reduce the relative number of errors you make.

Imagine that you're in charge of the word-processing division of a rapidly expanding company. Suddenly, within the space of a week, everyone in the division starts turning in documents filled with errors. You investigate their source and discover, with the help of a computer troubleshooter, that you have outgrown your computer's capabilities. Perhaps the computer hotshot says, "Gee, with equipment that old, mistakes were inevitable." Or maybe, "With so many people hooked up to the same system, mistakes were bound to happen."

In this situation, the technology at hand was insufficient to handle the demands of the work. But that doesn't mean that the rash of errors was unavoidable. Had the company expanded more gradually, or upgraded its equipment to meet the heightened demands that this growth placed on it, the errors might never have occurred. This doesn't necessarily indicate that the company *should* have upgraded its computer system earlier. Many other factors such as cost may have been involved, some of which might have encouraged even an error-aware manager to tolerate a few glitches on a temporary basis, until the company absolutely had to upgrade. But this, by no means, validates the assessment that the mistakes were inevitable.

Ironically, this half-truth is often offered in conjunction with a conditional statement that demonstrates the error wasn't at all inescapable. For example, "With that keyboard design, mistakes were inevitable." This plainly indicates that the mistakes could have been avoided through a different keyboard design. Like so many unquestioned half-truths, this statement serves as an excuse, rather than an explanation.

## HALF-TRUTH 2

*"It is costly to eliminate error in the input phase (or any other phase) of a system."*

No one can deny that the introduction of any special efforts to maintain (or restore) the accuracy of clerical work must add to operating costs and/or the time spent by an individual. That aspect of this half-truth is certainly true. Yet hidden in this half-truth is the following false assumption: *Not* making an effort to reduce errors in the input phase *won't* add to costs. The real significance of costs incurred in trying to eliminate errors surely depends on the degree to which they offset, or greatly reduce, the costs incurred by *not* maintaining accuracy—which, as we've seen, can be enormous. If efforts to improve accuracy prove even partially effective, the costs involved in the initial outlay may represent a great bargain.

## HALF-TRUTH 3

*"Making corrections involves going back and doing the work over again, usually out of the normal routine. And all too often, it requires the time and attention of higher-paid personnel."*

A great many companies have found this to be painfully true. And their experiences should serve as a strong argument for maintaining greater *initial* accuracy. After all, corrections won't be necessary if errors are avoided in the first place, or if they are caught by well-established interventions that help maintain accuracy. Besides, neglecting corrections can be very expensive indeed!

## HALF-TRUTH 4

*"Manual processing is strictly from the Stone Age: Automate as early, as extensively, and as intensively as possible."*

The validity of this credo, so widely held today it might almost be considered universal, needs to be carefully measured against the record of all those superbly updated systems (including NCR's doomed Warehouse Manager) that have somehow failed to live up to their alleged promise. After all, technological progress does not invariably lead to qualitative improvements. If it did, the market for hand-tailored suits—as strong today as it has ever been—would have collapsed with the invention of the sewing machine.

Are machines more accurate than human beings? Debate over that has been going on for at least 40 years. My simple answer: Machines depend on human beings. They are, therefore, as accurate—or inaccurate—as the humans who use them.

Obviously, automation offers advantages over human operators in certain cases, especially those that involve rapid processing of massive amounts of data and require sustained, focused attention. In operations in which the work is well-defined and highly repetitive, demanding neither flexibility nor creativity, computers can generally process the material more accurately (and definitely more quickly) than humans. Where human operators have demonstrated a high vulnerability to errors, their replacement with well-designed and applied technology may offer the best alternative to reduce the incidence of errors.

The accuracy of computer output, however, depends on the following three conditions:

1.  The data has been entered correctly.
2.  The software has been programmed correctly.
3.  The hardware operates properly.

Condition 1 is perhaps the most commonly ignored. Yet data-entry systems—in which the system input must go from data sources to tapes or discs or whatever—are particularly vulnerable to error. After all, computer operators are human and therefore just as subject as the rest of us to the influences and contributory causes that make us all vulnerable to errors (see Part IV).

The case of the current debate regarding the introduction of automated technology—tape recorders that may not yet have been perfected—to replace human court reporters, illustrates the necessity for properly programmed software. Those with unquestioned faith in technology, would assume that the use of mechanical tape recorders would provide, by far, the most cost-efficient and reliable records of court proceedings. But how complete and accurate are they really? Words like "inaudible" and "unintelligible" feature prominently in transcripts of tape-recorded court proceedings. And many other words represent guesswork on the part of the transcriber. In one recent test, two different firms transcribed the same tape-recorded proceeding. The result: over 1,000 discrepancies in a 200-page transcript. One example, as reported in the *New York Times*, (November 8, 1990) shows the impact that such differences could have on a court transcript:

TRANSCRIPT 1: "You're *allowed* to give an opinion as to that. . . ."

TRANSCRIPT 2: "You *don't have to* give an opinion as to that. . . ."

Critics contend that tape recording results in ambiguous, incomplete, and even inaccurate transcripts. The accuracy of new computer technology needs to be put to similar tests.

Hardware needs to function well too. Machines sometimes suffer from being too new or too old. In some cases, new technology is introduced before it is truly perfected. In others, old machines sustain wear and tear.

Computers, like people, can suffer from the effects of stress and fatigue when given too much to do in too short a time. And any of these conditions can lead to errors.

No matter how automated an operation becomes, it still links with and depends on human workers at some stage of the operation. And increased automation undeniably affects the people called on to deal with it. When a machine strips too much control from its operator, it can actually heighten the system's vulnerability to error. The most obvious vulnerability is the depersonalization of the job, the reduction of human function to little more than a passive, monitoring role.

For example, the newest models of passenger aircraft have become so fully automated that the airlines will be able to reduce the size of the crew to just two people. Computer improvements have all but eliminated the need for flight engineers on new planes. In his 1995 book, *Fatal Defects: Chasing Killer Computer Bugs*,[1] science journalist Ivars Peterson repeats a joke widely circulated in the aviation industry regarding the growth of aircraft computerization:

> Future automated airplanes will have only a pilot and a dog in the cockpit. The pilot will be included to reassure the passengers while the computers fly the plane. The dog is there to bite the pilot in case he or she touches anything.

Very few people in the aviation industry have bothered to ask about the human effects that arise through the reliance on technology. Will smaller crews with less work be safer? Well, less work can create new dangers—especially when people's lives hang in the balance. The task of monitoring instruments requires such a low level of attention that most people find themselves ill-suited for such an essentially boring task, especially when it comprises the bulk of their job. What impact will increased automation and reduced crew size ultimately have on aviation safety? History does not support an optimistic forecast.

Like workers on an assembly line, the computer operator and/or instrument monitor who has no control or influence over his or her work quickly becomes a servant of the system. Workers may end up relying *too much* on the automated system. If the equipment fails for some reason, the people who operate the machines may find themselves entirely unable to function without it. This impotence can instantly lead to disaster. In April 1990, for example, an Indian Airlines plane crash resulted when the crew incorrectly set the plane's altimeter. But they exacerbated their error by accidentally overriding the plane's computerized systems, which might have detected it. Through the combination of their human error and the crew's overreliance on a computerized system they had accidentally neutralized, the plane landed far short of the runway.

In addition, those who operate highly automated systems may lower their standards regarding output. They may accept whatever comes out of the machine, whether or not it precisely conforms to their needs, simply because changing the operation would prove difficult (or even impossible).

Rather than automating everything, we may find it more advantageous to rely on computers a little less freely than we do now. We may be putting too much power—and too much trust—into our technology.

## HALF-TRUTH 5

*"The computer is a tool of unlimited potential; programs can be designed to accomplish any desired result. So it is best to rely on computer edits and programmed substitutions ('plugging') to handle all input errors."*

Computer edit or plugging programs make automatic substitutions for data that they determine to be incorrect. Their design does indeed continue to improve. As a result, some edit programs and some system edit capabilities are more effective, better programmed, and more up-to-date than others.

Yet one must still be wary. The automatically plugged substitutions may not be any more "correct" than the erroneous input they replaced. Indeed, they can introduce into a system new errors that may go undetected forever. The substitution may be unsuitable or irrelevant to the purposes of your data-processing or information system.

For example, many computer plugging programs can now adequately deal with spelling. But because they do not have the capability of placing words in any meaningful context, they still sometimes substitute the wrong one because its spelling closely resembles that of the word they judge to be incorrect. Errors involving proper names and numbers can easily slip through such programs.

The imperfections in today's plugging programs notwithstanding, more advanced applications continue to be developed. Court reporters, for instance, currently have access to an advanced plugging program that substitutes English words for stenographic symbols. Despite the demonstrated inadequacy of current recording technology in courtrooms, reporters still fearfully anticipate being phased out in favor of tape-recorded transcripts. To ensure they don't become obsolete, they are trying to stay one step ahead of the new technology.

According to the *New York Times*, court reporters now have the ability to connect their stenographic machines to computers. "The computer, using a dictionary of stenographic terms, then translates the reporter's cryptic shorthand into everyday English." Court reporters can thus provide virtually instantaneous transcripts of court proceedings. But no one has yet answered some critical questions regarding these computer-generated transcripts: How accurate are the programs that substitute words for stenographic symbols? How many errors do the transcripts contain?

Worthwhile answers to these questions regarding the accuracy and effectiveness of computer edits and various plugging programs must come from detailed studies, not through the wishful estimates of industry spokespersons. A painstaking comparison of the errors and costs resulting from inappropriate plugs and those that would have resulted from accepting the original text would help accurately evaluate the overall effectiveness of any plugging program. Yet it would seem that very few users could or would bother to undertake a study of this magnitude. Sadly, we may never know how many unreported or entirely unnoticed errors fail to surface at all, or what cost or damage they incur.

More accurate, though also more time-consuming for the user than automatic plugging programs, are programs that call for the user to make the final decision about whether to substitute a new word for the original input. These programs not only require a thinking person to double-check before making substitutions, but in the course of doing so, may actually help improve the user's own performance—off line as well as on. As Donald I. Norman pointedly asks in *The Design of Everyday Things*:[2]

> Do I fear that I will lose my ability to spell as a result of overreliance on this technological crutch? What ability? Actually, my spelling is improving through the use of this spelling corrector that *continually points out my errors and suggests the correction, but won't make a change unless I approve* . . . . I get continual feedback about my errors, plus useful advice. [emphasis added]

To maintain and improve accuracy and a high level of performance, operators need to preserve a degree of control over automated systems. Indeed, designers and/or supervisors of jobs that require the hands-on involvement of both people and computers in any operations should recognize that we should not view workers as merely complementing or monitoring the functioning of the computers. Rather, the computers should complement and support the vigilance, decision making, and overall performance of the humans.

## HOW MUCH DO WE VALUE ACCURACY IN THE COMPUTER AGE?

Computers are no more accurate than the people who program or operate them. We can, therefore, no more rely on computerized systems to provide complete accuracy than we can depend on flawless performance from ourselves or others. Few of us would deliberately abandon the time-honored value of "accuracy"—a quality once regarded as so essential, it was indispensable. Yet in the fast-paced, quantity-oriented computer age, we have tried to shift responsibility for accuracy from ourselves to our computers. And, we have learned to value speed and efficiency above all else.

Computers undeniably allow greater "efficiency" in the processing of data. To justify the enormous and ever-growing investment in their development, purchase, and operation, computerized systems must furnish at least four important benefits:

1. *Volume.* The capacity to process enormous volumes of data that would, for purely quantitative reasons, be impractical to handle through earlier pencil-and-paper methods.

2. *Accessibility and Applications.* The ability to provide direct and immediate access to and application of extensive compilations of stored data.

3. *Speed.* The capability to compute and/or process data at great speed (a pace of an entirely different order from that achievable through manual procedures).

4. *Economy.* Monetary savings, in terms of cost per record or unit of data processed.

How well has the computer industry achieved these aims? Volume, speed, and accessibility have improved—and continue to improve—dramatically. Economy, which depends on speed and volume, is therefore also definitely on the rise. And the already wide variety of possible applications continues to expand rapidly as well. Sometimes these applications are introduced even before the new systems have been developed that can handle them, resulting in the inevitable and expensive problem of "outgrowing your own system."

For example, AT&T recently discovered that the company's computer system was inadequate to track the huge volume of transactions made by credit-card customers and major corporate customers. Just after introducing an ambitious credit-card program and offering special discount packages to big corporations, the company discovered that it had fallen months behind in its billings for these very accounts—as much as $5 *billion* in accounts receivable in each area. The computer inadequacy not only delayed AT&T's receipt of these billions but also created a nuisance for the affected customers. They couldn't pay their bills because they hadn't received them! And that meant they couldn't balance their own books until AT&T straightened out its computer problems.

New technology, though it may fulfill a valued function and even improve many aspects of performance, tends at the same time to introduce new ways of making errors. And when it comes to the "accuracy" (and therefore the reliability) of computerized systems' output, computerization has not achieved the degree of improvement that we so enthusiastically tout regarding their influence on volume, access and application, speed, and economy. Nonetheless, research and development in most of the computer industry continues to focus little effort on maintaining and improving accuracy.

Why then does the computer industry continue to devote most of its developmental efforts toward further improving the already significant advantages of productivity, access and application, rapidity, and economy? Almost invariably, computer users respond to questions about upgrading computer systems with a single sentence: We wanted the system to be able to process even more information faster and cheaper and/or in a different manner. Since most consumers don't demand greater accuracy, the computer industry devotes most of its resources to satisfying what they do demand. Yet since the high-technology elements of information and data-processing systems generally come into play only *after* data has been entered into the computer, this concentration of human resources ignores the parts of the system where most errors are introduced: the original source(s) of computer input and the point of data entry itself.

You may never have considered the question of accuracy in connection with upgrading your computer systems before. But, if you demand volume, speed, economy, and an expanding variety of applications of your computer systems, why not require accuracy?

A few innovators are beginning to focus some creativity on the problem of inaccuracy, and are even making some progress. Interleaf, Inc., for example, has developed a new computer technology called "active documents." This allows operators to insert programming into documents that enables them to "evaluate" the information they contain. Based on this evaluation, active documents will construct graphs, make copies, edit themselves, and send copies to appropriate recipients on the computer network. Interleaf claims that its sophisticated, almost "intelligent," active documents can prevent users from making errors (although the company concedes that their primary benefit lies in the increased productivity they provide).

If Interleaf's active documents not only increase productivity but also reduce or prevent errors, it will be an exceptional development in computer technology. Most recent computer developments, if they have improved accuracy at all, have done so only as a secondary benefit.

Despite their inherent limitations, computers can still offer us much more accuracy than they have provided to date. By applying the techniques and methods of error awareness—analyzing the nature, extent, cost, and source of inaccuracy in computer systems—we can develop and adopt measures that protect us against the damage that unchecked computer errors can inflict.

## LIMITING ERRORS IN PROGRAMMING

Since the computer industry concentrates virtually all its research and development efforts on improving applications, speed, cost-efficiency, and volume capacity, you may have left it to them to take care of these areas. It would, however, be overly optimistic to say that you could blindly trust the industry to police itself assiduously. Computer engineers and program designers can sometimes make mistakes—big ones. As Ivars Peterson explains in *Fatal Defects*,[3] "Software is the mental battleground where human needs, predilictions, and desires contend with brittle logic, mathematical rigor, and inhuman precision. Inevitably there are bugs." And, as Peterson points out later in his book, "nearly all software problems can be traced to faulty human reasoning."

As we have seen with NCR's Warehouse Manager, flawed programming can wreak havoc. And this situation is not unique. Another software firm was recently sued as a result of defects in a spreadsheet it had developed for building contractors to use in preparing and submitting bids. Errors in the program's basic math formulas caused contractors to grossly underestimate their costs. Users of the software won their bids, but subsequently lost their businesses—and sued the software manufacturer. (The suit was thrown out of court; software license agreements still strictly limit liability.)

This situation holds a valuable lesson. Whenever you introduce any new element into your system—whether hardware, software, or operating procedures—make sure initially to check the program for accuracy. Use a pencil and paper to figure the results (even roughly) of several different applications. Then regularly recheck it to ensure continued accuracy (depending of course on the accuracy of input)—especially when those results are particularly important to you or your business.

Moreover, until the reliability of any new system—especially a computerized system—can be established, you may find it helpful to maintain the old system temporarily and redundantly as a way of checking the accuracy of the new one. This also applies to cases in which new elements are introduced into the old system.

## CONTROLLING INPUT ERRORS

With the industry allocating most of its resources to the high-tech side of computers, there's a real need (and opportunity) for resourceful and creative systems designers to pay more attention to the garbage-*generating* segments of their systems. Controlling input errors, however, is something the industry virtually ignores. So we the users need to take care of this aspect ourselves. What are the two primary sources of input errors (Garbage In)?

1. The people and processes involved in translating source material into computer input.
2. The source material used to provide input.

The points at which people and computerized systems link are particularly vulnerable to error and demand careful design of both the workspace and the job task. In Chapter 13, we will look at some of the contributory causes of error—including flawed operating procedures and distractions in the work environment—that can lead to errors by computer personnel. In this chapter, we will examine errors that spring from the material used to provide input. Where does most of this raw material come from?

## UPSTREAM SOURCES OF COMPUTER ERROR

Unless your computer system is entirely self-contained, one of the most prolific garbage-generating segments tends to be upstream sources of data:

agencies, customers, clients, suppliers, carriers, other branches, outside data banks, and the like that provide you with the data you need to operate. This information may be furnished on forms such as cash or credit card receipts, bank checks, applications for various insurance policies, credit, loans, licenses, or permits, mail-order or other purchase forms, or many other documents. Yet all these forms introduce into the operations of the system material that is not subject to the same controls as the system itself. And, just as computers can infect one another with "viruses" in the course of routine communication, so can they introduce errors that can corrupt an entire database.

Although you have no direct authority over these upstream sources (do you know who your computer was sleeping with?), you may have substantial influence over the way in which you receive this input. The acquisition and accuracy of input from outside sources depends heavily on two factors:

1.  The *forms* on which upstream sources enter this data.
2.  The *instructions or other text* that accompany the forms and direct their completion.

You can therefore often exercise a positive influence on upstream sources of data—not only improving the accuracy of the material received, but also ensuring its relevance for your purposes—simply by altering the design of such forms or clarifying the instructions that accompany them.

Designers of most consumer product have long understood that they must incorporate design features in their products that prevent users from employing them improperly. Cars, for example, cannot be shifted into reverse while going forward at over five miles per hour. Fire exit doors open outward. An airplane must have its landing gear down before the engines can be reversed to slow the plane. These physical constraints force users to operate the product in the correct way. Yet computer systems designers have only very recently begun to apply their creativity, intuition, and practical experience to the way data are transformed into input. Even if the industry continues to advance in this regard, we need to apply our own error awareness and creativity to address these problems.

## IMPROVING LAYOUT DESIGN OF INPUT FORMS

The ideal input-acquisition form or format should model itself after a sensitive talk show host. Phil and Oprah know how to ask just the right questions and delicately guide a guest away from making embarrassing or inappropriate responses. Like the talk show host, a well-designed form or format should prompt the guest (the upstream supplier of information) to furnish the audience (both the computer processor and the use to which these data will ultimately be put) with all of the information it requires. At the same time, however the host (form or format) must protect the guest from making improper inputs, thereby safeguarding the integrity of the overall information.

Layouts of forms and computer formats—the arrangement, plan, design, and/or appearance—of the forms through which data are gathered can either enhance or detract from the mental and physiological activities involved in perceiving, converting, and transferring symbols accurately. Yet when forms fail to accomplish their purpose, most people tend to blame the stupidity of those filling them out, instead of examining the design of the inefficient form itself.

"Good design," notes Donald Norman, "exploits constraints so that the user feels as if there is only one possible thing to do—the right thing, of course." This applies to the design of forms as much as it does to the design of heavy machinery.

The following guidelines will help you redesign and rewrite the layouts of forms to safeguard against improper use. They will instead encourage and guide users to fill them out in the way that best suits your information needs. An ideal input-acquisition form should feature a number of essential elements:

*Title.* The form's title should clearly state its function. Assigning the form a number can also improve control.

*Comprehensiveness.* The form should cover all essential steps. You should have adequate prompts and space for all the information you need to solicit. Use complete terms like "birth date," "order date," "shipping date," or "reporting date," rather than ambiguous terms open to interpretation such as simply "date."

*Consistency.* Forms should avoid the use of synonyms. If you refer to an "order number" in one place, don't call the same information a "purchase number" elsewhere in the form. Use the same terms for the same items.

*Logical Order.* The design of forms and formats should follow a logical progression. The various functions (elements, questions, spaces to be filled in, and so on) should be placed in a sequence consistent with a normal, natural train of thought. Whenever possible, avoid placing distracting, unrelated information between items of related significance.

Double lines, thicker lines, boxes, or colored, shaded areas should be used to group related material into logical, clearly divided sections.

*Sequential Spacing.* Spacing should follow the order of the prompts or questions, providing ample room for each response. Forms intended to gather data must provide enough space for the entry of that data. (when building a mousetrap, leave room for the mouse)! Saving space seldom becomes so important that it justifies crowding the elements of the form or format or inhibiting the completeness of a response.

*Adequacy of Shape and Size.* The page, card, sheet, or computer format should not crowd elements. It should provide ample area to allow the choice of the size and design of type most suitable to making the form's text clear and easy to read. It should also provide adequate and even "invitational" space for each expected response. If appropriate, leave room for the user's additional comments.

*Logic and Visual Compatibility of the Layout to the Transcription Process.* The layout of the input-acquisition form should be logically and visually compatible with the way it will be processed by personnel *within* the system—especially with the specific requirements of the transcription activity. The form conveying data from the upstream source to your system should be parallel to the form in which the information will be transcribed. Because it simplifies the process of transcription, the more precisely these layouts parallel each other, the less likely users will be to make errors of omission, position, or relevance.

*Room for Error.* Since everyone makes mistakes, we need to *design everything*—forms included—*with error in mind!* The well-designed form makes it easy for users to correct inaccurate entries.

*Appropriate Paper.* The weight and grade of paper for the forms should be suitable for the intended handling. The color should allow for easy photocopying, even if users are expected to retain a carbon of the form. Carbons, if supplied, should be color coded (and titled) to help ensure that each is forwarded to the proper recipient.

## IMPROVING TEXT ON FORMS AND FORMATS

The most suitable language for any form ensures that those filling it out find that they can readily do whatever they are asked to provide the desired information. Ideally, this text should encourage sources to provide precisely the information you want in just the way you need to ensure optimum functioning of the system that processes this information.

*Write from the Users' Point of View.* Ask yourself what the users will want and need in reading the instructions (and the prompts on the form itself). Include everything that the users will need to fill out the form correctly and appropriately.

*Use Simple Language.* Since about 4 percent of the population has some difficulty in reading, the writing style should not place inordinate demands on the user's reading ability. Forms and accompanying instructions should explicitly, simply, and clearly state precisely what the user is expected to do. Complete sentences are not always necessary.

*Write with Clarity.* Avoid ambiguities of terminology or sentence structure. All words should be familiar to the person completing the form. In addition, short, simple sentences help prevent confusion. The affirmative works better than the negative. The active voice works better than the passive.

*Apply the One Item/One Question Rule.* It is best to avoid questions involving more than one criterion. Use two or more simple questions instead.

*Break the Material into Sections.* Underscored or highlighted headings and even subheadings that separate the form into different "sections" can often be employed to good effect in guiding the data source toward making appropriate responses.

*Keep to the Point.* Provide users with all the information they need, but don't give them more than they need. Instructions should be comprehensive, covering all relevant situations, but should not include extraneous and distracting information.

*Follow a Logical Order.* Whenever filling out a form calls for sequential activities, all references to them in the instructions should conform to the order of actual (or desired) occurrence. In other words, write, "Do this, then do that!" rather than "Before doing that, do this!"

*Identify the Source and Purpose of the Form.* Your instructions should not merely tell users how to fill out the form, but also what to do with it after completing it. State where the form came from and where users should send, return, or forward it. Make sure you have supplied the current address. Provide the name or number of a contact person if the users have questions about the form. Explicitly state whether users are expected to send the original or a copy. Include instructions on how users can attach additional information or explanations regarding unusual items. Also make sure to include a deadline for response time, if applicable.

It pays to scrutinize any forms and formats you use. In many situations, especially if the form will be used in great volumes, it will be worthwhile to develop one or more "trial" forms. Actually testing their appropriateness with a sample of prospective users large enough to be properly representative can provide considerable insight into what works best. Such a trial form offers the opportunity to discover and eliminate "built-in" causes of error *before* they affect the processing system. Then you can incorporate revisions and retest the form, repeating as necessary to allow it to evolve into the ideal document for your purposes.

Everyone in your organization should systematically categorize and analyze errors that occur despite the preventive measures in the design of layouts and instructions of forms and formats. The insights and error awareness developed this way should then be used to guide the development of further error-preventive measures that address the specific causes of these errors.

## FAULT-TOLERANCE PRINCIPLES

One measure to protect against computer errors in general centers on the creation of "fault-tolerance" principles or computerized safeguards against errors in the development and installation of most computerized systems. NASA engineers, for example, incorporated fault-tolerance principles in the Magellan spacecraft, orbiting Venus, 155 million miles away from Earth. By duplicating essential hardware and designing computer programs to recognize and ignore erroneous instructions, whether arising from within the spacecraft or without, they have protected the craft from the introduction of errors. The Magellan stops to ask *human* operators to make a final decision before following an order it regards as damaging or otherwise incorrect.

NASA engineers have recognized that, as the late Heinz Pagels once wrote in the *Washington Post*, "It is the better part of wisdom today to make sure that people, not computers, stand behind decisions." Computers are by no means infallible. Not only the people who enter data, but the designers of programs themselves, are subject to human errors. For this reason, it's a good idea to protect yourself against these computer errors by instituting double-checking systems, redundancies, or fault-tolerance procedures of the kind adopted by NASA. Because we cannot blindly trust machines to do what we want them to do, we need to monitor them carefully—not only to protect against machine error, but to protect against human error as well.

# HEIGHTENING YOUR ERROR AWARENESS

## HOW DO YOU USE YOUR COMPUTER?

Keeping in mind that computers are a vital part of the future, list any error-awareness methods that you think might improve the way you program or operate your computer system.

## BELIEFS ABOUT COMPUTERS

List some general statements that reflect your opinions or beliefs regarding computers. Have you ever tested or thoroughly explored these statements? How did you formulate these beliefs or opinions? Do you consider them facts? Were these conclusions taught to you or are they based on your personal experience, your subjective feeling, or generally held assumptions that you've adopted unquestioningly? Are they the whole truth or simply half-truths?

## THE VIRTUES OF LOGICAL SEQUENCING

Imagine that you manage a fast-food hamburger restaurant. Your preparation area has three countertops in front of the grill. The first countertop has bins of lettuce, pickle slices, and onions. The middle one features stacks of cheese and bottles of ketchup and mustard. The final countertop has bags and bags of buns. Your customers consistently complain about missing ingredients on their burgers. How would you correct the high incidence of errors in burger assembly? How can you apply this information to the design and development of computer input forms?

## HOW DOES THE STATE FARE?

Carefully examine your state's income tax form and the book of instructions that accompanies it. Based on my discussion of the layout and language of forms, circle the design elements or text that could stand improvement.

## COMPUTER EDITS AND PLUGGING PROGRAMS

How many and what kinds of errors still pass through computer edits and plugging programs undetected?

Have you detected any errors that slipped through plugs or edits? Have you discovered any errors that resulted directly from incorrect plugging programs? How much did these errors cost you? Or how much would they have cost you had you not noticed them?

## WHAT YOU LOOK FOR IN A COMPUTER

Have you or your company upgraded your computer system, mainframe, or micros within the past five years? What were you looking for in your new system that your old system couldn't offer? How have you benefited from the introduction and application of the new system?

## COMPUTER ACCURACY

Are you satisfied with the accuracy of your computer output? Have you ever explored the possibility of improving the accuracy of computer output? Have you ever even considered this question? What factors might be involved in reducing the number of errors in computer output? Do you tend to blame yourself or the incompetence of the data processors working for you for any inaccuracy in computer output? What are other possible sources of computer errors? Can you do anything about them?

## IT'S A QUESTION OF DESIGN

Think of a consistent source of errors in your life or work. Is there some way you could redesign the operating systems (DOS or equivalent) or materials or formats to better facilitate accurate performance of the task?

# NOTES

1. Ivars Peterson, *Fatal Defect* (New York: Random House, 1987).
2. Donald A. Norman, *Design of Everyday Things* (New York: Doubleday & Co., 1987).
3. Ivars Peterson, *Fatal Defect* (New York: Random House, 1987).

# THE HIGH COST OF ERRORS

# 7

# THE
# SNOWBALL
# EFFECT

**VERY SIMPLE IDEAS LIE WITHIN THE REACH OF
COMPLEX MINDS.**

**—ANONYMOUS**

On August 29, 1988, a Soviet spacecraft, having traveled 12 million of 111 million miles on its journey to the planet Mars, fell victim to a simple clerical error. The ground control operator was to transmit a complex message that consisted of a series of digital commands. Usually, backup systems are in place to detect any errors or faulty programming. However, that evening, the redundant computer was disabled, and the operator who normally would have double-checked any transmissions was off duty. Contrary to Soviet mission control's policy, the ground control operator decided to transmit the instructions anyway, oblivious that he had omitted a single letter in one of the commands.

What happened after that is a textbook case of how a single, simple clerical error can snowball into a catastrophe. The spacecraft's computer misinterpreted the erroneous message to mean that it should shut off its thrusters and abandon its guidance system. It began to drift, aimlessly. Within several hours, it turned over, its solar power panels facing away from their source of energy. Without the sun, the batteries could not recharge, and quickly ran down. By August 31—only 48 hours later—the probe's systems had frozen, and it had, according to a Soviet space official, fallen into a "deep, lethargic sleep."[1]

Not all simple clerical errors result in such disasters. In fact, countless probably entail no serious consequences or costs at all. But every error has the potential to lead to misfortune. And a careful analysis of errors shows that, except in their consequences, no qualitative difference exists between those that result in serious damage and those that lead to little harm. Given enough errors, however, one or more will surely lead to grievous damages.

What is the cost of a simple error? One not entirely facetious response would be: How high can you count? The exact cost of a specific error, as you will see throughout this chapter, depends greatly on both the context in which it is made and the context in which it is discovered. Undoubtedly, however, one tiny error can sometimes lead to enormous—and even tragic—losses.

## THE IMMEDIATE EFFECTS OF SIMPLE ERRORS

Before delving into some of the possible long-term outcomes, let's look first at the immediate effect of clerical errors that can snowball into costly or even disastrous consequences. The possible immediate effects of simple transcription errors may include one or more of the following:

- Wrong numeral.
- Wrong letter.
- Wrong quantity.
- Wrong identification number.
- Wrong word.
- Wrong column.
- Wrong line.
- Wrong total.
- Wrong meaning.

These immediate effects are by no means mutually exclusive. A single transcription error, for instance, can result in the immediate effect of a wrong letter. Yet this simultaneously produces the wrong word, and possibly the wrong meaning as well. Similarly, when an error results in the immediate effect of a wrong numeral, it also brings about the wrong number (such as a quantity or an identification number), the wrong meaning and, if further calculations are performed, the wrong total.

Many people might be tempted to minimize these effects, using one or more of the following arguments:

- If a letter or numeral gets changed here or there, it can't really matter. Who could possibly care?

- Even if an occasional amount is changed, or a customer or product identification number is entered incorrectly, why make a big deal out of it? After all, if a mistake is made, somebody else will catch it eventually.

- A customer can always return an incorrect order. All errors tend to even out in the end anyway.

Let's tackle some of the assumptions presented in these arguments one at a time:

## FAULTY ASSUMPTION 1

*It can't really matter if a letter or numeral is transcribed inaccurately.*

Although this statement may be true in the abstract, most clerical errors don't remain abstract; they are not merely typographical. The consequences of immediate transcription errors can produce real, concrete, and harmful effects on you or your business. And when they do, they will not seem so trivial.

For example, an error was recently made in addressing a shipment of components to a laboratory for analysis. No big deal, perhaps. Yet it took two and a half months for the shipment to arrive at its correct destination. And in the meantime, the shipper—NASA—flew five shuttle missions with cracked or damaged fuel sensors. Analysis of the components revealed irregularities that, if discovered earlier, would have prompted the examination and testing of all similar components in all the shuttlecraft. Fortunately, none of these five missions ended in disaster, and the sixth mission was scrubbed when the same problem was discovered yet again prior to the launch. Yet had these leaky sensors broken off and dropped into the orbiter's fuel line during a mission, it could have triggered an emergency landing or even an explosion that might have destroyed the shuttle. So much for the "trivial" impact of clerical errors.

Even if you're not an astronaut, clerical errors can have a powerful impact on you. What if the "wrong identification number" means that one of your suppliers sends someone else the shipment that you need to fulfill a contract you have with your own customers? What if the "wrong meaning" causes you to operate your electric hedgeclippers in a dangerous manner? Or if the "wrong total" causes you to underpay your income tax, with all the penalties and interest that can bring? What if the "wrong quantity" specifies how many cubic centimeters of insulin or morphine you are to receive intravenously during a hospital stay?

## FAULTY ASSUMPTION 2

*Somebody else will eventually catch the error.*

This is not always true. Some errors escape notice forever. (This last statement can not be proven since any example of an error that "escaped notice forever" would have to be caught first. Nonetheless, we can safely assume that some errors elude us entirely.) Even errors that are detected may be discovered far too late to undo the damage.

Consider what would happen if the "wrong word," for example, is your first name, and the error causes you to receive the wrong medical treatment while in the hospital? Impossible? You'd like to think so. Yet not too long ago, a veteran's hospital in Albuquerque, New Mexico, admitted two patients with the same surname, resulting in a tragic mixup. Following a rare blood procedure, the hospital injected one man with the AIDS-tainted blood of the other—simply because they failed to get his first name right! Somebody eventually caught the error, but this didn't prevent the damage from being done.

## FAULTY ASSUMPTION 3

*Errors tend to even out in the end.*

Do you have blind faith in this assumption? Do you neglect to balance your bank statement with your record of transactions? Do errors made in your favor tend to balance out those that work against you?

In May 1991, Mark Green, Commissioner of the New York City of Consumer Affairs, released the results of a study of supermarket scanners. The study found that while scanners in the five boroughs of New York City undercharged on just 1 percent of all sale items, they overcharged on 10 percent of these items. This means that the scanners were 10 times more likely to overcharge consumers on sale items than to undercharge them.

As Green suggested, such a great and systematic disparity may indicate that some of these errors were either intentional or grossly negligent. Yet it should also serve as a warning to those who blindly trust errors to even out in the end. Besides, even if, in the larger scheme of things, errors did even out, why would you want to depend on chance instead of taking charge by increasing your error awareness?

## HOW LITTLE TRANSCRIPTION ERRORS
## CAN LEAD TO BIG DISASTERS

Clerical errors seldom remain benignly on the paper or screen where they were first made. To an accountant or invoice clerk, an "error on paper" can lead to serious undercharges in preparing bills or overpayments in writing checks. A similar error in information systems may lead to wrong, and potentially damaging, decisions. Tiny clerical errors in a product's instruction manual can endanger every consumer who buys the product and then assembles or uses it incorrectly, leading to lawsuits, damage awards, and the destruction of a company's image.

It is amazing how a simple error in the recording of symbols can produce disastrous results. Think of data processing operations, for instance. Anyone who has ever let an error slip past the entry level of a database knows the damage such tiny errors can do. They exercise an exponential influence on an entire database, corrupting it and perhaps rendering it completely unusable.

When an error moves into a system—whether your tax return or checkbook, an accounts receivable ledger, or a computer data bank—it enters along with the enormous bulk of correct material that accompanies it. If uncaught, the error can therefore corrupt much of this otherwise correct material, distorting the entire system through the unchecked combination and application of both correct and incorrect material. This combination and further application only magnifies the harmful effects. In multistage processes, a single error made in an early stage invariably insinuates itself into all subsequent stages, influencing and ultimately invalidating all conclusions.

The difficulty of tracking down these kinds of errors after the fact is just one indication of how errors can snowball in multistage processes.

## THE POTENTIALLY HIGH COST OF ERROR

How much do such clerical errors cost us? That depends largely on the importance of what those symbols represent (or were *meant* to represent before the error occurred). In some cases, errors cause little more than an-noyance and wasted time. "Tiny" clerical errors can cost much more than that, however: huge sums of money, ruined reputations, and even death.

In 1986, Prudential Insurance Company of America discovered that a secretary at its corporate law firm — Haight, Gardner, Poor & Havens — had made a typographical error several months earlier. In calculating a lien on eight huge container ships owned by the United States Lines, Inc., the typist omitted three critical zeros:

The sum that *should have been* entered on the document: $92,885,000
The sum that *actually was* entered                              92,885
**Cost of the Error**                                       **$92,792,115**

Had it gone undetected, this simple yet horrifying error in the recording of symbols — subsequently repeated on almost 100 different documents, each time escaping the notice of both Haight, Gardner's lawyers and Pru-dential's in-house counsel — might have cost Prudential over 92 million dollars! Even in detecting it, however, Prudential paid an enormous sum.

Ultimately, Prudential settled out of court with U.S. Lines — which contended that under the clear terms of the lien, Prudential's interest in its ships amounted to thousands, rather than millions of dollars — for "only" $11,400,000. And that didn't include the millions spent in "sec-ondary" costs: tracking down the error, preparing to litigate, holding on to and maintaining ships it would have sold except for ongoing litigation, and attempting to restore both the insurer's and the law firm's reputation. Prudential itself estimated that the typo had cost the company at least $31 million. (A $62 million lawsuit filed by Prudential against Haight, Gard-ner for the damages resulting from the typist's error was settled out of court, with the terms of the settlement shrouded in secrecy.)

As the *New York Times* summed up this disaster, "The omission of three figures from a routine mortgage agreement, . . . a mistake over-looked by numerous supposedly crackerjack lawyers . . . , has generated a spate of litigation, hundreds of thousands of dollars in legal fees, millions of dollars in damages and an untold fortune in embarrassment."

The costs of error, as Prudential's misfortune vividly demonstrates, can be enormous indeed. This example, chosen for its dramatic impact, is not intended to represent the *average* cost of an error, but rather the po-tential *extremes* to which this cost may rise. Yet how rare are such $90 mil-lion errors? Not nearly enough, as both Prudential and Haight, Gardner would agree. And ubiquitous New York City politician Carol Bellamy would back them up in this assessment.

In 1983, Bellamy, at that time the City Council President, submitted a proposal to balance the budget by imposing a surcharge on the city's high-income earners. As she later explained in a letter sent to the mayor, "A failure to program several zeros into the computer" had left her proposal seriously flawed. The tax surcharge would yield just $37 million rather than the $128 million Bellamy had originally quoted—a $91 *million* error! So much for balancing the city's budget.

## IT'S A QUESTION OF CONTEXT

As you can see from these examples, it's not the prominence of the person who makes the error, but rather the context in which the error is made, that most forcefully determines its ultimate cost. Clerks such as the one at Haight, Gardner, as well as maintenance technicians, machine operators, and cleaners have just as much potential to cause million-dollar errors and significant personal and financial injury as those in the executive offices of businesses or government, or space-exploration mission controls.

The context in which an error is committed helps determine the enormity of the damage and the ultimate cost to the error-maker (and/or his or her organization). If you dial a wrong telephone number, the results are often trivial: You hang up and dial again. However, if you make the same error in writing down the telephone number of someone who has called you, you may find it difficult or even impossible to reach that person again, thus suffering more serious consequences.

A recipe in the *New York Times* once called for ¼ cup (rather than ¼ teaspoon) of black pepper; cookbook author James Beard once published a recipe that called for 11 jalapeño peppers instead of just the one he intended. While typographical errors of this kind would certainly have an incendiary impact on the digestive tracts of those who tried these recipes, the identical errors in a different context—the label on a pharmaceutical product, for example—might have resulted in even graver consequences. Depending on the context then, an error may cost only pennies—but it might also cost hundreds, thousands, or even millions of dollars.

Sometimes the context can be helpful, blunting some of the error's damaging impact. For example, in 1991, AT&T was saved from even more disastrous consequences by the context (timing) of a failure in service. A breakdown occurred at 4:50 P.M. on Yom Kippur Eve. Many businesses—including the stock markets—had already closed for the day. The same disruption two hours earlier might have had an even more damaging impact on the company's customers and its reputation. AT&T was also fortunate that the resultant crippling of the air-traffic control centers did not cause any airline accidents, which, in all likelihood, would have forced the FAA to seek redundant systems from other telecommunications companies.

## THE HIDDEN COSTS OF ERRORS

In addition to the actual, direct, measurable losses, which can often be great, errors can also entail more remote and indirect costs. And these hidden costs — the wasted time and effort that went into making the error and the time and trouble demanded to correct it or undo its adverse effects — can be even greater.

Any estimate of indirect costs would have to consider those involved in handling customer complaints, maintaining customer service centers, performing warranty work, expedited service, computer downtime, computer reruns, correcting (or never detecting) billing errors, and so on. Some management experts estimate that these costs can represent between 35 and 50 percent of operating expenses in the average organization. Wouldn't some of this money be better spent analyzing and avoiding errors in the first place?

Think of all the functions and activities that must be performed in an organization as a result of getting things wrong:

- Specialist and management time is unexpectedly allocated to correct the error.
- Material is wasted.
- Extra paperwork and phone calls are necessitated by the error.
- Customers require apologies or demand discounts.

Adding it all up, management experts estimate that the unmeasurable indirect costs of error may be as much as 10 times greater than the measurable costs. And don't discount the secondary losses that can arise out of error: the damage to confidence, status, and reputation.

Take the case of the Heinz Food Company. It manufactures pork and beans and vegetarian beans. Only the latter, of course, qualify as being kosher. The cans which do not contain ham feature a U, a symbol that indicates the contents are kosher. Several years ago, some Orthodox Jews who maintain the kosher tradition, discovered ham in a can of Heinz beans with the U symbol. Apparently, inadequate control of labeling in the production line had resulted in the incorrect labeling of many cans of beans. This typographical error seriously damaged the company's reputation, especially among its kosher consumers.

Your errors can also cause your customers or clients to suffer serious losses. A power failure that went unnoticed for far too long crippled an American Telephone and Telegraph Company switching station in lower Manhattan on September 17, 1991. As a result, half the company's long-distance phone traffic was cut off for several hours including telephone and computer links between the three local airports and regional air traffic control installations. Virtually all air traffic into and out of the city ground to a halt, resulting in the cancellation of about 400 flights and the stranding of tens of thousands of air passengers. In addition, the safety of planes flying through the region was surely compromised.

The breakdown of AT&T's long-distance service brought the company's reliability into question among government regulators as well as corporate customers. The error, the third significant disruption of long-distance service for AT&T in less than two years, embarrassed the company and further tarnished its reputation for dependability and up-to-date technology.

In fact, the reputation for ineptness that AT&T had earned through the error made it an easy target for its competitors. Within a week, MCI had begun a series of advertisements attacking AT&T's self-proclaimed reliability and urging large corporate and government customers to split their phone business between AT&T and MCI as a hedge against another wide-scale breakdown. In initiating its new advertising campaign, MCI trumpeted its earlier success in winning long-distance business with General Electric, Merrill Lynch, Revlon, Woolworth, and NASDAQ in the wake of a similar breakdown in January 1991.

The negative impact of your errors on your customers may end up costing you even more than the original error did. You may lose your client's or customer's business, fail to close a deal, or suffer from the ill effects such errors have on references or recommendations. You may also lose countless other advantages that you anticipated such as potential agreements, sales, or promotions. Errors may even cost you benefits that you hadn't considered or expected.

Because the ramifications, direct costs, and indirect consequences of error vary widely according to when and where the error is made, detected, and corrected, determining the "true" cost can never be more than a speculative exercise. Yet even the incomplete estimates that we can calculate should provide sufficient motivation for us to cut down on our errors and guard against those of others. Our errors have untold costs.

## CURTAILING THE HIGH COST OF ERROR

To attract participants to my seminars on The Art of Negotiating,® I often advertise through direct mail. Like all direct mailers, I am constantly testing new lists to determine which are most cost effective. Although other direct mailers have different standards, I consider a list successful if I receive a return of one per thousand.

One year, I decided to test a new list by mailing brochures to a sampling of 5,000 *Playboy* magazine subscribers. At the end of the seminar season, I was informed that we had received a return of 16 per thousand! Everyone in my office attempted to justify these astonishing figures, suggesting, for example, that the readers of such sophisticated men's magazines were highly interested in negotiating and other business skills. If the figures could be believed, the total mailing list—a million and a half subscribers—represented a marketing bonanza, and I considered making the investment.

Before initiating such an ambitious undertaking, however, I had my office staff investigate a sample of the 16 people from the test list who had signed up for the seminar. This revealed that one company, alone, had signed up eight people—still not a bad return as it was nonetheless eight times as successful as I needed it to be. But since my suspicions had now been raised, I demanded that my mailing-list service recheck with the computer house to see exactly how many *Playboy* readers had actually responded to this mailing, to which they had assigned a code of 106.

This investigation revealed that the results sent to me had been assigned the wrong number. Code 106 actually had nothing to do with *Playboy* magazine, but rather, was a combination of two other larger mailings. The mailing-list service never could tell me how many of the 5,000 *Playboy* readers had responded to my direct mail advertisement. But had I taken the original figures at face value and mailed to the million and a half *Playboy* readers, I would have soon been out of business.

In such cases, when through luck, circumstances, or early detection of the error, you have managed to avoid the worst possible consequences, estimating the actual cost may not sufficiently motivate you to avoid repeating the error. For this reason, you might want to construct a worst case scenario that considers what *might* have happened as a result of the error. Recognizing the potential damage that might have ensued, as well as the actual costs incurred, should prompt you to take action to avoid making the same error again.

The ultimate cost incurred through any error depends on all its direct and indirect consequences. The context in which the error is made plays a critical role in determining these consequences. The other important factor that determines the result of an error and how many people pay for it is the context in which the error is discovered. The components of this context include *whether*, *when*, and *by whom* the error is caught.

## WHETHER THE ERROR IS CAUGHT

Real-life examples of unnoticed errors do not (and cannot) exist without being detected. Yet hypothetical illustrations suggest that errors, which cost us dearly whether or not they are caught, probably entail greater costs if they go undiscovered. Prudential, for example, might have lost the entire $92.8 million had they not caught the typo. In addition to the high financial costs, uncaught errors may injure other people and cause further errors (or even disasters) down the road. For this reason, one tiny error that goes unrecognized may end up affecting dozens, hundreds, or even millions of lives depending on its context.

## WHEN THE ERROR IS CAUGHT

Assuming an error is detected, its ultimate consequences and the number of people affected by it will be determined by when it is found. An error can be detected:

1. When it's already too late to prevent the worst consequences.
2. When it's not too late to correct the error and mitigate the dire results.

As Pearl Buck wrote in *What America Means to Me*,[2] "Every great mistake has a halfway moment, a split second when it can be recalled and perhaps remedied." When further processing, calculations, or even major decisions have been based on the erroneous material, it may be much too late to correct it. New York City Council President Carol Bellamy discovered her own error in time to prevent a $91 million shortfall. Had she not caught this error until later, however, the budget might have been saddled with a crippling deficit, plunging the city into a financial crisis seven years prematurely.

On the other hand, in the September 1991 disruption of AT&T's long-distance service, technicians had every opportunity to catch the failure before it escalated to a full breakdown. A key generator in its switching station had failed six hours earlier. When the generator stopped, the switching station began operating on batteries, which could keep it going for approximately six hours before requiring a recharge. Shouldn't alarms have warned AT&T employees that the station had changed to batteries as its source of power? Of course. But some alarms had failed, some had been disconnected, and some were located in areas seldom patrolled by technicians. When a worker finally noticed the loss of the generator, at about 4 P.M., the batteries were almost completely drained. It was too late to avoid the disaster. The switching station shut down, not simply because of the error, but also because it had escaped detection for six critical hours.

Most individuals and organizations can—and should—employ procedures designed to check, proof, review, or otherwise detect errors *after the fact*. Of course, catching and correcting mistakes after they have been made usually entails certain additional costs. In fact, as Rep. Don Ritter of Pennsylvania suggested to *Quality Digest* (May 1991), "Here in America, because of the way we manage the work process, up to a quarter of our employees do nothing but fix the mistakes of co-workers." Certainly we could do better on this score. Yet despite these costs, it is much better to catch an error soon after the fact, before it leads to even worse consequences.

The National Aeronautics and Space Administration, so highly praised years ago for the Apollo program, has suffered one blow after another to its reputation in recent times. Many of the agency's current problems stem from budget constraints that have caused NASA to cut corners, especially in the field of error detection and correction. In the construction of its GOES-NEXT weather satellite, for instance, NASA saved money by testing components only after the completion of the assembly process. When the agency finally did test the instruments and discovered a serious defect in the power of its sensors, it had to disassemble the satellite in an attempt to find and correct the errors among thousands of disparate parts—at a much greater cost than would have been incurred with earlier tests.

Apparently, NASA has learned less than it might have from past mistakes. For, in allowing budget pressures to shortchange prelaunch testing intended to detect and correct errors in the GOES-NEXT weather satellite (as well as in the Hubble Space Telescope blunder), NASA is employing the same strategy that helped lead to the space shuttle Challenger disaster in 1986. Here again, designers skipped essential tests that might have foretold the disaster and, even worse, ignored the warnings of its own engineers regarding flaws in its solid-fueled rocket booster joints. Had NASA allocated timely funds for error detection and correction, the disaster might have been averted and the lives of the seven astronauts saved.

The sooner an error is detected, the better. It can save millions of dollars, for example, to discover an error before shipping a product line rather than after the products have been shipped and sold, a circumstance that can force a costly product recall. The later the correction of an error, the higher the cost—in dollars, reputation, effort, and perhaps lives.

## WHO CATCHES THE ERROR

It's bad enough when you suffer due to your errors. But when others suffer because they depended on you to provide accurate information or error-free performance and you failed to do so, that makes it even worse.

Let's look at a less tragic example than the Challenger space shuttle. Suppose you make a "simple" error on a business proposal, or a bid for a contract, or a cost estimate. The error, if contained in material that will be used directly or indirectly in other levels of your organization, may be relayed from person to person throughout the company. And it may have serious repercussions, inflicting a cost not only on the organization as a whole, but possibly on every individual who lets it slip past.

No matter what your business, you will probably be held responsible not only for your own errors, but also—if you pass on uncorrected data to a customer, a client, or someone else in your organization—for the error of *not detecting someone else's error!*

# WHO PAYS FOR ERRORS?

Everyone does. We pay for our own errors, the errors of our colleagues, the errors of the manufacturers whose products we use or the professionals whose services we employ. On the other side of the coin, your colleagues, your company, and your customers all pay for your errors, too. Each of us is connected in so many direct and indirect ways to so many different people, companies, and institutions that we cannot help but suffer for their mistakes.

Who has ultimately paid for the monumental error made by Haight, Gardner and Prudential (and would have paid even more had it eluded detection)? Prudential carried the initial burden—a cost Haight, Gardner shared as a result of litigation. But in the end, Prudential will pass the cost of this error on to its customers (and the rates of competing insurers will doubtless follow suit).

Examples like these demonstrate that everyone has a stake in cutting down on their own errors, in encouraging others to do the same, and in protecting ourselves from those who resist this encouragement. Certainly we need to scrutinize the performance of others and guard against falling victim to their errors as well as our own. But we would also do well to work on developing the habit of accuracy in our own use of units of meaning. At first we will work just on detecting and analyzing these errors. But in time this new awareness of errors—and the factors that contribute to causing them—will allow us to suppress errors even before we make them.

The habit and practice of accuracy depends on this kind of cultivated sensitivity to error, and the understanding of how to prevent it. What is sensitivity to error? It is the driving force of error awareness—the first step toward reducing the errors in your life.

# HEIGHTENING YOUR ERROR AWARENESS

## ASSESSING ERRORS

How can transposition, omission, insertion, repetition, or substitution influence arithmetic, spelling, and overall meaning? What immediate effects can transcription errors produce?

## THE IMPORTANCE OF "TINY" ERRORS

Do you agree with arguments that minimize the importance of clerical errors? Why or why not? Reexamine each transcription error with an eye toward uncovering some of the hidden—or even explicit—assumptions concealed in them. Are all the assumptions valid? Can you think of examples that would contradict any of these assumptions?

Now think of situations or experiences—from your own life, related to you by others, or widely publicized through the media—that illustrate some of the disastrous consequences that can spring from "simple" errors.

## PLAYING TELEPHONE

Get together in a group of 10 to 12 people. Have one person write down two or three sentences on any subject. Then, without revealing the actual sentences to anyone else, whisper them—once and only once—to one of the other people in the group. This person will in turn whisper it to the next person in the group and so on, until everyone has heard the sentences. Make sure that none

(*continued*)

of you stop to repeat yourselves or clarify any possible misunderstandings that might arise. The sentences should be restated, no matter how little sense they seem to make. The last person in the group should then write down what he or she has heard. You may be amazed at the discrepancies between the sentences written down by the first and last persons in the group.

## TELEPHONE REVISITED

After you have completed the preceding exercise, trace the succession of errors to their sources. (In all likelihood, more than one error will occur because one person's misunderstanding will fuel the next.) Have everyone in the group write down what they thought they heard. Can you see how one tiny error in a multistage process not only subverts all the stages that follow it, but often prompts further errors as well?

## CORRUPTING THE DATABASE

Intentionally introduce a small "error" into a database used in one of your critical operations. While duplicating the operation without the error, trace the consequences of this error over a day, a week, or more. (*Note:* Although it will probably not have as strong an impact, you might prefer to do this exercise using an old database that you no longer employ in actual operations. This will allow you to see some of the consequences that might have resulted if the error had been introduced. Distance may, however, prevent you from recognizing or acknowledging some of the mistaken decisions or judgments you might have reached as a result of trusting this faulty database.)

## PINPOINTING ERRORS

Think of the last time your personal checking account or business ledgers did not balance, or the last time you noticed something amiss in one of your databases. No matter how many times you recalculated the sum of your outstanding checks, you found it impossible to make the balance of the checkbook equal the closing balance on your bank statement until you *pinpointed the error—*

(*continued*)

(*continued*)

the missing check or the check that you entered incorrectly. So how long did it take you—or your employees—to find the original error(s)? How long did it take to correct the effects of the error(s)?

## ASSESSING THE COST OF ERRORS

Establish criteria by which to judge the seriousness of an error's actual and potential consequences in terms of monetary and human costs. Following an error (whether made by you or someone who works for you), work with a group that includes, but is not limited to, the person who made the error, one or more colleagues, his or her immediate supervisor, and a higher-echelon manager—to assess the outcome of the error according to:

1. Its *actual* impact (in terms of money, time, reputation, safety, human lives).
2. Its *potential* impact (in terms of money, time, reputation, safety, human lives).

## PREVENTING THE SNOWBALL EFFECT

Think of examples from your business or personal life in which you suffered because you let someone else's error slip by you. Are there situations in which others unwittingly suffered the consequences of your error? In either case, how could you have caught the error earlier, before further damage was done?

## THE IMPACT OF TRANSCRIPTION ERRORS

List some situations in which you made the following types of transcription errors in arithmetic, spelling, or conveying overall meaning:

1. Transposition.
2. Omission.
3. Insertion.
4. Repetition.
5. Substitution.

(continued)

Now that you are aware of the potentially high cost of these errors, do you see any steps that you might take to minimize these errors, or at least catch them before they get out of hand? Do you know of any new computer programs that might help accomplish these ends?

## THE SNOWBALL EFFECT

Have you ever made what at first seemed like a tiny error, only to see it snowball out of control? What were the circumstances surrounding the error? What factors exacerbated the error's destructive impact? Did you first recognize the error as such *before* or *after* it got out of control? If before, did you take any steps to curtail its damaging effects? If after, how did it escape your attention for so long?

## NOTES

1. Roald Sagdeev. *The Making of a Soviet Scientist: My Adventures in Nuclear Fusion and Space from Stalin to Star Wars.* Cited in Ivar Peterson, *Fatal Defect: Chasing Killer Computer Bugs* (New York: Wiley, 1994) pp. 195–196.

2. Pearl S. Buck, *What America Means to Me* (London: Methuen, 1944).

# 8

---

# WHAT IT COSTS WHEN
# WE DON'T LEARN
# FROM OUR MISTAKES

## A CRITICAL LOOK AT
## AIRLINE ACCIDENTS

IF ERROR IS CORRECTED WHENEVER IT IS
RECOGNIZED AS SUCH, THE PATH OF ERROR
IS THE PATH OF TRUTH.

—HANS REICHENBACH

C haucer once observed, "Many small make a great." Yet, when we make a slip, error, or mistake in judgment, it's human nature for many of us to put it behind us as quickly as possible. Because we want to move on to new tasks, to "get on with our lives," we tell ourselves that we can't let our errors slow us down.

In some respects, this is a healthy, positive attitude. Certainly we shouldn't wallow in the past. At the same time, however, we must not ignore its lessons. We need to make sure that we don't move on *too* quickly. By stopping to analyze and correct our mistakes, errors, and slips, we can learn from them. And by increasing our awareness, we will simultaneously decrease the likelihood of repeating them.

Although as the philosopher Hans Reichenbach noted, corrected errors lead to truth, many of us fail to correct errors when we recognize them. Some of us don't identify our errors at all, while others never try to right them. Still others attempt to rectify them too late, long after the damage has been done and the lessons that might once have been gained have all but been forgotten. For these uncritical millions, the path of error becomes the path of folly.

## THE PATH OF FOLLY

Those who never fully examine or learn from their errors make the same mistakes more than once. Nowhere does this seem as true as in the airline industry. The following is a selective list of airline accidents that occurred during the 1960s and 1970s, before today's advanced computer technology. This small sample dramatically illustrates how the *same types* of mistakes can recur if uncorrected—and how that recurrence carries increasingly severe consequences.[1]

- On February 2, 1964, a Comet aircraft heading for the Nairobi Airport in Kenya touched down a full nine miles away from the nearest runway! The most significant factor contributing to the error was the incorrect setting of the altimeter. Accordingly, the instrument provided an altitude reading 3,000 feet higher than the plane was actually flying. The pre-flight and flight crews had failed to perform essential instrument checks satisfactorily.

- On September 1, 1966, while on its landing approach into Ljubljana, Yugoslavia, a Britannia plane crashed short of the runway. Again, an incorrect setting of the plane's altimeter contributed to the crash. The captain had not reset the altimeter to account for the local barometric pressure at the Ljubljana airport—information which had been properly supplied by the airport's Air Traffic Control. Furthermore, this error was then overlooked in routine prelanding checks.

- On December 23, 1969, a Boeing plane flying over Surrey, England just barely missed crashing into another plane. The captain of the Boeing had failed to reset the plane's altimeter at the flight's transition altitude.

- On January 10, 1967, a Piper Apache overshot the runway and hit an obstruction when the port engine failed to respond during a simulated single engine approach. In all likelihood, the accident resulted from the failure of the instructor to return the fuel mixture control lever of that engine to the correct position during the landing approach.

- On June 18, 1972, a Piper Twin Comanche crashed in Newbury, England due to a power loss in one engine after the plane's initial climb. Investigators determined that the loss of power probably resulted from a misalignment of the engine fuel selector cock.

- On June 4, 1967, an Argonaut aircraft crashed on its landing approach to Stockport, England. An inadvertent fuel transfer during the flight had resulted in fuel starvation, causing a loss of power to both starboard engines.

- On December 23, 1967, an HS 125 aircraft crashed in Luton, England, immediately following a practice engine failure after takeoff. Apparently, after closing one thrust lever to simulate the engine failure, the pilot had accidentally shut down the other engine as well.

- On January 14, 1969, a British Airways plane crashed in Italy immediately after takeoff. This time the engine failure was not the result of a simulation. The plane's number two engine failed as a result of an inadvertent displacement of the throttle control, which resulted in a drastic reduction of thrust in that engine. Not only did the crew fail to recognize their mistake, they then mistakenly closed the throttle of the number one engine—leading directly to the crash.

- On March 20, 1970, an HS 125 crashed at the Turnhouse Airport in Edinburgh, Scotland, again the result of a simulated engine failure immediately following takeoff. The pilot apparently attempted to apply power of the failed engine rather than the working one. Investigators suggested that the pilot, knowing that one engine would fail in the simulation, unconsciously anticipated the failure of a specific engine—the wrong one.

- On June 29, 1972, a Hausa aircraft crashed in Blackpool, England, after failing to leave ground during takeoff. The failure to remove an elevator gust lock during preflight checks had prevented the takeoff. The error was compounded by the plane's crew, which had abandoned takeoff at too high a speed.

As you can see, the same kinds of errors occur repeatedly. Three different pilots erred in setting their altimeters. Others incorrectly positioned one or more of the levers regulating the supply of fuel to their engines, resulting in a disastrous loss of power. Still others crashed because, after losing power in one engine, they accidentally turned off the other. These errors recur because no one took the time to investigate their causes—and then *to take action to eliminate them.*

Because the airline industry has done a poor job of learning from its mistakes, the same kinds of accidents continue even today. Several years ago, a Seattle air traffic controller's transmission of descent instructions to the *wrong plane* resulted in the Olympic Mountains crash of an Air Force jet transport carrying 16 persons, all of whom died.

A Delta 767 had reached an altitude of 1,700 feet in its ascent from Los Angeles International Airport in June 1987. The pilot, responding to a fuel control warning light, reached down to deactivate the switch and accidentally shut down both engines instead. The plane lost 600 feet before the crew could restart the engines.

On January 10, 1989, according to the *New York Times,* investigators found that a British airliner had crashed in central England, killing 44 people, due to an unexplained shut-down of one of the plane's engines. Most safety experts determined that ". . . the crew, for unknown reasons, shut down the wrong engine." It had apparently made precisely the same error as the pilots of the Luton crash and the British Airways disaster in 1969.

The National Transportation Safety Board (NTSB) estimates that 90 percent of all plane accidents are due to pilot error.

## HAS COMPUTERIZATION ELIMINATED ERRORS?

In an industry thus plagued with repetitive blunders, one would hope that the advent of computerization would help eliminate their deadly consequences. Wrong! As we have seen in Chapter 7, many of us would like to rely on computers alone to reduce or sidestep human errors. But far from doing so, this technology has actually created *new ways* for people to err.

A series of scathing articles in the *New York Times,* for example, documents how air traffic control centers have broken down at least 11 times between August 1994 and August 1995, "robbing controllers of the tools they use to keep airplanes separated and on course, sometimes leaving them completely deaf, mute, and blind." The culprit? An aging computer system—more than 25 years old—that should have been replaced decades ago.[2]

## $500 Million Is Wasted System for Air Traffic Control Will Still Be Outdated Once Long Project Is Done[2]

By Matthew L. Wald

WASHINGTON, Jan. 28—Stymied by mismanagement, the Federal Aviation Administration has squandered 15 years and at least half a billion dollars on a new air traffic control system that is still years from completion and already obsolete.

In 1981, when President Ronald Reagan dismissed 11,000 striking air traffic controllers, the Government pledged to replace many of them by overhauling and modernizing the system that guides planes from takeoff to landing.

But today, in aging control centers across the country, overworked controllers direct tens of thousands of flights each day with the same screens that were out of date 15 years ago. So fragile is the equipment that technicians who open it for maintenance fear doing more harm than good. During breakdowns, which are more and more frequent, controllers carry slips of paper around darkened control rooms or read commands aloud, instead of sending computer messages or clicking on symbols on a screen. At such times, skill and luck substitute for technology.

Even when the system works, controllers are using screens so old, that they "look like all the 'Victory at Sea' movies," as the head of the biggest pilots union, J. Randolph Rabbitt, has put it.

Both the F.A.A. and the airlines say there have been no accidents they would attribute to system breakdowns. But about two dozen times in the last two years, the 25-year-old mainframes that drive the controllers' screens at five of the busiest centers have failed, delaying hundreds of planes each time, sometimes for hours. In Chicago, at the busiest center, there were seven failures last year alone, including three in mid-July.

The major airlines say that even when things run normally, there are about 20,000 delays a day due to air traffic control. Although most are short, the delays cost them up to $5 billion a year the airlines say.

## AMBITIOUS UPDATE OF AIR NAVIGATION
## BECOMES A FIASCO

No accidents *but* delays. This is a typical case where traffic controllers realize that their computer systems are not working, therefore not reliable. They do not depend on systems.

The FAA now has a real opportunity to solve these problems by using the salami strategy. A little slice at a time. They are trying to solve all these problems at once. This has failed over and over again.

See what works in the field and use it.

According to reporter Matthew L. Wald, these computers dating from the 1960s "have such limited memory (the host computer has 1 percent or less of the memory in a modern desktop computer) that they sometimes fail to put any information about a plane on the screen. At other times, they lose the ability to predict conflicting paths, which could result in a collision, or to show, at the touch of a button, where a plane is headed." And sometimes, a controller watches a "ghost" of a plane on the radar screen—a phantom aircraft "created somewhere in the center's cluster of computers," that is not a plane at all![3] The FAA has neither the money nor the manpower to monitor, service, or upgrade these increasingly deteriorating and dangerous systems.

Moreover, a 1989 FAA safety review of air traffic control in the Northeast region concluded that "the most significant factor in terms of providing services to the air traffic control system is the reliability of the telecommunications network." The review suggested that the air traffic control system depended too heavily on a single telephone circuit for all its telecommunications and cited "a strong need for backup contingency systems."

So what did the FAA do about it? Not a thing. The agency neither required AT&T to provide redundant systems, nor did it establish backup systems through other telecommunications companies. The agency's failure to take action had a predictable result. From August 1990 to July 1991, 114 major telephone failures, lasting an average of six hours, disrupted air traffic control, leading to flight delays, increased workloads, and concerns regarding safety. In the wake of yet another serious disruption caused by an AT&T failure on September 17, 1991, which resulted in the cancellation of 400 flights into and out of New York airports and inconvenienced tens of thousands of passengers (see Chapter 7), New York Senator Alphonse D'Amato posed a critical question to the *New York Times* (September 19, 1991): "How many more shutdowns do we need before a terrible tragedy occurs in our skies?"

Because computers are no more accurate than the programmers and operators who use them, we need to maintain control over operations while still taking advantage of the benefits that they can offer. We need to watch over the computers that are watching over us. When computers and automated warning systems fail us, our lives hang in the balance.

When a Northwest Airlines MD-80 jetliner crashed at Detroit Metropolitan Airport on August 16, 1987, 156 people were killed. Due to incorrect setting of the wing flaps, the plane could not lift off the runway during take-off. Northwest attempted to blame the manufacturer, McDonnell Douglas, because an alarm system that should have warned the crew of improperly set flaps and slats failed to go off. However, the National Transportation Safety Board (NTSB), and later a jury, attributed the crash to the flight crew's negligence and the airline's negligent training and supervision.

On June 30, 1991, two jets traveling at a combined speed of over a quarter of a mile per second came within one and a half miles of each other over North Carolina. That's a mere six seconds away from disaster! One of the most disturbing factors in the near-collision was the failure of a new anticollision system on one of the planes, a system that the government required to be installed in all planes by 1994.

In the mid-1980s, the U.S. Army's new UH-60 Blackhawk helicopters would sometimes pitch down without warning. This malfunction caused nearly two dozen accidents, including one crash that killed 12 crew members. What caused the downward plunges? Whenever a Blackhawk flew near power lines, radio towers, or other sources of electromagnetic interference, the interference would garble the computer instructions that controlled a critical horizontal tail flap.

When computers and computerized warning systems fail to function properly, we usually absolve the machines for the disasters that follow. We rightly feel that pilots (or more generally, computer users) must take responsibility for ensuring that the information furnished (or *not* furnished) is accurate, and for the actions they take based on this judgment. We cannot excuse our errors by blaming them on the technology that we too often trust blindly. While taking advantage of available technology, we must maintain control (and responsibility) over all the operations and uses to which that technology is put.

## GOING ON AUTOPILOT?

Computerization of airplanes can further compound problems by encouraging crew members to relax their vigilance. Because machines control virtually everything in the modern-day cockpit, today's pilots need to be fully versed in computerized technology while at the same time maintaining some control over the machines.

Because most of us tend to rely too much on technology, however, we often allow computer-generated errors to go unchecked or unnoticed until it is too late (see Chapter 6). Overtired, inattentive pilots sometimes depend on their autopilot systems. And as modern flight crews have relinquished more of their power to omnipresent and almost omnipotent cockpit computers, they have little left to do (except during takeoff and landing) beyond sitting back, monitoring instruments, and occasionally updating flight information. As a result, the crew's vigilance as well as their ability to prevent accidents, has diminished significantly.

The usurpation of flight crews' power to prevent accidents by computers was tragically demonstrated when a Lauda Boeing 767 crashed in Thailand on May 26, 1991, killing 223 people. Austrian investigators concluded that a computer malfunction had switched one of the engines into reverse. According to a statement released by the Austrian Transport Minister, Rudolf Streicher:

> One of the two engines that were computer controlled during ascent was suddenly switched to reverse. The pilots tried to solve this totally unforeseen problem with the aid of the flight manual, but were unable to do so. The plane became unpilotable, stalled, and broke apart.

Picture a desperate crew, rendered impotent by the current technology, thumbing frantically through a manual as their computer-controlled plane crashed into the jungle. Rather than improving human performance, computers, in this deplorable set of circumstances, crippled it.

Today's commercial flight crews have to clear virtually every maneuver they make through a computer that either approves or rejects the chosen course. Some pilots complain that computers can prevent them from making certain maneuvers that, though unsafe in "normal" flight conditions, may be the only way to save the plane from a deadly crash. Yet pilots have little ability to disconnect the automatic pilots as soon as they suspect malfunction or when they *need* to take control in an *emergency* situation. With so little control, it's no wonder that the alertness of flight crews to the details of piloting has given way to a certain degree of complacency in recent years.

The dependence on computerization can make human pilots reluctant to take charge in a crisis situation. In February 1985, a China

Airlines 747 carrying 274 passengers and crew dived 32,000 feet (over six miles) and just missed crashing into the Pacific near San Francisco, in part because the pilot failed to disengage the autopilot when trouble first developed. As Stephen Barley assessed the near-disaster in the *San Francisco Examiner's Image* magazine, "[The pilot's] performance was not *impaired* by boredom, monotonous environmental conditions, fatigue, overreliance on automated systems and the effects of lengthy and dull monitoring duties, but these factors might have *contributed* to his apparent reluctance to re-enter the 'control loop' and take active command [emphasis added]."

An *underreliance* on computerized systems can present just as serious a problem as overreliance. When unreliable automatic warning signals set off false alarms—crying "wolf" too often—pilots become accustomed to ignoring them or even disconnecting the systems entirely before flight. The earliest systems, intended to warn flight crews of a plane's proximity to the ground, for example, tended to sound inadvertently.

In 1983, the ground-proximity warning system on an Avianca 727 flying over Spain went off. "Pull up. Pull up. Pull up. Pull up," the machine droned. The pilot, no friend of modern technology, apparently lost his patience and shouted at the annoying machine to shut up. Ignoring the warning, the pilot crashed the plane into a mountainside, killing 148 people.

As National Airlines Flight 193 headed into Pensacola, Florida, on May 8, 1978, the ground-proximity warning system deployed. A red light on the instrument panel flashed a warning and the sounds of a whooping siren and a mechanical voice shouting, "Pull up, pull up!" filled the cockpit. Believing he was acting on the pilot's orders, the flight engineer turned the warning system off after nine seconds. Nine seconds later, the plane plowed into Escambia Bay, a full three miles short of the runway! Three passengers drowned in the accident.

The NTSB cited several factors that contributed to the crash. Disengaging the warning system was one error. But the failure of the crew to monitor the plane's altitude and rate of descent were equally critical. The crew had not used all the instruments available to gauge the plane's altitude.

The dependence on technology not only to monitor, but to control operations is not confined to the airline industry. In most businesses that have introduced computerization, the staff becomes overconfident and relaxes its vigilance. Error awareness is impossible since employees view the computer as a savior that will protect them. To make matters worse, automation changes the prevailing working conditions, in many cases resulting in decreased autonomy and increased boredom and fatigue. In the case of the airlines, the results of such a dependence on machinery coupled with an abnegation of personal responsibility are dramatic and frightening: A simple error can easily lead to a blunder of catastrophic proportions.

Certainly, we should take advantage of the technology available to us. But we should heed the warnings of Captain Eric Pritchard, chair of England's Air Safety Group, who insists, "A pilot must monitor the systems and know where he is at any given moment, for if he's complacent, and something goes wrong, there's no time to go back to basics."

We cannot continue to rely on computers alone to correct our mistakes. Although computers—and the machines, like airplanes, that depend on them—have been built to tolerate quite a few mistakes without breaking down, we should avoid becoming so reliant on technological safety nets to catch and correct our errors that we take dangerous liberties. Despite advances in technology, we still need to examine the errors we make, discover their causes, and attack those causes by instituting specific changes. These are the fundamental principles of error awareness.

## THE AIRLINE INDUSTRY'S FLEDGLING ATTEMPTS AT ERROR AWARENESS

In the wake of far too many airline disasters that computers did not eliminate, the National Transportation Safety Board has begun its own error-awareness program. In 1990, John H. Cushman Jr. of the *New York Times* discussed error awareness in the airline industry with the National Transportation Safety Board's John Lauber. "Basically the system, the way we're operating it, almost demands error-free performance," Lauber acknowledged. "And that just isn't the nature of the beast . . . . Human beings are subject to various kinds of errors in various situations, and the challenge is to design a system . . . which is tolerant of those errors when they do occur and which detects and traps them before we have near-collisions or, quite obviously, actual collisions."[4]

Lauber expresses the fundamental principles of error awareness: increasing our understanding and awareness of errors, making changes and redesigning systems or protocol in ways that will show more sensitivity to—and provide greater protection from—errors, and catching or preventing future errors before they lead to disaster.

One of the most important (though perhaps least surprising) of the NTSB's findings is that overtired, inattentive pilots sometimes depended too much on their autopilot systems.

A system currently under development allows pilots to fly their planes under the "watchful eye" of a computer that monitors in-flight decisions as well as the plane's overall flight pattern. The computer would thereby provide an "electronic cocoon" that protects against human error. At the same time, however, it *leaves the pilot in full charge* of the flight and therefore more closely attuned to the flight's progress. If the computer noticed an error on the pilot's part, rather than usurping control completely, it would warn the pilot and suggest ways of correcting it *before* the situation becomes critical.

Such early-warning systems will have to prove themselves accurate before pilots will trust them enough to rely on them. When technology is introduced before being perfected, users sometimes become conditioned to expect—and ignore—malfunctions.

After examining the *causes* of pilot error, the agency has recognized the *need for specific changes* in training, flight protocol, and cockpit design, among others. This kind of AWARENESS is extremely helpful in suggesting the best course of ACTION to follow. For example, the NTSB concluded that poor cockpit design played a part in the two near-accidents in which pilots inadvertently cut off their own plane's fuel supply. As a result, they recommended moving the switches for some automatic systems to a different place on the control panel.

Recognizing the value of error awareness, pilots and manufacturers have begun to cooperate in order to reduce errors. Rather than simply blaming each other for accidents, they have taken action to find out what caused the errors—and then cut down on them. Boeing is currently using the new error awareness gained through the NTSB analysis to develop a plan to sharply reduce the number of airline accidents and casualties. Boeing recommends and is helping to institute the following measures:

- Installation of safety-enhancing equipment.
- Better pilot training.
- The correction of design or construction flaws.

The airline industry merely serves as one of the most dramatic illustrations of the consequences that follow when we fail to learn from our errors. Any one of us who ignores or attempts to belittle our errors might fall into the same trap. And as a result, we make the same errors over and over again. The NTSB and Boeing have set an example that all of us would do well to emulate. Though your own mistakes may not exact a deadly toll, they nonetheless cost you—and those who depend on you—dearly. For this reason, we all need to try to learn from our mistakes. That's the best way to ensure that they *won't* recur!

# HEIGHTENING YOUR ERROR AWARENESS

## YOU'RE IN THE PILOT'S SEAT

Consider the following errors that led to airline accidents: inaccurate altimeter settings, incorrect positioning of fuel levers, shutting off the wrong engine, and poor communication. If you were investigating these crashes for the National Transportation Safety Board (NTSB) and had isolated these errors, what sorts of questions would you still want answered? What would you want to know about the flight crew's operating procedures? Would you investigate the layout of the instrument panels and/or controls? Would you want to know what instruments were located next to the fuel levers or altimeter? Would you have any questions about the crew members' experience, training, or personal habits? Would you want to know whether any of the flight crew had been drinking or taking drugs prior to takeoff? What other factors might have contributed to the errors that resulted in the crashes?

## COMPUTERIZED OPERATIONS

What effect do you think computerization of instrument panels and controls might have had on the incidence of error in piloting aircraft? Has computerization improved accuracy? Why or why not?

## LEARNING FROM MISTAKES

Have you ever experienced or read about any situations in which the same kinds of errors kept recurring? Do the same errors ever recur in your life or work? Have you (or anyone else) ever stopped and questioned why these errors repeat themselves? Might any of these errors have one or more causal agents in common? To develop your error awareness, consider what you might have done to stop this vicious cycle.

*(continued)*

(*continued*)

**GLOSSING OVER ERRORS**

Think back on some of your own errors. Can you identify any that you now think you glossed over or moved past too quickly? Were there any errors that you not only failed to learn from, but didn't even try to examine critically? Although the passage of time may have blurred their lessons, examine these errors now to see if they still have anything to teach you.

**YOU AND YOUR COMPUTERS**

Has computerization resulted in a significantly lower incidence of errors in your business or personal life? Can you think of possible solutions to prevent overreliance on computers to protect against errors? Can you think of ways to guard against computer errors going unnoticed? Would any of these methods apply to your own computer operations?

## HOW TO BE A BETTER INFORMED PASSENGER ON AIRLINES AND STAY IN THE 80 PERCENT SURVIVAL LEVEL[5]

1. When flying, know the airline safety record and its equipment. This information is available from the F.A.A. and on W.W.W.

2. Wear clothes that cover the body, allow for free movement, and are not fire hazardous, like nylons for women.

3. Choose an aisle seat toward the center of the plane and accessible to an exit.

4. Read and listen to safety instructions. Remember that instructions differ for each flight.

5. Always buckle up tightly when instructed.

6. Keep informed about hazardous weather conditions.

7. When instructed to leave the plane do so immediately, in an orderly fashion, and without taking any carry ons.

U.S. airlines can also help to change regulations by following the Swedish study on crew sleep patterns. Allow crews on long flights to sleep on the jobs during the flight (30 to 90 minute naps) with controls attended by other crew members. This cuts down on jet lag and gives better performance.

## NOTES

1. These examples of airline accidents have been drawn from reports prepared by the Accident Investigation Branch of Great Britain's Civil Aviation Authority, published by Her Majesty's Stationery Office, London, England.
2. Matthew L. Wald, "Aging Control System Brings Chaos to Air Travel," *New York Times*, 20 August, 1995.
3. Matthew L. Wald, "With 'Ghosts' and Other Evils About, Controllers Must Sift Fact from Fiction," *New York Times*, 20 August, 1995.
4. John H. Cushman, *New York Times*, 10 December, 1990.
5. From a television program titled "Why Planes Go Down," aired April 22, 1996 on Fox Broadcasting Company. Based on Ralph Nader and Wesley J. Smith's book *Collision Course* (New York: McGraw-Hill, 1993).

# 9

## WHAT IT COSTS WHEN WE DON'T PROTECT OURSELVES FROM OTHERS' ERRORS

### A CRITICAL LOOK AT MEDICINE

THE CAUTIOUS SELDOM ERR.

—CONFUCIUS

In some respects, our relationship to doctors mirrors that which we have with airline pilots. We have little choice but to entrust our lives to their care. As writer Stephen Barley described this relationship in the *San Francisco Examiner's Image* magazine:

> We trust the pilot. We have no choice. We must live (hope to live) with the assertion that the pilot is a highly trained professional who can do his largely monotonous job, cope with his own very ordinary human failings and work in constant readiness to deal with the unexpected.

The same could be said of doctors. Most of us blindly trust them, refusing to admit the possibility of error. And physicians must do their best to live up to this trust. As caretakers of our lives, medical practitioners have a tremendous responsibility to be as error-free as possible. After all, in such a profession, an error could cost a limb or a life. For this reason, most doctors do everything they can to avoid tragic errors. Indeed, some want so badly to be error-free that their shame makes them reluctant to admit errors when they actually make them.

## AN INSIDE LOOK AT SOME ERRORS IN THE MEDICAL PROFESSION

By far the greatest cost involved in errors made by doctors or other hospital staff is the havoc they wreak on the health of patients: the unnecessary operations, the medical emergencies, and even death. No one knows exactly how often patients pay with their lives for errors made by medical personnel. However, according to a recent Harvard study, errors in drug therapies alone account for more than 200,000 injuries to hospital patients annually.[1] As seventeenth-century poet Francis Quarles wrote, "Physicians of all men are most happy; what good success soever they have, the world proclaimeth, and what faults they commit, the earth covereth."

The newspapers are filled with anecdotal evidence of people maimed and lives lost due to medical practitioners' mistakes. In the first nine months of 1995 alone, more than a dozen were reported in the *New York Times*. Here's a sampling:

- On April 25, 1995, two patients who had arrived simultaneously for relatively minor surgeries at Long Island Jewish Hospital suffered disastrous consequences as a result of mistakes made by anesthesiologists. One of the patients died less than two weeks later; the other suffered severe brain damage and fell into a deep, permanent coma.[2]

- Health writer Betsy Lehman died at Dana-Farber Cancer Institute after having received an overdose of chemotherapy to fight breast cancer. As Natalie Spingarn, Vice Chairwoman of the National Coalition for Cancer Survivorship wrote in a letter to the editor about this case, "Grossly swollen, vomiting up, as her husband (himself a Dana-Farber scientist) put it, the 'lining of her gut,' this 39-year-old mother of two young children called her caretakers' attention to her misery, as did her husband. Despite her status as a sophisticated, well-known health consumer, doctors and nurses obviously did not take her complaints seriously. She called a social-worker friend at another hospital and left a frightened message pleading for help. By the time the message was picked up, it was too late."[3]

This is not as rare as one might think. On June 18, the *New York Times* reported on another cancer patient—this one living in Des Plaines, Illinois—who died of a chemotherapy overdose.

- In a highly publicized case, Dr. Rolando R. Sanchez, a surgeon in Tampa, Florida, amputated the wrong leg of a diabetic. According to the doctor, the blackboard in the operating room at the University Community Hospital and the hospital computer slated the wrong leg for surgery. Hospital personnel had already prepped and draped the leg by the time Sanchez had entered the operating room.[4]

- On September 2, 1995, the *New York Times* reported that Memorial Sloan Kettering Hospital had notified Dr. Ehud Arbit, its chief neurosurgeon, of its intent to dismiss him after he had mishandled two brain operations. In both he had operated on the wrong side of the brain. The dismissal was under appeal.

Some medically related errors have long-term social implications, as well. For example, in August 1991, a Long Island woman reached an out-of-court settlement estimated at $400,000 after suing a Manhattan doctor and a local sperm bank. The woman's late husband had deposited sperm there prior to chemotherapy treatment for cancer. As a result of a mistake at the facility, another man's sperm was apparently substituted for her husband's. Consequently, this white couple gave birth to a black child. The lack of a resemblance between mother and child, the mother claimed, had subjected her daughter to taunting and racial prejudice.

## HOW WIDESPREAD IS ERROR IN THE PRACTICE OF MEDICINE?

Too widespread, I'm afraid. A 1990 study of prescription errors made at a teaching hospital counted 905 errors in a single year. This figure represents about one-third of one percent of all prescriptions written by doctors at the hospital during that year. A relatively low rate of error perhaps, but this "good" record would be of little comfort to the 905 patients affected, perhaps adversely, by these errors.

A doctors' legal insurance society in London attests that over the 18-year period from 1962 to 1979, 482 swabs and 946 other objects (such as surgical instruments and needles) were *reported* to have been left inside surgical patients in London alone. If these objects (74 a year!) represent the errors that were caught, how many *unreported* objects may have gone undiscovered? And how many of London's surgical patients are carrying objects inside of them to this day?

A 1989 study of interns and residents at teaching hospitals found that 90 percent admitted (at least on a confidential questionnaire) making errors that resulted in "serious adverse outcomes" for patients, such as complications, longer hospital stays, or even the ultimate in adverse outcome—death.

A Harvard study of medical malpractice reviewed the records of over 30,000 hospital inpatients and found that 4 percent of them suffered a disabling injury as a direct result of their medical treatment.

The Royal College of Physicians of London estimates that 20 percent of all British death certificates cite the incorrect reason for death, and that 25 percent contain other errors.

A recent study at the University of California-Los Angeles (UCLA) found at least one error in the medication histories of a frightening 60 *percent* of hospital patients 65 years old or older! Admitting physicians either omitted prescription drugs from the histories or included drugs that the patient no longer took. And when over-the-counter medications were included, errors occurred in 83 percent of the histories.

The UCLA study found that these errors most often stemmed from two factors. The first involves the demands and time constraints that admitting physicians experience. As a result of this pressure, doctors too often devote little effort to obtaining accurate medication histories from patients. The second centers on the condition of the patients themselves, whose illnesses or injuries may prevent them from providing comprehensive medication histories when being admitted to hospitals.

Given this alarming rate of error, Dr. Mark Beers, the author of the UCLA study recommends that everyone, young or old, carry a current and regularly updated list of medications. Although we may have little power to ease the time constraints and other pressures on doctors, we can take steps to eliminate *our* part in causing errors in medication histories.[5]

We sometimes forget that doctors are human, too. Most of us tend to look on them as infallible authorities rather than as human beings capable of making mistakes like the rest of us. Whatever our physicians say we regard as God's word, never considering the possibility of error. And while some doctors arrogantly welcome this perception, others feel both uncomfortable and inadequate trying to live up to their patients' idealized expectations of perfection.

# LEARNING FROM A DOCTOR'S COURAGEOUS STAND

In a courageous and insightful 1976 article for the *New York Times*, Ray Gambino, MD recalled three major errors he had made in his medical career. By analyzing his medical mistakes, we can learn about some of the causes of errors in general—and begin to develop ways to minimize them. Even if we are not medical professionals, all of us can learn from him.

## THE WRONG BLOOD

Gambino's first error involved mistakenly transfusing a patient who had Type O blood with Type A. Fortunately, the patient only suffered mild chills as a result. The error had its source in the hospital's blood bank, where a clerk erred in filling a requisition slip that clearly called for Type O blood. Yet rather than simply laying blame, Gambino correctly held himself responsible for overlooking the clerk's mistake.

Gambino then analyzed the error in an effort to increase his awareness and prevent it from recurring. As he noted, "That week our regional blood bank had adopted the new national standards for colorcoding, sizing, and shape of identification labels on units of blood. The new 'A' labels were very different from the old labels. Furthermore, the printing was so poor that the yellow 'A' was nearly invisible."

He made an excellent point. Each of us needs to exercise care *at all times* when we are performing essentially routine tasks, but especially when acclimating to a new clerical or operating procedure. As Gambino remarked, "A time of change is a dangerous time because habits are hard to break."

Too many costly blunders stem from a failure to pay attention to details. Whenever processing new data—or old data in a new format—it's important to read what's printed. Moreover, when we perform routine tasks, rather than seeing only what we expect to see or operating by rote, we must keep our eyes open and look critically at what is in front of us. We cannot assume that others have completed their tasks correctly, especially when they may be just as unfamiliar with a new system as we are. Failure to exercise *extra* caution to compensate for unfamiliarity can cause serious errors—in Gambino's case, an error that might have had dire consequences.

This is not so far-fetched. In August 1991, a heart transplant team in Portland, Oregon, made a similar mistake. As a result of mislabeling, a patient with Type O blood received more than a mere transfusion of Type A. He was also the recipient of a heart from a donor with the wrong blood type! Since the risk of rejection increases sharply in the case of a mismatched heart, this error had a fatal result. Of the eight known cases of incompatible hearts in transplant operations worldwide, only one patient is known to have survived.

## THE WRONG BODY

Gambino's second error sprang from a failure to follow established procedure. He described a long and busy night in the hospital's pathology department, during which he performed "four autopsies—one right after another." Just after completing the final operation, "I did what I usually do at the *beginning* of the case," he wrote, "I looked at the identification wristband. 'Good God,' I said. 'It's the wrong patient!'"

Assuming that the right body had been delivered to him, Dr. Gambino had blithely performed the unnecessary autopsy. Not only was this autopsy unnecessary, however, it was actually offensive to the patient's husband. As Orthodox Jews, this family had refused to permit an autopsy, since this procedure runs counter to religious laws and traditions.

There is another valuable lesson here for us. We should read everything at our disposal and employ all available double-checking measures, especially in performing operations of critical importance or tasks under circumstances that correspond to a higher incidence of error. Whenever established procedures exist to guard against errors, we must observe them rigorously, never departing from them, especially if we are tired or otherwise working under unusual circumstances. Indeed, when tired, pressured, or rushed, we should exercise particular care, since these conditions are particularly conducive to errors.

## THE WRONG GAS

Gambino's third major error involved a tank of gas ordered for an operation. Gambino found that no matter how much force he applied, he could not remove the protective cap on the gas outlet of the tank. As he and two colleagues struggled to loosen the cap, he even laughed off the observation of his semiconscious patient, who tried to tell him that the tank had a left-handed thread. When he called a clerk to find out what the problem might be, Gambino discovered that "the tank contained 12 percent carbon *monoxide*," a fact he confirmed when he actually took the time to read the label. Fortunately, tanks with lethal carbon monoxide feature "left-handed threads and different size connectors . . . to prevent the potentially disastrous consequences" of just such an error.

In not making the "extra effort" to check the label of the tank for accuracy, Gambino might have made a fatal error. But, the mistake might not have been his alone. The person who completed the requisition slip obviously erred in requesting carbon monoxide. Gambino's colleagues never noticed the label either. One of the key lessons of error awareness is that others make errors, too. Fixing the blame on someone else, however, does not solve the problem or eliminate the consequences. If Gambino had actually given the patient carbon monoxide, he would have been just as dead, no matter who had made the original mistake. Moreover, numbers do not guarantee safety. Three or four people had an opportunity to catch the error, but none did. Similarly, Gambino notes that in the case of the incorrect blood transfusion, three people who looked at the bottle in the operating room failed to notice the discrepancy on the label.

Is Ray Gambino the only medical doctor who makes errors or merely one of the few courageous enough to admit to them? Sadly, I suspect it's the latter. In his confessional report, Gambino demonstrates a degree of error awareness uncommon not merely among his medical colleagues, but in our society. Yet that certainly doesn't mean he is the only one who makes errors. Indeed, his systematic pursuit of error awareness no doubt means he makes *fewer* errors than most of his colleagues.

## DESIGN CONSTRAINTS CAN PREVENT ERRORS

Dr. Gambino's experience with the carbon monoxide tank suggests the importance of design consideration in *safeguarding* against error: Whenever possible, *physical* constraints should be put in place to distinguish one routine task from another.

Physical safeguards are relatively easy to design and implement, and they require no special training for the user. Yet since they limit the number of possible actions a user can take or physically direct the user to the correct action, they can significantly reduce the number of errors. Virtually every product, system, or technique demands that it be designed with error in mind. As Donald A. Norman points out in *The Design of Everyday Things:* [6]

Errors are an unavoidable part of everyday life. Proper design can help decrease the incidence and severity of errors by eliminating the cause of some, minimizing the possibilities of others, and helping to make errors discoverable, once they have been made.

Designers should expect human beings to err. They should make every product or system capable of tolerating a certain number of errors without malfunctioning, shutting down, and/or injuring its users. Designers of WordPerfect and other word processing software, for example, took this to heart when they inserted double-check commands such as REPLACE FILE? (Y/N) N or DELETE FILE? (Y/N) N, with "No" as the default command. This requires the user to *stop and choose* the correct action intended. Some self-proclaimed "efficiency experts" might object that it takes one more keystroke to do what you want. Yet the safeguard more than compensates for the extra second it takes to save or delete a document. Anyone who has ever "lost" a document knows that those extra few keystrokes can save a great deal of time and trouble.

British Airways recently employed a similar strategy in modifying its fleet of two dozen 757s. To avoid the all-too-common incidence of pilots mistakenly switching off engines, the airline fitted protective plastic covers over the fuel control switches on all its 757s. Yes, when a pilot actually *wants* to turn off the plane's engines, it will take an extra second. Yet these covers will prevent a score of devastating errors and ultimately save thousands of lives, more than compensating for the slight inconvenience.

The design, adoption, and practice of double-check systems can also help prevent inadvertent errors. For example, in the medical field, assigning patients numbers as well as names—and instituting the practice of carefully checking *both* before performing any less-than-routine procedure—could prevent many tragedies. The use of color-coded labels to indicate the hospital floor and/or wing could reduce the likelihood of a drug being administered to an individual with the same last name as the one for whom it was intended.

All of us, whether or not we work in a medical profession, could benefit from using double-checking procedures. Companies that rely too heavily on customer numbers—to the exclusion of all other identifying references—should find ways of combining two or more references to make sure the right order or invoice goes to the right customer. Many of us could also benefit from establishing color-coding methods or other visual signals that cue certain operations, functions, or applications. These signals would cause us to freeze in our tracks if we diverge from the specific tasks associated with them.

One caveat, however. Whenever you introduce a new double-checking, classifying, or function-indicating system, you will need to pay special attention until the system becomes entirely familiar. Errors are much more widespread when new procedures, operations, or materials are introduced into any process.

## ASSERT YOURSELF! PROTECT YOURSELF FROM THE ERRORS OF OTHERS

We need to lower our expectations, recognize the possibility of physician error, and do what we can to eliminate or minimize the chances that it will happen to us. Good patients make their doctors look good just as good defendants or litigants make their lawyers look good or good customers make salespeople look good. To accomplish this end, we owe it to our doctors, others, and ourselves to prevent them from making mistakes in treating us, and to point out any errors that we notice as soon as we discover them.

I once had a secretary who had just been admitted to the hospital for a bypass operation. No sooner did Ethel Gross settle into her room, however, when a nurse came in and told her that she should go home. (Another patient with the same name and operation was to be discharged on the same day my secretary was admitted.) Although Ethel briefly argued that nothing had been done for her yet, in the end she meekly retrieved her bags and left, only to return later that afternoon.

The nurse made the original error, but Ethel acquiesced to it—*even though she knew the nurse was wrong!* As a good patient, she had the responsibility to point out the nurse's error, but she did not have the courage of her conviction. If we *know* that someone is mistaken, it's our responsibility to draw attention to it and fight for our beliefs.

The tendency to acquiesce to others' errors affects us not only in our interactions with doctors, but also in many of our other relationships: as customers, clients, coworkers, or just good friends. Quality management consultant Robert P. Reid recently told *Quality Digest* (May 1991):

> We are bad consumers in this country . . . . The average guy goes out to dinner, and if the dinner's burnt or not right, he'll sit there and eat it and not complain . . . . It's the consumer's fault as much as it is the producer's fault . . . . We just consume stuff, and we're not critical as to what we buy. If it breaks, we'll buy another one."

In our culture, we may feel uncomfortable pointing out others' errors. Perhaps we feel too humbled that all of us make mistakes, or we believe H. G. Bohn's addage: "Wise men learn by other men's mistakes, fools by their own." Rather than helping one another improve our performance, we ignore or excuse the errors of others even when they have a negative impact on us.

For example, when Japanese customers complained to the Tennant Company about hydraulic leaks in its floor maintenance equipment, the company's CEO, Roger Hale, assumed that the defects must have somehow originated during shipping. As Hale described it in his book, *Quest for Quality*,[7] however, he soon discovered that "the leaks weren't just happening in Japan. Machines we sold here at home were leaking too. U.S. customers accepted the leaks. If a drop of oil appeared on a freshly polished floor, they simply wiped it up."

Too many of us don't know how to offer constructive criticism or how to accept it without defensiveness. Yet we need to work on both of these complementary skills if we want to minimize the incidence and impact of errors in our lives. Tom Peters, author of the bestseller *In Search of Excellence*, goes so far as to suggest that it's our patriotic duty to point out error whenever we see it. "If you want America to stay atop the economic charts," he wrote in the May 1991 issue of *Quality Digest*, "change your ways and start howling—over even the slightest product- or service-quality lapse."

Many people don't feel comfortable challenging or even questioning the assessment of colleagues either. Dr. Ray Gambino attributes errors repeated by a group of people in succession to a kind of herd mentality. Because most of us feel uncomfortable sticking out our necks, "all of us are more likely to follow a group's consensus than our individual opinions."

The reluctance to question or challenge colleagues is especially prevalent in relationships with those who have authority over us. Yet such healthy skepticism can often help prevent errors and/or mitigate their damaging consequences. Stephen Barlay includes a tragic case of failing to question authority in his book on aviation errors, *The Final Call*:[8]

> The captain was not only a very experienced, grumpy old pilot, but also the company vice president. The first officer was a very young one . . . who knew his future would depend heavily on the impression he made. They had been flying together for some 11 hours, so by now he saw that the warnings he had received from colleagues were correct: The captain did not bother to give

proper responses to the challenge-check routine of running through the checklist. Now they were on approach to their home base.

The first officer began to make his callouts according to the book, but got no response. Not a word. Not a grunt. He saw they were descending a bit too steeply, but he was not going to question his boss's flying abilities or to leave a final impression of being a fusspot. So rather than say anything, he kept his head down and let the old man get on with it—all the way into the ground. The copilot survived, the captain did not. The autopsy revealed that the captain had been killed not by his injuries, but by a massive heart attack: He had been dead, in fact, for quite some time before the crash.

The reluctance to stand up for one's convictions and point out colleagues' errors is common in virtually every business or professional arena. A Boeing study of accidents caused by flight crews found that crew members not charged with flying the aircraft almost always had the chance to effect corrective action yet failed to do so. The same could be said of errors in business, medicine, and other professions. In most cases, colleagues have a chance to catch and correct the error, yet too often they don't. Herd mentality may not always have fatal consequences. Yet all of us who blindly or blithely go along with it implicate ourselves.

To guard against error then, each of us needs to work on developing the courage to stand by our own convictions. Rather than saying, "They must be right!" or "They can't *all* be wrong!" we need to say, "I'd better see if I'm right." When in doubt, check your observations, readings, judgments, or understanding against those of other people—they may have erred.

To foster this kind of vigilance on a widespread basis, training programs for most jobs or profession should encourage and teach assertiveness. In a recent report on crew-induced airline accidents, the National Transportation Safety Board recommended "assertiveness training [as] part of the standard curricula [for pilots and flight crew members], including the need for individual initiative and effective expression of concern." The same recommendation could be made to medical residents and interns, not to mention aspiring junior executives in any business.

## ASSERTIVE COOPERATION: TAKING MATTERS INTO YOUR OWN HANDS

A colleague once told me about a client for whom he had filed a negligence suit because she had had a varicose-vein operation performed on the wrong leg. On the morning of the surgery, the woman's doctor had prepared her for surgery by outlining the veins to be removed on her right leg with a marking pen. Because the operating room had become so busy that day, the woman had to wait on a stretcher in a hot corridor for several hours before the surgery. Occasionally, to ease her discomfort, she turned on her side. Finally, she was taken into the operating room.

Imagine her surprise and discomfiture when she discovered that although the surgeon had marked the correct leg, he had operated on the wrong one! Apparently, while lying on her side, waiting her turn, the markings on her perspiring right leg had been transferred to the left.

Given this story, when I was scheduled for a hernia correction on the right side several years later, I was concerned about the possibility of error. And so I decided to take matters into my own hands. As the orderly wheeled me into the operating room (under just a local anesthetic), I lifted my head from the gurney and announced, "All right, everyone, repeat after me: It's on the right side!" They all laughed, but they also got the point. And they operated on the right—that is, correct—side. (Most operating teams use the term "correct" rather than "right" while in the operating room to avoid this kind of right/left confusion.) I took the initiative to communicate my concerns in a manner that neither alienated nor offended the members of the surgical team.

The majority of doctors (even those who lose malpractice suits) are not incompetent, but human and therefore just as fallible as the rest of us mortals. Recognizing this truth, good patients (clients and/or customers) do everything they can to ensure that their physicians (attorneys, suppliers, and/or salespeople) do not err. This strategy serves the interests of everyone! And the best way to accomplish this involves assertive cooperation.

You have a much better chance of getting what you want if you act assertively, informing people of it and also letting them know when you are dissatisfied. Tell salespeople as precisely as you can what you want. Let attorneys or doctors know exactly what you expect of them. If the person you are dealing with depends on you for certain information, *cooperate*, hold up your end. Acquire and supply complete and accurate information regarding your medical history to your physician. Share all the facts of your case with your attorney. Let your suppliers know any circumstances that might affect your needs for their supplies.

The kinds of errors detailed throughout this chapter affect all of us, everyday. For this reason we need to take them personally. Whether the errors are made by our physicians, attorneys, suppliers, accountants, or retailers, they can have a direct and negative impact on us. It's our responsibility to catch, examine, and prevent not only our own errors, but those that others make too. That's what error awareness is all about.

# HEIGHTENING YOUR ERROR AWARENESS

### DEALING WITH OTHERS' ERRORS

Write down any errors made by others that have affected you (or people you know) in:

1. Medicine.

2. Any other field of importance to you (like banking, insurance, or law).

List anything that you would do differently *today* to handle these errors, either by preventing them *before* they occurred or minimizing their effect *after* the fact.

### THE WRONG BODY

Based on your growing knowledge of error awareness, come up with a solution that might reduce or eliminate "mistaken identity" errors such as Dr. Gambino's mistaken autopsy.

### THE WRONG DRUGS

Given the causes of errors in medication histories, can you think of any course or action to minimize the chances of this kind of error affecting you? (Keep in mind that medication errors could lead to medical complications, prolonged hospital stays, and perhaps even death.)

### SAFEGUARDS AND DOUBLE-CHECKING

Look over some of the errors that you've described previously in using this book. Can you think of any physical safeguards that you might introduce to protect against an error you (or those who work for you) commonly make?

### PREVENTING MEDICAL ERRORS

Can you come up with any methods or suggestions that doctors— or their patients—might take to help eliminate some of the other errors detailed in this chapter?

## NOTES

1. Ron Winslow, "Hospitals' Weak Systems Hurt Patients, Study Says," *The Wall Street Journal*, 5 July, 1995.

2. Elisabeth Rosenthal, "Deaths after Surgery Prompt Inquiry at a Queens Hospital," *New York Times*, 1 August, 1995.

3. Natalie Davis Spingarn, "Doctors Can Prevent Errors Just by Listening," *New York Times*, 25 July, 1995.

4. "Doctor Who Cut Off Wrong Leg Is Defended by Colleagues," *New York Times*, 17 September, 1995.

5. *New York Times*, December 18, 1990.

6. Donald A. Norman, *Design of Everyday Things* (New York: Doubleday & Co., 1987).

7. Roger L. Hale, *Quest for Quality* (New York: Monochrome Press, Inc., 1987).

8. Stephen Barley, *The Final Call* (London: Sinclair-Stevenson, 1990).

# PART IV

# THE CAUSES OF OUR ERRORS

# 10

---

# WHY SIMPLE TASKS
# ARE SO HARD
# TO DO RIGHT

DO WHAT IS EASY AS IF IT WERE DIFFICULT, AND
WHAT IS DIFFICULT AS IF IT WERE EASY.

—BALTHASAR GRACIAN

Think of a relatively easy, routine task involving symbolic units of meaning (letters, numerals, words), something you do every day at work or at home. It may be dialing a telephone, typing a letter, or entering income and expenses into a ledger. Maybe it's ringing up a sale on a cash register. Whatever you choose, ask yourself the following two questions:

1. "Do I have the ability to perform the task correctly?"
2. "Do I know how to do it?"

If you've answered "yes," then ask yourself a critical question: "*Why then, do I sometimes make errors in performing these simple, everyday tasks?*"

Why do we dial wrong numbers when we've dialed correctly hundreds of times before? Why do we strike the wrong key on a keyboard or cash register? Or enter the wrong figure (or the right figure in the wrong place) in a ledger? If we have the knowledge and the ability to perform the task correctly every time, then why don't we? Shouldn't we know better—or don't we know enough to avoid these errors?

Errors made in performing routine, familiar operations such as clerical tasks are not unlike accidents that occur in the home. Just as we generally assume that our residences are the safest places imaginable, we tend to disregard the possibility of errors in the performance of routine tasks. The truth is, we relax our vigilance in performing familiar activities and fail to pay close attention when an activity is routine.

This chapter will illustrate how error awareness works to isolate and attack the causes of errors. We will begin by examining the general task itself. Then we'll explore the composition of that task—its component aspects. Next we will identify the kinds of errors that can arise from lapses in any aspect of the task. Finally, we will consider possible solutions that might eliminate the errors or catch them soon after they occur.

## HOW SIMPLE ARE "SIMPLE" CLERICAL TASKS?

When we perform the same activities over and over again, our brains have stored the knowledge of how to execute them correctly: how to coordinate our senses (such as our eyes and ears) with the parts of our bodies—usually our hands—that carry out the operation.

Since we have absorbed the knowledge of *how* to do such tasks, we tend to think of them as simple, even mechanical. Clerical tasks involving identification numbers—especially because these symbols have no intrinsic meaning (semantic content) for those working with them—can become a quasi-mechanical process. Yet even this most mechanical of clerical work is not really mechanical at all. Leaving aside the fact that human beings do not function with the level of predictability and reliability that we think of as mechanical, the work performed is *not* truly mechanical either. Because the symbols themselves vary, referring to different items, people, or companies, the content of each unit of work varies too. In fact, this combination of mechanical and nonmechanical processes—the need to apply the same essential procedure to each *new* (and therefore unique) unit of transcription—helps make them much more vulnerable to error than they would be if they truly were mechanical tasks.

# WHAT IT TAKES TO PERFORM A "SIMPLE" TASK

When examined thoroughly, clerical tasks (like most routine activities) reveal themselves to be neither mechanical nor simple. They actually involve a synchronized complex of activities, on several different levels of knowledge and competence. Though listed below as separate steps, we perform them as one, simultaneously coordinating the four (or more) different types of brainwork.

In typing, for example, we have ingrained knowledge about how to gather through our eyes (or ears or touch) all the information essential to the task and how to coordinate the muscles that enable our fingers to enter this data on the keyboard. Yet no matter how practiced and skilled we are, each time we type, the brain must function in several different ways simultaneously:

1. *Recognition.* Recognition requires the coordination of two distinct types of brainwork. To recognize something, you must first perceive the symbols and then identify them—and their meanings—in the "source material."

2. *Segmentation.* You perform the task detail by detail, dividing the work into segments or units to process each one separately.

3. *Processing.* Processing, like recognition, generally requires the coordination of two types of brainwork: production and integration. You correctly apply your knowledge and understanding of the task and the *general* method or procedure to be followed to the *specific* requirements indicated by the numbers and/or letters in each segment of the source material. That's production. At the same time, however, you also integrate the processed segments in a way that makes sense in the context of the final product.

4. *Manual Skill.* If you are using a keyboard, you will need to apply some degree of "know-how." This includes familiarity with the keys and their arrangement as well as experience, competence, and skill in using the keyboard or any related equipment.

No matter how familiar you are with the task or how well you are *able* to perform it, you still have to coordinate these distinctive elements. Usually, the immediate cause of the error is either a lapse in one of these discrete functions or a failure to synchronize them. Somehow, our hands and/or eyes (or ears) fail to function properly in conjunction with our brain and nervous system. Yet this failure stems not from inability or lack of proficiency, but rather from a glitch somewhere in the complex totality of the nervous system.

## THE ERRORS THAT STEM FROM LAPSES

Specific clerical errors can stem from a lapse in the performance of each of the four types of brainwork. Some of the many possibilities are detailed in the following list:

- *Misperception.* You misperceive the symbols, incorrectly identifying them, perhaps because you are anticipating something else rather than simply looking at what is in front of you. This can result transposition, omission, insertion, and substitution errors.

- *Getting Ahead of Oneself.* This involves biting off more than you can chew, segmenting a task into units too large to be handled comfortably. This most commonly results in errors of omission, although it can also lead to transposition or substitution.

- *Babying the Material.* Segmenting a task into units that are too small commonly leads to errors of repetition or insertion. You lose your place and process the same material more than once.

- *Poor Processing.* Wavering of concentration or short-term memory lapses can cause you to enter the wrong symbols, resulting in transcription errors.

- *Misplacement.* A processing error can also involve entering the right symbols on the wrong line or column. Misplacement is essentially a transposition error in which a set of symbols is transposed with a blank space.

- *Miscalculation.* If processing involves an arithmetical calculation, a processing error might center on an incorrect calculation.

- *Poor Skills.* Setting one's hands on the wrong keys can produce major substitution errors. On a less grand scale, hitting one wrong key (or worse, regularly hitting wrong keys) can produce more isolated substitution errors.

## RECOGNITION ERRORS

You probably find it easy to recognize almost without thinking symbols (numerals, letters, and punctuation) and their many arrangements (numbers, words, even phrases), as long as they're in our own alphabet and language. Despite our essential familiarity with these symbols, however, we can still make recognition errors. Symbols used in higher mathematics, for example, may seem foreign to us; letters from other alphabets and words from other languages stymie us.

For example, in July 1945, the Japanese were deliberating over the ultimatum issued by the Allies in Potsdam: Surrender or face overwhelming force. The Japanese cabinet, perhaps trying to buy a little more time to consider the terms of the demand, released a statement using the word *mokusatsu*, a term that unfortunately has two meanings: no comment and ignore.

Although the Japanese cabinet apparently intended the statement to be translated as "The cabinet *refrains from comment regarding* the demand to surrender," the translation that went over the wires read, "The cabinet *ignores* the demand to surrender." The cabinet could not recall the statement without losing face. Sadly, their refusal to acknowledge the error (even though it was not *their* error) cost the Japanese much more than face. The correct—or corrected—translation might have halted the war sooner, which would have prevented atomic bombs from devastating Hiroshima and Nagasaki, stopped the Soviets from establishing footholds in Manchuria and Korea, and perhaps even avoided the Korean War. Talk about consequences that can spring from one simple clerical error!

Even in our own language, words exist outside our vocabulary. And when we confront such a situation, our unfamiliarity may cause us to err. Even when we are fully familiar with both the basic and the semantic symbols, we may fail to see what's right in front of us. Simultaneous translators, for example, perform a function not entirely unlike that provided by data processors. Almost without thinking, they synchronize the fundamental brain functions of recognition (of the language used by the speaker), segmentation (into words, phrases, or entire concepts), and processing (translating into a second language and communicating it in this new format to the audience).

A Spanish translator I once hired for a Central American seminar on negotiating performed brilliantly, with one notable exception. He did not understand when, just before the lunch break, I told the seminar members to "caucus" in teams for an hour after the break, starting the negotiating exercises.

The translator then compounded what had been a simple functional error (a lack of recognition) with a mistake (an error in his chosen intention). Rather than admit his understandable ignorance—the word "caucus," which as it turns out has no easy Spanish translation, was outside his experience—he chose not to translate the instruction at all. I returned from lunch to find everyone sitting in exactly the same seats where I had left them two hours earlier!

Admitting a lack of recognition was hard for my translator, just as admitting errors of any kind is difficult for many of us. Perhaps he regarded it as unprofessional or inadequate not to know one of the English words I had chosen to use. Yet admitting his lack of recognition was the only way he could actually help *avoid* error, or at least avoid compounding it and curtail the error's negative impact. This is true not only of recognition errors, but most other errors as well. They cannot be corrected until they are acknowledged and revealed.

Errors due to lack of recognition are perhaps the most difficult to avoid, yet the easiest to correct. You can seldom know beforehand what symbols you will be unable to recognize. But whenever you do come across an unfamiliar symbol or arrangement of symbols, all you need to do is *familiarize* yourself with it. Go back to the source—your boss, your employee, the author of the handwritten material, or the book. *Ask* what they intended or what they think the author meant. If the source is unavailable or inaccessible, consult some other resource: a dictionary, colleagues, friends.

## UNDERSTANDING RECOGNITION HABITS

In general, it's easy to pinpoint errors due to failure of recognition. Most of us, know immediately when we encounter an unfamiliar symbol. Sometimes, however, we fail to recognize even the most familiar of symbols. Try the following exercise:

How good an inspector are you? Read through the following paragraph just once and count all the f's that you see:

The necessity of training farmhands for first-class farms in the fatherly handling of farm livestock is foremost in the minds of farm owners. Since the forefathers of the farm owners trained the farmhands for first-class farms in the fatherly handling of farm live-stock, the farm owners feel they should carry on with the family tradition of training farmhands of first-class farms in the fatherly handling of farm live stock because they believe it is the basis of good fundamental farm management.

Total Number of F's _____

We'll get back to your answer shortly.

The brain tends to establish habitual patterns in approaching similar tasks. For the most part, these patterns facilitate performance, making it easier for us to tackle similar tasks. Yet they can also hinder performance by setting up a *general* habitual pattern that does not apply to the *specific* task we're working on. In this way, simple habitual patterns can interfere with the way we see or approach new objects—and lead us to error.

Now try this exercise:

Do the following questions and answers contain any errors?

| | |
|---|---|
| What does a comedian tell? | A joke. |
| What's the nickname for Coca Cola? | A Coke. |
| What's the white of an egg called? | A yoke. |

Rhyming words like "joke" and "Coke" can set a generalized pattern that we would like to apply to the next words in the series. So although generalized patterns cannot be applied in every instance, we condition ourselves to write "yolk" instead of "albumen"—and furthermore to write it as "yoke" instead of "yolk."

Similarly, the way we habitually read certain words can prevent us from fully recognizing them. How many f's did you count in the first exercise? If you found less than 36, you missed some. From my experience, many readers count just 27: They miss fully one-fourth of the f's in the paragraph. (If you take special care to count the f's in the word "of," you will probably locate the ones you had missed.) Unlike "forefathers," the word "of" doesn't sound as if it has an f in it, so our minds don't associate f with "of." This habitual reading causes most of us to miss the connection, and fail to recognize the otherwise familiar symbol.

Old habits are hard to bring to consciousness, much less break. However, habitual mistakes can be caught long before they lead to disaster. Instead of reading through the paragraph in the F Exercise, this time scan it backward, letter by letter, beginning at the last word (management) and ending with the first (The). When you actively dissociate the letters from the sounds of the words that contain them, the f's become much easier to spot.

Moreover, our education causes most adults to see letters as integral parts of words, virtually inseparable without a great effort of concentration. Yet if you took segmentation one step further and read through the paragraph as a small child might, letter by letter instead of word by word, you also would have found the f's. This solution, however, which calls for babying the material, can cause just as many errors as it prevents—or more.

Seeing things in habitual ways can cause you to fail to recognize even the most familiar objects. Knowing this underlying cause of errors, however, suggests one way to catch them. Perhaps we need to train ourselves to look at the objects or materials of our routine daily tasks in new ways, especially in double-checking the accuracy of our performance (or the performance of others). Although such errors may be difficult to prevent, the best approach to catching them quickly involves using a checking procedure that does *not* follow the standard processing procedure.

## ERRORS CAUSED BY
## IMPROPER SEGMENTATION

Now try this exercise. Look up an unfamiliar telephone number in the local phone book and quickly dial it. Stop. Did you memorize the whole number, then dial it after a single glance? Or did you copy the number down on a piece of paper and then dial it two or three or four digits at a time?

Recalling and dialing a telephone number illustrates the importance that segmentation plays in the accurate performance of a clerical task. Consider the number 986,745,312. Imagine how you would copy it if you were a small child. You would probably segment this nine-digit number into nine distinct units of transcription, writing the digits one at a time. If you actually try transcribing the original nine-digit number in this one-at-a-time way, you will almost definitely avoid making any substitution errors. And you will certainly not make any transposition errors, which, by definition, involve the processing of more than one character at a time.

But most of us try to transcribe several digits at once. And indeed we *should* move beyond single-symbol segmentation. Ergonomics experts have shown that transcribing multidigit numbers one digit at a time is not only inefficient, but highly vulnerable to inaccuracy as well. Single-digit transcription makes us function much more slowly than necessary, requiring us to go back and forth for each digit from source material to end product. Moreover, each time we return to the source material, we make ourselves vulnerable to error again. If we turn back to the wrong page, wrong line, wrong column, or wrong place, we will be working with the wrong digit and hence make an error of omission or repetition.

Think of that small child again, this time painstakingly copying the word "FARMER" on a piece of paper. How often will the child, despite all the care and effort that goes into getting it right, write "FRMER" or "FARMR" or "FAMER" instead? Parents of small children know that this kind of error is not at all rare. It's easy to lose your place when you segment a task into too many steps.

The way we break up a task can either enhance or detract from the performance of memory—the vital link between segmentation and processing. Although most clerical tasks do not put an enormous strain on the memory, short-term memory come into play in transferring symbols correctly from the source material to the end product. And segmentation of source material into "units of transcription" (which may be just one basic symbol, a single semantic symbol, or a collection of several symbols) can exercise a powerful influence on the accuracy of short-term memory.

How many symbols you can copy accurately at one time by writing down the following four catalog numbers?

3956187739486BL      839X749B841R33L

00034839252013X      624BAD937DOG790

How did you choose to segment this task into manageable units of transcription? Did you break the numbers into groups of three or four symbols at a time? More? Less? If you used groups of three or four, try this task again, this time tackling groups of five or six symbols. Did your transcription become less accurate? Did you find any of the four catalog numbers easier to remember than the others? Which were easiest for you to recall? What made them so?

The solution to this problem naturally depends on the nature of the material involved. Let's look at words first. The strong semantic content of words often makes them much easier to remember than numbers, especially nonquantifying numbers, which generally have less meaning. So if the material consists primarily of words, we can segment the task into semantic symbols rather than basic symbols. Words have such a strong semantic content that we can often segment the material into clauses or sentences: collections of semantic symbols. Because they usually mean something to us, inefficient segmentation seldom results in processing errors when a clerical task involves only words.

Not so with numbers. Except for the smallest or roundest of numbers, few of us can remember more than one or two full numbers at a time. And when the numbers get up into the thousands and millions, most of us have difficulty even tackling the semantic symbol. We need to break the number into collections of numerals to transcribe it. This brings us back to the problem of how many symbols we should attempt to tackle at once.

Bookkeepers, accountants, clerks, and others experienced in maintaining records in which numbers represent quantitative units have become accustomed to dividing numbers into intervals of *three*. Whether you're writing about dollars or dozens, pounds or tons, yards or yen, reams or riyals, grosses or guilders, commas are used to separate the hundreds from the thousands, the thousands from the millions, the millions from the billions, and so on. This method of segmentation, whether exercised by custom or design, actually enhances the accuracy of various number crunchers.

Most identifying numbers—which use letters that don't form words, mix alphabetical and numeric symbols, or use seemingly random arrangements of numerals to signify people, places, or things—do not have the same long-standing traditions that quantifying numbers do in regard to where they should be broken up. The arbitrary relationships established by such systems further complicate the performance of simple tasks. Despite this extra complication, however, good design can help minimize the problems experienced by those who use these systems.

In general, identifying numbers, exactly like quantifying numbers, should be segmented into units of just three or four basic symbols. Results of short-term memory studies indicate that although capacities vary widely with each individual, the upper limit of short-term memory is about 5 to 7 items. (This limit can be increased to 10 to 12 if the person has the chance to rehearse, mentally or verbally repeating the items to be remembered, an opportunity seldom available in everyday situations or work-related tasks.) The average person, however, can consistently and accurately remember just 3 or 4 items at a time. And as you may have discovered in copying the catalog identification numbers, whenever we try to process more symbols than we can handle precisely, we heighten the risk of making errors.

## DESIGNING SYSTEMS THAT MINIMIZE SEGMENTATION ERRORS

In fashioning Social Security numbers in successive units of three, two, and four digits and telephone numbers into units of three, three, and four digits, the government and the telephone company—whether by accident or design—have reflected the average individual's ability to remember numbers. Many credit card providers have followed suit, using hypens to segment the numbers into several units, none longer than four numerals.

Any error-resistant system will segment alphanumeric sequences into units small enough to be handled accurately, yet not so small that they destroy efficiency or increase the users' vulnerability by losing their place. Therefore, to stay within the capabilities of *most* users, units of transcription—with the exception of certain sentences or phrases that have strong semantic content—should be no longer than three or four symbols. Studies have shown that the first three or four symbols in any sequence are the *least* likely to be transcribed erroneously.

This finding should offer some guidance if you want to design error-resistant information systems or data-processing procedures. Encourage segmentation into units of three or four symbols each, a strategy that essentially makes every three or four symbols the "first" three or four symbols in a new sequence.

You can arrange identifying numbers in a way that suggests how best to segment them. Longer sequences should incorporate spaces, hyphens, dashes, or other nonalphanumeric symbols to segment the array into manageable units. This will encourage users to break up the numbers. Don't require a person to remember more than four (or at most, five) items at one time. By prompting the user to automatically segment the identifying number into three- and four-character strings, you will make them easier to remember and transcribe correctly.

In addition, letters of the alphabet provide a powerful way to break up sequences of numerals that have little or no meaning on their own. Letters inserted as part of an sequence become especially easy to remember when they form words (or at least quasi-words that lend themselves to enunciation). For example, in the catalog numbers I asked you to copy earlier, the numbers in the second column employ letters to suggest where users should segment them. The first item in the second column (839X749B841R33L) uses discrete letters to break the long catalog number into four units of three or four alphanumeric symbols each. The second item in the column (624BAD937DOG790) was probably even easier to remember. In addition to breaking the numerals into units of three each, the letters "spell out" words. This strategy enables users to break up the catalog number into longer (six-character) segments when transcribing it—for example, 624BAD followed by 937DOG, and finally 790.

Using letters in this way can enhance recall and thereby reduce processing errors. But no matter how you go about it, *imposing* segmentation into three- or four-digit units of transcription will minimize the susceptibility of your system to error. By inserting symbols that tell users where to break up a sequence, you eliminate their need to figure out where best to segment the array. And this will minimize errors by overeager users who try to bite off more symbols than they can accurately chew as well as those by overcautious users who baby the numbers in your system.

The preceding strategies will help guard against the segmentation errors of others that might affect you or your business. But you can also tackle your own segmentation errors. No matter how much ability you currently have, you can improve your memory. And one of the best ways to develop the ability to make less errors is to build your memory gradually while performing the task correctly (see Chapter 15). Practice really does make perfect—even if you have to begin with small segments.

You can begin to minimize errors by confining your segmentation to reflect your current abilities. Limiting your segmentation will train you to better coordinate recognition and perception of the source material with the processing task, and thus to perform with greater accuracy. Enhanced coordination and accuracy will then allow you to tackle increasingly larger groups of symbols while retaining your improved reliability and your confidence.

## MANUAL SKILL ERRORS

If the source of a clerical error involves a lack of manual skill, the prescribed treatment is obvious: improved training to break bad habits and dedicated practice. Training that not only improves speed and productivity but skill as well can have an immediate and positive impact on accuracy. Indeed, certain computer-based training programs now on the market claim not only to improve familiarity with the alphanumeric elements on a standard keyboard, but also to signal users to errors made during training and direct them to remedial exercises designed to eliminate them. Since most training programs of this kind take only 20 to 40 hours to complete and can reduce errors by 50 percent or more, many users find them well worth the effort.

The benefits of improving manual skill go well beyond the increase in accuracy and productivity. When you can perform a routine task without really thinking about its manual aspect (such as keyboarding), it frees your mind to be more creative and flexible in responding to the specific demands of the task. As Alfred North Whitehead once observed, "It is a profoundly erroneous truism . . . that we should cultivate the habit of thinking of what we are doing. The precise opposite is the case. Civilization advances by extending the number of important operations that we can perform without thinking about them." In improving your manual skill, you will free your mind to concentrate on the other elements of brainwork involved in the task.

## MENTAL JUGGLING

Even if you improve your manual skill and enhance your knowledge and ability to perform these various types of brainwork with enough competence to handle the task, these efforts do not guarantee lack of error. You may recognize and feel fully familiar with all the symbols in your source material. You may segment the task into the most efficient units of transcription. And you may know how to process and integrate the material in accordance with the task at hand. Yet you still need to coordinate all three elements of brainwork (as well as the fourth if you need manual skill) so that they work together smoothly, efficiently, and accurately. If these different elements get "out of sync" for any reason, you will make errors.

In the F Exercise, for example, you certainly had the ability to recognize the letter f, and also the skill needed to break the paragraph down into units small enough to pinpoint the f's. Yet for most people taking this test, segmentation (into words) interferes with recognition of the f's. And this interference in turn affects the ability to process the task correctly.

Having two elements of brainwork out of sync can often set off a chain reaction that affects all other types of brainwork as well. Most errors in the performance of routine tasks or skills stem from just this sort of coordination lapse. The different levels of mental activity required to complete the task correctly are out of sync. Attempting to keep the various functions of the brain in harmony is therefore one of the key strategies we must adopt to reduce or eliminate error. In Chapter 12, we will explore these strategies more definitively.

# HEIGHTENING YOUR ERROR AWARENESS

### THE BRAINWORK OF SIMPLE TASKS

Think of any routine task that you perform in which you apply all of the following elements:

1. Recognition.
2. Segmentation.
3. Processing.
4. Manual skill.

Do you tend to make more errors in exercising one of these functions than the others? Applying your newly enhanced error awareness, what plan might you come up with to decrease the errors you make?

### CLERICAL ERRORS

Identify some of the kinds of clerical errors that might stem from a lapse in the performance of each of these four types of brainwork.

### ERRORS THAT STEM FROM LAPSES

Consider the various types of errors that stem from lapses: misperception, babying the material, getting ahead of oneself, miscalculation, poor skills. What remedial solutions might eliminate or significantly reduce any of these?

### LACK OF RECOGNITION ERRORS

What would you do to correct an error due to lack of recognition? Think of a time when you came on a word or other symbol that you didn't recognize in reading a report or a memo, or an occasion when someone used a word or made a reference in conversation that you were unfamiliar with. How did you respond to this lack of recognition?

(*continued*)

Can errors due to lack of recognition be prevented? What technique would allow them to be caught before they got out of hand?

## TELEPHONE ACCURACY

The method you chose to use in the telephone exercise is probably your habitual way of dialing a new number. How often do you get the wrong number using this method? Can you think of any changes you might make in the way you look up, record, or dial/touch-tone the number to improve your accuracy?

## SEGMENTATION ERRORS

How many symbols should we attempt to tackle at once? How can we best segment a clerical task to reduce the chances of making processing errors while still maintaining efficiency?

What errors have you made due to improper segmentation? What methods might you now employ to decrease the errors you make as a result of poor segmentation?

# 11

---

# HOW TO CUT DOWN ON READING ERRORS

... THE DEPTH AND BENEFITS OF READING VARIES
IN PROPORTION TO THE DEPTH OF ONE'S OWN
EXPERIENCE.

—CHANG CH'AO

D o most of us know the letters and numerals that we are reading now on this page? Of course we do. We are entirely familiar with virtually all the symbols we use on a day-to-day basis. Yet despite this familiarity, we occasionally fall prey to errors caused by their misidentification.

We read a letter or a numeral as something other than what the person who originally recorded it intended to represent. (Mis)taking one symbol for another, we distort the author's intention. We create a semantic gap — a significant difference between the meaning the author wanted to convey and the one we actually received.

Why might we misidentify such common symbols? With a foreign alphabet, recognition errors are immediately understandable, even if we have worked to learn the language. Yet with letters and numerals we use daily, an explanation seems somewhat more elusive. Shouldn't the universality of symbols and the regularity of our perceptual patterns protect us from virtually all errors of misidentification? What possible factors might cause us to err in recognizing all-too-familiar letters and numerals? If not unfamiliarity, then what?

To begin exploring these questions, let's look at another example of the failure to recognize a familiar object. Have you ever walked past someone you know without recognizing him? Perhaps he stopped you to say hello and only then did you recognize him. Or maybe you heard later that you had passed him on the street, entirely oblivious of having failed to identify him. Why does this occur so commonly? Several possibilities suggest themselves:

1. You weren't paying attention to the person you were passing. If he stopped you, however, you no doubt focused on him, and this shift in concentration prompted recognition.

2. The context of being on the street was too foreign from situations in which you had previously met. Context can help recognition. When you walk into a business meeting with people you've met only once before, your anticipation and the surrounding context make it easier to place them.

3. The person had a new hairstyle, wore new clothes, or sported a "new look" that sharply differed from the last time you met. The image of the person you passed on the street therefore did not match the memory you had of him.

4. You had forgotten to wear your glasses or contact lenses, making it difficult to see buildings, much less recognize faces.

5. Perhaps you had only met this person once or twice before. Though he was somewhat familiar, you weren't entirely familiar with him. It's relatively common to fail to recognize people you've met only a few times.

Could any of these explanations also apply to situations in which you do not recognize a numeral or letter? Certainly the first four might:

1. A lapse in concentration can cause errors of all kinds, including but by no means limited to recognition errors. Fully focused attention could thus help eliminate many recognition errors.

2. Context can either enhance or detract from recognition. For example, if you saw a Z or an I or an O in midst of an array of numerals, you might easily make the mistake of reading it as 2 or 1 or 0.

3. Letters or numerals with a "new look" can easily be misread or mistaken for others. An elaborate or otherwise unfamiliar typeface or a hastily written, barely legible scrawl might make recognition more

difficult. This failure of the symbols to match accepted archetypes is perhaps the foremost cause of recognition errors involving alphanumeric symbols.

4. Poor vision can certainly be a cause of recognition errors. In fact, it probably ranks as one of the top two causes.

The fifth explanation, however, though it might account for the failure to recognize a passing acquaintance, definitely does not apply to the use of common letters and numerals. The fact that you are reading this book indicates that you have more than a fleeting familiarity with English letters and numerals. So you cannot point to this as a reason for your recognition errors.

Of the four factors listed, one may do us little good. We have little control over the context in which alphanumeric symbols appear. To convey a specific semantic meaning, basic symbols must appear in a certain order. We may be unable to alter their context without sacrificing accuracy or clarity. However, we can exercise considerable influence on the other three factors.

And, although factors that contribute to lapses in concentration can exacerbate the likelihood of recognition errors (see Chapter 12 for more on this), most errors of this kind arise due to an unfamiliar new look, poor vision, or a combination of the two. The rest of this chapter will explore these two causes of recognition errors in reading symbols and point toward some solutions that might reduce or eliminate them.

## THE IMPACT OF ILLEGIBILITY

The sheer illegibility or ambiguous legibility of source documents, especially handwritten ones, can cause a degree of unfamiliarity that differs so significantly from the intended symbol that it muddles or even defies recognition. Poor legibility is the most common cause of misperception and misidentification of symbols. It may render symbols either indistinct from others or almost entirely meaningless.

To minimize the possibility of recognition errors, symbols must therefore be both legible and *easily* identifiable. A hard-to-recognize symbol or set of symbols, however, fails to meet one or both of the following criteria:

1. *Basic Legibility.* The arrangement of lines—or dots on a computer monitor or printout—intended to represent a specific symbol must be recognizable as such.

2. *Symbolic Differentiation.* The arrangement of lines or dots intended to represent a symbol should be distinctive. To differentiate among the symbols, the physical characteristics of the archetypes themselves must also be unique.

Illegible symbols are like blurry photographs of your spouse and children. No matter how well you know your family, you may fail to identify them in a folio of blurred photographs. So it is with alphanumeric symbols that fail to meet the criterion of basic legibility. And, if some of your children were identical twins or triplets, the lack of "symbolic differentiation" might make recognition more difficult. Although you might have little difficulty recognizing which kid is which in person, you might still make some errors in identifying their photographs.

## THE PERILS OF SCRIPT

Without a doubt, cursive handwriting or script is most susceptible to illegibility and therefore has the highest vulnerability to error. The prevalent use of handwriting is the single greatest enemy of basic legibility and symbolic differentiation.

Script prizes speed over accuracy. Especially when written hastily or under extreme pressure, some cursive symbols—and even entire words— fail the basic legibility test: They appear to be meaningless scribbles, making them all but indecipherable.

Consider the most notorious of all handwriting samples: physicians' notes on patients' medical charts. In a hospital setting, doctors always work under severe time constraints. Most use rapidly scrawled script in entering their medical notes and writing prescriptions. Although other medical professionals and staff members become quite adept at deciphering physicians' scratches, the illegibility of these notes often results in delays of treatment and/or time wasted by other staff members trying to make sense of them. Occasionally, it leads to even more serious consequences, such as inappropriate treatments or incorrect prescriptions.

The overreliance on script exerts a paradoxical effect on speed and efficiency. Although quicker to produce than handprinting, script increases the vulnerability of documents to errors of recognition or interpretation, and this increased likelihood hampers any later use of the document. So the time saved by writing in script all too often costs time in *reading* it or in checking one's reading with others. Pity the poor hospital staff (and their patients) who need to decipher doctors' notes. At the very least, the use of script can cost more time, and even then, the reading may be inaccurate.

If you've never seen it before (and even if you have), I recommend that you rent Woody Allen's early film *Take the Money and Run*. If you can stop laughing for a few minutes, pay particular attention to the scene in which the hapless Allen tries to rob a bank by giving a teller a handwritten note. The illegibility of the note soon demands the consultation of a dozen bank employees, causing such a delay that the police arrive and make the arrest. Although Allen plays the scene for laughs, it highlights the wasted time and heightened frustration that illegibility can incur.

Cursive handwriting also fails to fulfill the second criterion of legibility: symbolic differentiation. The various symbols employed in standard script lack distinctiveness. Some lower-case letters are particularly ill-defined. For example, although many cursive symbols are vulnerable to misidentification, the most susceptible are lower-case g's and q's, m's and n's, and y's and z's. Lower-case c's, e's, l's, and b's—all of which involve the same curving stroke—are often mistaken for one another, as are lower-case i's, u's, w's and r's.

Like all symbolic systems of conveying information, our alphanumeric system is inherently vulnerable to error. Since many of the symbols share a number of similar, or even identical, physical characteristics, symbolic differentiation often poses a problem.

## SOLUTIONS TO HANDWRITING PROBLEMS

Can we apply error awareness to illegibility and poor symbolic differentiation to cut down on recognition errors? Of course we can.

The particular vulnerability of cursive writing to errors of recognition or interpretation suggests a relatively easy cure. People who have poor handwriting should handprint, type, or keyboard *everything*—all business correspondence, interoffice memos, personal letters, notes to themselves or others—but their signatures. And, if you have difficulty reading the handwriting of others, advise them to do the same.

Research by Bell Laboratories several years ago revealed that most handprinting errors (in telephone operations) involve differentiation problems, usually the substitution of one letter or numeral for another. At the same time, they found that some symbols are much more vulnerable than others to misperception or misidentification.

Most substitution errors result from (mis)taking one symbol for another that *strongly resembles* it: An I looks like a 1, which also resembles a 7. A Z looks like a 2; an O resembles a 0. These seven symbols, which account for just 19 percent of the alphanumeric system, caused well over 50 percent of the errors in the study. Although we use these symbols every day, most people don't stop to analyze their relative vulnerability to error. For this reason, the same errors keep recurring.

Obviously, we need to adhere more strictly to the principle of symbolic differentiation. We should incorporate this principle in our handprinting, as well as printing done by machines. While not at all abandoning the symbols to which we have grown accustomed, we must work at developing characteristics that more distinctively convey these symbols' *unique* identity. For example, for six of the seven troublesome symbols, the solution involves a simple stroke of the pen. Most Europeans habitually attach a crossbar when they make a Z (Ƶ) or a 7 (7̶). This tiny stroke makes it easier to distinguish Z's from 2's and 7's from 1's that feature a serif. Similarly, the habitual addition of a diagonal slash to a 0 (0̸)—a practice long observed in the computer industry—would help differentiate it from the upper-case O. In the case of 1's and I's, a serif on the 1's, common among machine-printed typefaces but less widely used in handprinting, would help distinguish them from I's.

The extra strokes may add a little time to the process of handprinting. However, the time "lost" will actually be significantly less than the time "gained" through the avoidance of symbolic ambiguity and the necessity to correct errors caused by indistinctly rendered symbols.

Naturally the fault does not always lie solely in the symbols themselves. Sometimes it lies within us. The Bell Labs research also suggested that the individual styles of particular workers can influence vulnerability to error. Some workers can make 10 to 20 times more handprinting errors than others. This suggests that these individuals might benefit from better training as well as the introduction of more uniform handprinting procedures designed to minimize substitution errors. If some workers still have a dramatically higher incidence of errors despite these corrective measures, managers will need to work on cultivating more careful methods of selecting their staffs.

## MAKING MACHINES MORE ACCURATE

Most printers use the same alphanumeric system we do. The problem of symbolic differentiation is so pervasive, however, that even mechanically or electronically produced symbols, though seldom rendered as meaningless blurs, can fall victim to mistaken identification. Although the danger of mistaking one symbol for another varies with the typeface or design, all systems are vulnerable.

While encouraging the uniform adoption of new archetypal characteristics among ourselves and our employees, we should therefore also attempt to do the same with our printers. Designers of type should maximize symbolic differentiation. To protect against errors of misidentification, crossbars, slashes, and serifs should be incorporated not only into handprinting, but also into typefaces. The widespread introduction of these distinguishing characteristics would not only accomplish this end, but would also produce the additional benefit of reinforcing these features in handprinting.

The continued development of computers that can "read" handwriting will not eliminate the problem of recognition errors caused by inadequate symbolic differentiation and poor legibility. When ambiguity exists, machines cannot make the same kinds of inferences and deductions that we do to help us determine an intended but indistinct symbol. This limitation will leave machines crippled when confronted with illegibility or symbolic ambiguity. So advancements in programs that can read handwriting will, in fact, only make symbolic differentiation and basic legibility even more critical in our efforts to avoid error.

## THE INFLUENCE OF POOR VISION

Inadequate vision can also account for the failure to recognize familiar symbols (or familiar people). In particular, the poor vision of the person responsible for processing—or strained vision due to haste, deadline or quota pressure, poor lighting, and so on—can lead to errors in recognizing common symbols. And sadly, elements of the work environment all too often make already existing vision problems worse.

How much do we use our eyes in performing clerical tasks? Almost all the time. Indeed, optometrist Dr. Melvin Schrier, director of Vision Efficiency—a firm that specializes in the assessment and improvement of factors that affect visual performance in office operations—estimates that the average office worker uses his or her eyes at least 85 percent of a normal working day. Clerical workers need acute visual skills not only to read source materials, forms, lists, and other information, but also to guide, check, and edit the data they have written, or otherwise transcribed, recorded, or transmitted.

The quality of an individual's vision affects the rate of errors he or she makes. Yet most people overlook the obvious. They slight the connection between vision and error, either failing to recognize this connection at all or not fully appreciating its significance. Yet defective vision, often inadequately counterbalanced by corrective glasses, handicaps the performance of millions of people.

The crash of National Airlines Flight 193 into Florida's Escambia Bay in May 1978 (see Chapter 8) resulted from a combination of diverse pilot errors. Implicated as one of these causal factors, however, was inadequate vision. Captain George Kunz, the plane's pilot, later testified that he had not been wearing his glasses. As a result, he had misread the altimeter—believing it to be 1,500 feet when it actually registered an altitude of just 500 feet. At a descent rate of 2,000 feet a minute, this 1,000 feet of altitude makes an enormous difference!

Adequacy of vision influences not only accuracy, but also overall productivity. Poor vision can exacerbate other causes of error. Efforts to compensate for visual inadequacies can trigger strains that induce undue fatigue, at the very least. According to Dr. Schrier, the tension induced through visual inadequacy can also result in headache, eyestrain, general fatigue, double vision, sleepiness, or drowsiness. These, in turn, can account for irritability and tenseness as well as decreased production, unsatisfactory work, or deficient performance (see Chapter 12 for more on the influence of fatigue).

Sadly, poor vision can wreak havoc on accuracy. Since vision tends to deteriorate gradually, most of us remain unaware when inadequate vision afflicts us. Though we depend on the proficiency of our eyesight to complete our work accurately, the extent of the problem escapes us. Yet the findings of a detailed study of banking employees who work within the Rockefeller Center complex in New York City indicates that poor vision is all too common.

Among all employees tested as part of the study, examiners classified 35 percent as having inadequate vision. An additional 40 percent had vision considered doubtful. Only 25 percent of all employees had "adequate" vision. What's more, although 50 percent of the subjects had received eye exams within the previous year, only 25 percent of these people had adequate vision while wearing their glasses or contact lenses. This means that the mere wearing of corrective lenses does not ensure adequate vision.

This realization should motivate you to have your vision tested regularly, and corporations to have their employees' vision checked as well. An effective screening of employees' visual capabilities can be conducted on the premises of virtually any business. Only by first discovering if a vision problem exists can we then take appropriate actions to correct it and thus prevent the numerous future errors it might cause.

The need for regular vision checks increases in importance with age—our own as well as that of our steadily aging workforce. After age 40, *presbyopia* (farsightedness) makes it difficult or even impossible to achieve a sharp focus in close-up vision and reading. This normal part of aging demands that we expend more energy to do routine visual tasks, which can lead to additional strain, headaches, and fatigue.

## OTHER FACTORS THAT CAN AFFECT VISION

Recognizing and correcting poor vision will not eliminate all visually based recognition errors. External conditions in the workspace can further detract from one's performance. In particular, lighting can exercise a powerful influence on the proper functioning of one's eyes. This can, in turn, affect accuracy.

You can take a number of corrective steps to minimize the negative influence of poor lighting on vision and accuracy:

- Accuracy and minimal eyestrain demand lighting of appropriate intensity, not so bright that it causes the eyes to strain against the glare and not so dark that the eyes must strain in to focus.

- Most ergonomics and vision experts favor lighting from a single source that approximates the characteristics of sunlight.

- The source of light must be placed in an appropriate location so that it illuminates materials without creating glare.

- Light fixtures demand regular cleaning to remove light-absorbing dust accumulations and replacement whenever old, dim, and/or flickering.

Other external conditions can also influence the functioning of vision to a lesser degree. These include the size and design of symbols, the reflectivity of the paper or video screen, and the distance between the eyes and the work materials. In addition, the condition of working surfaces, background color and color contrasts, and the general decor of the workspace can also influence vision.

The practical application of office ergonomics can make our environments much less conducive to errors. Taking action to improve lighting and other environmental conditions will invariably enhance vision. And this will in turn help cut down on the errors.

It's also wise never to rely solely on your own evaluation of your senses. Regularly test the acuteness of your senses against an objective standard by having your vision or hearing tested professionally. Have your employees had recent checks of their vision and hearing? Maintaining keenness of perception—or becoming aware of deficiencies that exist and then correcting them—is key strategy in cutting down on errors.

# Heightening Your Error Awareness

### ERRORS IN RECOGNITION

Of the four explanations of recognition errors involving the use of symbols—a lapse in concentration, context, a "new look," and poor vision—which do we have the most power to correct?

### LEGIBILITY

Which system is most vulnerable to illegibility and therefore to recognition errors: handprinting, handwriting, dot matrices, type, laser printers?

What changes can you make in the way you write or print to improve legibility?

Which cursive symbols would you suspect are most commonly misidentified?

Write lower case g's and q's; m's and n's; y's and z's; c's, e's, l's, and b's; and i's, u's, w's and r's quickly and see for yourself how similar they are. Then write a few words with some of these letters in them. Ask a friend to assess your handwriting.

### PRINTING ERRORS

Of the 36 basic alphanumeric symbols, which do you think are most vulnerable to substitution errors when handprinted? Can you identify several pairs of symbols that might easily be mistaken for one another?

Given your awareness of poor symbolic differentiation as a prominent cause of recognition errors, what might you do to attack this problem head-on?

Can you develop a method that might help further distinguish the seven most problematic symbols (I, 1, 7, Z, 2, O, 0) from one another?

*(continued)*

*(continued)*

## MACHINES AND RECOGNITION ERRORS

Are machines exempt from the problem of symbolic ambiguity? If not, what can be done to produce greater symbolic differentiation in machine-printed documents?

In light of the increase in international trade, how can you make the symbols you use on a regular basis more universally acceptable?

## THE VISUAL CONNECTION

Can inadequate vision account for more than recognition errors?

Recognizing that impaired or inadequate vision can lead to serious errors that can, in turn, incur grave repercussions or astronomical costs, what solution would you propose?

List physical improvements you can make in your immediate environment to help stop errors.

## ASSESSING YOUR SENSES

Consider how inadequate perception can lead to errors no matter what senses you may be using. Build an awareness of the functioning of all your senses, becoming especially sensitive to any possible shortcomings. Ask yourself, "Where do my senses fail me?"

## APPLYING WHAT YOU HAVE LEARNED

The examination and treatment of recognition errors in this chapter provide a good overview of how error awareness can work for you. We first explored some of the possible causes of recognition errors. Then we narrowed the list to causes over which we had some influence. Next, we explored the nature of those causes further to isolate specific problem areas. And finally we developed strategies designed specifically to correct those problem areas.

Can you apply the preceding methodology to errors of other types? Choose some errors that regularly afflict you and see whether you can suggest possible causes. Focus on the ones you can attack, and then analyze and correct them.

# *12*

---

# CONCENTRATION

## FOCUSING ON THE JOB AT HAND

WHEN A MAN KNOWS HE IS TO BE HANGED
IN A FORTNIGHT, IT CONCENTRATES HIS MIND
WONDERFULLY.

—SAMUEL JOHNSON

O ur brains function best—and therefore we perform most efficiently and accurately—when we can *concentrate* on one subject or task at a time. We all have the ability to juggle several
activities at once. However, although we may engage in simultaneous actions, further analysis invariably shows that we can only *concentrate* on
one at a time. As Donald A. Norman succinctly described it in *The Design of Everyday Things*,[1] "We can do more than one thing at a time only
if most of the actions are done automatically, subconsciously, with little
or no need for conscious attention."

Certain actions—some of them job-related—may require our full
conscious attention as we learn them, but eventually they become so
routine and automatic that we can safely engage in other activities at the
same time. For example, after mastering the essential skills, we can
drive a car while talking or listening to music. But we actually attend to
such skills very little while performing them. Only when something disrupts the normal routine do we return the focus of our attention to the
now automatic task.

Bill Cosby, for example, once noted that the first thing most people do when they realize they've gotten lost is to turn off the car radio. It's as if the radio waves have distorted our ability to concentrate on the road. Our conscious attention is limited to one task at a time; trying to divide it among two or more tasks almost always leads to errors.

Any lapse in concentration, no matter how brief, can result in a failure to coordinate our senses, especially sight, but occasionally hearing, with the activity—typing, steering a car, counting inventory, dialing a phone, resecting a bowel, tightening a nut—necessary to complete the task. And whenever concentration wavers, errors almost always ensue. Although we would do best to concentrate on just one thing at a time, however, very few of us find ourselves in positions that allow us to focus *exclusively* on one task without considering other responsibilities as well.

It takes enormous concentration to keep the various brain functions "in sync." By improving your ability to concentrate, you will therefore reduce the number of errors you make. And by removing distractions and stimulating or reviving interest in their work, you can cut down on the errors of your employees or other members of your department.

## CONCENTRATING ON THE JOB

In most jobs, workers must simultaneously divide their attention among three types of activity—the primary activity, secondary activities, and monitoring of other operations:

1. *The Primary Activity.* This is the conscious focus of our attention. In general, the more we find the primary activity important and relevant, the more attention we devote to it. Employers hope their employees consider their primary activities to be the focus of their attention, at least during work hours. Tasks that are perceived as unimportant or as "grinds," however—though they may command a great deal of attention during the learning stage—command less attention and invite concentration lapses once they have become routinized.

2. *Secondary Activities.* Skilled tasks, once mastered, often fall into this category. These do not command as much attention as the primary activity. Since we devote little conscious attention to them, yet still perform them and our primary activity simultaneously, they must be both familiar and routine. This is beneficial whenever a job entails another task that should properly be regarded as the primary

activity. However, in any job that centers on such a skilled task, it *should* occupy the focus of attention. If the jobholder relegates it to secondary status due to its familiarity and routine nature, the mind becomes open to all sorts of error-producing distractions. The jobholder may actively search for some other primary activity that might engage his or her mind and command more attention.

3. *Monitoring.* This involves routine checking to make sure that the activity going on around you conforms to your expectations. Monitoring seldom demands rigorous attention unless and until something goes wrong—the computer starts beeping, the assembly line stops, the fax machine bursts into flames. At that point, it generally supersedes the primary activity and becomes the new focus of attention.

## THE ENEMIES OF CONCENTRATION

Since concentration lapses play such an important role in causing errors, let's apply the aims and methods of error awareness to analyzing what causes them. In so doing, we can reveal the source of many errors.

A wide variety of factors may play a part in concentration lapses that lead to errors. But chief among these are the following four great enemies of concentration:

1. Haste.
2. Fatigue.
3. Boredom.
4. Distraction.

These may themselves arise from an earlier chain of causal factors. Yet by themselves or joined together, any of these enemies of concentration can help lead to significant and costly errors.

A British study of errors in the workplace provides one indication of the critical role that haste, fatigue, boredom, and distraction play in the production of errors. The British firm asked workers to cite the reasons for their errors. The causes suggested most often were:

- Excessive workload (Fatigue + Haste).
- Trying to do several things at once (Haste + Distraction).
- Boredom (Boredom).

- Emotional pressure—from the boss (Haste + Distraction).
- Time pressure (Haste).
- Interruptions (Distraction).
- Environmental pressures—noise, temperature, lighting (Distraction).
- Feeling tired or sick (Fatigue).

How do these enemies undermine concentration? Let's look at them one at a time.

## HASTE

The rush to complete a task can often render concentration virtually impossible. You cannot focus on the *process* involved in doing something and each of the steps necessary to get it done right if you are already focusing on having it over and done with.

A nineteenth-century British surgeon, Robert Liston, prided himself on the speed of his surgical performances. Yet his haste resulted in several notable errors. In one case, he amputated a gangrenous leg in just two and a half minutes. Unfortunately, he amputated the patient's testicles at the same time. In another case, he amputated a leg in even less time. Sadly, he also amputated the fingers of his surgical assistant, who later died from gangrene (as did the original patient.) Who was it who coined the phrase, "Haste makes waste?"

Certain deadlines and timetables are inevitable. The rush to implant a donor heart in a transplant recipient cannot be averted; magazines must meet their publication dates; advertising agencies must have a presentation to show a client at the next meeting; attorneys cannot file continuances indefinitely. Yet many of us have the tendency to impose arbitrary and quite unnecessary time pressures that lead to haste and consequently to sloppiness and error.

On December 23, 1933 a dense and treacherous fog settled down east of Paris, France. With their visibility obscured, the crew of a local train from Paris to Nancy exercised caution, slowing the train considerably. An express from Paris to Strasbourg failed to exercise the same degree of care, however, continuing to chug along at over 60 miles per hour despite the unsafe conditions. In a suburb just 15 minutes outside Paris, the express train plowed into the back of the local, killing 230 people and injuring 500 more. The thick fog had prevented the crew of the express train from seeing the local train's signal.

Why had the engineer of the express train not exercised more prudence in such dangerous conditions? The investigation identified haste as one of the prime causes of the engineer's recklessness. The express train was late in leaving Paris, and the engineer had hoped to make up time in order to receive the standard railway bonus for punctuality.

The moral of this story: Instead of rewarding speed, we should reward accuracy. What good is it to get something done quickly if you don't do it right? And bonuses for speed or on-time performance can contribute to erroneous performance.

In a more contemporary case, Domino's Pizza has come under a lot of fire recently for their guarantee of delivery in 30 minutes or less. This kind of assurance, critics charge, can and has fostered reckless driving. And the outcry over this issue has certainly hurt the company's public image.

## FATIGUE

Medical residents can work, on average, between 80 and 120 hours a week. Bleary-eyed airplane pilots and frequent flyers zigzagging around the globe can cross many time zones daily. Night shift workers at nuclear power plants and car assembly factories fight their natural biological (circadian) rhythms, and force themselves to stay alert at 4 A.M., the moment at which their bodies most crave sleep. These individuals' job descriptions must include the fatigue factor. For the rest of us, exhaustion is simply an outgrowth of our stressful lives and careers. Indeed, as *New York Times* health columnist Jane Brody points out, although we need about eight hours of sleep daily, "it is not uncommon for top executives to attribute their success to the fact that they sleep only three or four hours a night."[2]

Tiredness exacts a physical toll, making it difficult to keep the mind sharp and focused. And though some might admit that fatigue makes them perform more slowly, studies have shown that fatigue detracts not merely from pace, but from accuracy and vigilance as well. The Federal Department of Transportation, in a year, attributes 200,000 car accidents to the driver falling asleep at the wheel. And the National Transportation Safety Board has found fatigue-related factors in nearly one third of all trucking accidents that were fatal for the driver.

"Night shift workers are being asked to do the impossible," explained Matthew Weisman, president of Light Sciences, a company that created a lighting system to help space shuttle astronauts adapt to their round-the-clock schedule. In a *New York Times* interview, he stated, "They are asked to work at a time when their brains are telling them to go to sleep and to go to sleep when told to stay awake. It is no accident that people make more mistakes at 3 or 4 A.M. than at 10 A.M."[3] Is it any wonder, then, that disasters like Three Mile Island, Chernobyl, Bhopal, and the Exxon Valdez oil spill all occurred in the wee hours of the morning?[4]

One study examined the effects of fatigue on subjects' ability to detect visual signals and found that those who had lost a night's sleep detected only half as many of the visual signals observed by fully rested subjects. And a Scandinavian investigation of passenger train night-shift drivers found that many seem to operate on a kind of automatic pilot. One out of six train drivers, although alert and awake enough to keep the train going at full throttle, failed to notice a series of red stop signals.

Since fatigue consistently impedes concentration, it disrupts the brain's ability to keep its various functions in equilibrium. And as I described in Chapter 10, most errors in the performance of routine tasks arise because the different levels of mental activity required to complete the task correctly are out of sync. As one respondent to a recent survey on job-related stress acknowledged, "I feel run down all the time. I can't concentrate. I make more mistakes on the job."

A 1989 survey of hospital residents and interns, as you'll recall from Chapter 9, found that 90 percent admitted making serious errors. An astonishing 65 percent of these doctors specifically mentioned overwork— feeling fatigued and having too many other things to do—as causes of their errors.

Fatigue is also a common problem and consistent complaint among international pilots, whose erratic hours may include two 14-hour flights in a 48-hour period. The stress of pilots' schedules often produces a cumulative sleep loss that results in both fatigue and diminished performance. "The whole environment is conducive to making silly mistakes," Captain David Linsley of the Air Line Pilots Association recently admitted to the PBS program *Innovation*. "You end up just shaking your head to keep alert all night long. And the last two segments at the end of an all-nighter are just brutal." It's not surprising then to hear stories of pilots who not only make stupid mistakes due to fatigue but actually fall asleep in the cockpit!

Just as fatigue detracts from accurate performance, feeling well rested can improve it. Recent studies suggest that most Americans do not get enough sleep in their day-to-day lives. Can anyone deny the influence of this epidemic of fatigue on the plague of errors that bedevils our performance of both simple and complex tasks? Although adequate rest will not get rid of all errors, it will certainly eliminate those caused primarily by fatigue.

But the rest must be well planned. Most athletes and sports physiologists do not regard the night before an athletic contest as the most important one in eliminating the fatigue factor. The key is to get plenty of rest *the night before the night before* the performance. So if you have a critical task to perform, plan to rest in advance.

Also, take advantage of your coffee breaks by trying something more stimulating than caffeine: Take a nap. Since most of us don't get enough rest at night, we need to try to make up for it during the day. Even without actually falling asleep, just lying down or sitting back and closing your eyes for 10 minutes will clear your mind, eliminate some of your fatigue, and allow you to return to the task with a renewed vigor and sense of purpose.

To combat the effects of fatiguing pilots' schedules, many European airlines—and their nations' regulatory agencies—actually encourage pilots to take turns napping in the cockpit. U.S. Air Force pilots also commonly employ this fatigue-busting tactic, which the FAA has yet to sanction. Advocates of this policy insist that as long as the pilots are flying in crews, nap one at a time, and are alert before initiating landing procedures, safety will not in any way be compromised.

Moreover, new technologies are being developed to assist night shift workers and frequent flyers adjust their circadian rhythms. Companies such as Circadian Travel Technologies of Bethesda, Maryland, and Light Sciences in Braintree, Massachusetts, have developed battery-powered visors that shine simulated sunlight into a traveler's eyes, fooling the brain into believing that night is day.[5] In addition, Light Sciences has developed and installed computerized lighting systems to help night-shift workers modify their biological cycles.

## BOREDOM

Ennui erodes your motivation to concentrate. It makes you more open to outside distractions, more likely to succumb to fatigue, and more apt to want to hurry through a task, to get it out of the way. For this reason, few people perform well at activities that bore them.

I once hired a group of intelligent, educated, and alert students for summer office jobs. Many of the clerical tasks I asked them to perform were simple, routine, and repetitive—as so many office duties are, especially in entry-level positions. The jobs demanded a methodical, indeed almost mechanical, approach that followed a standard procedure.

These highly creative students all too often found such repetitive jobs boring. The undemanding tasks allowed thoughts about other matters to intrude constantly. The students may have begun to wonder about the whys and wherefores of the task, and what it was intended to accomplish. Or they may have entertained thoughts about unrelated matters. And some of these thoughts no doubt distracted them from what I had hired them to do. Since their jobs did not demand their full attention, these people needed to make a special effort to maintain concentration.

None of us can avoid the occasional, or even frequent, necessity to handle a tedious, inherently dull task that nevertheless calls for scrupulous accuracy. Under such circumstances, we too usually need to make a special effort to focus our flagging attention on what must be done. If the satisfaction of doing the job right is not enough to motivate you, you might find it helpful, when faced with such a task, to promise yourself some sort of reward when you finish the job and do it right.

## OUTSIDE DISTRACTIONS

Distractions disrupt concentration and often require significant recovery time. With our on-the-job attention already overtaxed by primary and secondary activities and monitoring tasks, one would think that we would have no more attention to devote to anything else. Yet certain sensations can still intrude on our consciousness, distracting us from our job responsibilities.

Sudden and powerful provocations—such as pain or a strong stimulus to one or more of the five senses—captivate our attention, no matter how focused we may be on our primary activity. And no matter how brief the interruption, these disruptions can cause errors of omission, sequencing, or timing.

It's the rare mind, for example, that can remain focused on work as a car crashes outside an open window. Who has never been in a workplace where everyone suddenly stopped everything to wonder, "What was that noise?" or "What's that stench?" or "Did you see *that?*"

In addition to sudden and dramatic distractions (loud noises, flashes of light, noxious odors, chest pains) many subtler distractions can also eat away at one's concentration. These may include irrelevant yet attention-stealing external stimuli (a humming generator, a persistently flickering light, a constant flow of traffic through or past one's workspace) as well as intrusive thought that can make it difficult to concentrate. Intense emotion experiences, especially unpleasant or dangerous ones (in contrast to those which are familiar or pleasant), can command so much primary attention that it becomes difficult to concentrate on anything else.

These distractions, many of which can be eliminated fairly easily from the workplace or other performance arena, have a powerful negative impact on accuracy. For example, in 1972, while circling the Miami airport in a holding pattern prior to landing, the entire crew of an Eastern Airlines plane focused on the changing of a small lightbulb. The distraction prevented anyone from noticing that the autopilot's "altitude hold" function had inadvertently been turned off, which led to an accident.

The recognized danger of distractions led the Federal Aviation Administration to mandate a "Sterile Cockpit Rule" during takeoffs, landings, taxiing, and other urgent phases of a flight. This rule bans all nonessential activities—including talking with stewardesses or passengers, using the intercom to direct passengers' attention to sights of interest, eating, drinking, and reading—that might distract the crew's attention during these sensitive phases.

## ENHANCING CONCENTRATION

On their own, each of the four enemies of concentration have a remarkably damaging impact on accurate performance. But to make matters worse, these enemies often work together. The negative influence of one strengthens or complements the others. Boredom, as noted earlier, breeds both fatigue and distraction as well as impatience to get the whole thing over with. And fatigue can lead to boredom and a propensity for distraction.

By contrast, if you are truly interested in what you are doing, you will find it more stimulating than fatiguing. In addition, you will be less likely to rush through it, and you will attack it intently rather than succumbing to distractions. One of the best ways to minimize errors caused by lack of concentration, therefore, involves stimulating interest in the task. All of us must regularly perform certain activities for which we are overqualified, whether at work or at home. But if we can find a way to make the task more interesting, it will seem less like a chore. And this will have a positive impact on our accuracy.

General Motors and many other corporations have found that they can improve the performance of assembly-line workers by familiarizing the employees with other aspects of production. By periodically taking workers off the assembly line, varying their jobs, and permitting participation in different stages of the development of an automobile, management has permitted the employees to recognize the importance of their job—and their performance—in relation to the final product. The workers' renewed sense of importance and relevance, increases the attention they devote to their primary activity. Becoming involved in (or at least familiar with) the full production of an automobile or other product heightens workers' interest in their own jobs. And this interest tends to improve their concentration, making errors due to boredom or distractions far less frequent.

Overall performance improves through fostering interest.


## SETTING A PACE

The correct performance of a routine task requires the coordination of the mind and the body: Physical activity and mental activity need to remain in sync. Physical activity needs to follow a pace that virtually parallels the activity of the mind, which, in turn, provides the intention, direction, and control of the total process.

But the impatient, bored, tired, or distracted mind can destroy this synchronization. Instead of taking each stage of the task a step at a time, it may try to perform certain elements of the process earlier than they should take place. In this way, a lapse in concentration may cause the mind to "skip ahead" of the physical activity. Alternatively, the impatient, tired, bored, or distracted mind may perform the wrong steps or perform the right ones out of order.

The adoption of a pace that forces the focus of attention to move in proper synchronization with the related physical activity will help eliminate such errors. If we (or others who depend on us) have a stake in performing a particular task correctly, we should not rush through it in an effort to make sure that it gets done, period. On the contrary, we should make sure that it gets done *right*.

Music can help set an appropriate pace for clerical, assembly-line, or other "rhythmical" work. Many individuals and employers have found that the use of music that features a tempo appropriate to the actions performed can help focus one's pace and improve overall performance.


## HELPING OTHERS WITH THEIR CONCENTRATION

You have the power to eliminate the enemies of concentration that detract from your own performance. You can get proper rest, adopt an appropriate pace for the work, eliminate distractions, and drum up interest in tasks that might bore you. Yet which of these performance-enhancing methods can you do for others?

Certainly, you cannot force someone else (except, perhaps, your children) to get enough rest. But you can take steps to eliminate environmental distractions. In many cases, you can also encourage those who work for or under you to take the time they need to do the job right, rather than just doing the job. And finally, you can provide incentives and motivation to stimulate interest.

To improve the job performance of my summer help, I had to supply these students with motivation to stimulate their concentration. I chose a positive approach, similar to that employed by General Motors. I took the students into my confidence and demonstrated the importance of their jobs, showing them how the little details they handled played a critical part in achieving the ultimate objectives of the firm.

Their increased understanding and sense of their own importance in the overall functioning of the office improved their attitude and performance. This strategy also allowed me to take advantage of the many creative suggestions they offered.

A lapse in concentration is generally only the immediate cause of error. But fatigue, boredom, haste, and distraction themselves are not (usually) the ultimate causes. Other factors may exert their influence. Some environments and conditions, for example, are far more distracting than others. A "sick" office building in which sealed windows prevent fresh air from circulating can create headaches, nausea, high blood pressure, and respiratory symptoms.[6] Age can also play a part. Haste may result from pressure from above to finish the job to meet a quota or an urgent deadline. And fatigue may stem from family worries or domestic concerns. The next chapters will examine these contributing causes in more detail.

## HEIGHTENING YOUR ERROR AWARENESS

### THE ENEMIES OF CONCENTRATION

To which of the following enemies of concentration are you most susceptible?

- Haste.
- Fatigue.

*(continued)*

(*continued*)

- Boredom.
- Distraction.

What *errors* do they cause? List what you have done in the past to help you overcome these enemies of concentration.

## CONCENTRATION

What tasks and activities, especially on the job, but in other arenas as well, demand your attention? How well does each command it?

Think of some examples in which you made an error due to a lapse in concentration. For each error, list some of the circumstances or causal factors that might have contributed to the lapse.

## HASTE

What makes you rush through a task? What can you do to alleviate these pressures or other influences? If you can't, what strategies can you employ that will help you adopt a measured pace suitable for the accurate completion of the task?

## FATIGUE

What causes you to feel fatigued? What can you do to eliminate some of these factors? If you cannot eliminate them, how can you sharpen your mind to improve your focus on the tasks you must complete with accuracy?

## BOREDOM

What unavoidable tasks bore you? What can you do to make these dull chores more interesting? If you can't, how can you facilitate extra effort at focusing?

(*continued*)

### DISTRACTIONS

What outside objects, influences, or circumstances most often distract you from tasks you need to complete accurately? What can you do to eliminate these distractions? If you can't get rid of them completely, what can you do to minimize their influence?

What's the biggest distraction in your work environment? What can you do to eliminate it or reduce its influence? What is the one thing you would change in your work environment to make your work (or that of your employees or subordinates) proceed more smoothly, efficiently, and accurately?

### ENHANCING CONCENTRATION

How can you invest routine tasks with more interest? In a managerial capacity, how can you make the work of those you supervise more compelling for them? What strategies or techniques have you discovered or read about that can help employees become—and remain—interested in their work?

## NOTES

1. Donald A. Norman, *Design of Everyday Things* (New York: Doubleday & Co., 1987).
2. Jane Brody, "Health Alarm for a Sleep-Deprived Society," *New York Times*, 19 January, 1994.
3. Barbara Presley Noble, "Staying Bright-Eyed in the Wee Hours," *New York Times*, 13 June, 1993.
4. Jane Brody, "Heath Alarm."
5. "Technological Tacks to Battling Jet Lag," *The Wall Street Journal*, 1 March, 1994.
6. Amal Kumar Naj. "Squabbles Delay Cure of 'Sick' Office Buildings," *The Wall Street Journal*, 26 October, 1995.

# 13

## CLASSIFYING THE CAUSES OF ERROR

THERE MAY BE SAID TO BE TWO CLASSES OF PEOPLE
IN THE WORLD: THOSE WHO CONSTANTLY DIVIDE THE
PEOPLE OF THE WORLD INTO TWO CLASSES, AND
THOSE WHO DO NOT.

—ROBERT BENCHLEY

Knowing *that* an error occurred, and even understanding its consequences, is significantly different from knowing *why* it happened.
When you identify the origins of your errors, you'll be better
equipped to implement appropriate changes that can avert like problems
in the future. Even without this understanding, you might be able to *correct* some errors; but you cannot *prevent* future errors of a similar nature
from occurring.

At 6:43 A.M. on May 22, 1915, a troop train carrying 500 men steamed
into Quintinshill station outside Gretna Green, Scotland, at 40 miles per
hour. The chugging train plowed into a local that was waiting on the
same track. The engines and trailing cars of both trains crumpled and
tumbled off the track. A couple minutes later, an express roared through
the station, smashing into the wreckage. Fire quickly spread throughout.
227 died and 246 more suffered injuries—at that time the worst rail accident in history.

Most errors cannot be attributed to a single, definitive cause. Rather,
they result from the conjunction of a number of factors, which come

together inauspiciously. In this train wreck, for example, we would need to know why the signalman placed three trains on the same track at once. Although his shift had actually begun at 6 A.M., he had not started work until 6:38—just five minutes before the first crash. In fact, he had ridden to work on the very passenger train that was waiting on the track he had later okayed for the troop carrier. But, as he later told investigators, "I forgot about the local train."

Obviously, the signalman suffered from a concentration lapse. But what caused that lapse? It might have involved the combination of fatigue, the distractions involved in settling into the day's work, the secret arrangement he had with the night-shift signalman to allow him to show up half an hour late on a regular basis, and the unusually high degree of traffic through the station during wartime. On their own, not one of these factors had the power to cause the horrible accident. Yet combined, they led to disaster.

## DEFINING RELEVANT CAUSES OF ERRORS

Just as all errors can produce double-barreled effects, one immediate and the other more far-reaching, so apparent causes, such as the signalman's lapse in concentration, may be based on a variety of antecedents.

Attacking the immediate cause without at the same time eliminating the underlying factors will only result in wasted effort. If you want to improve yourself and your overall performance through error awareness, you'll need to take the time to evaluate the full string of causes that lead up to an error. This evaluation will then allow you to initiate the most effective measures to correct the error now and prevent similar ones in the future.

In analyzing the causes of your errors, however, you have to know where to draw the line between relevant and irrelevant information. "Relevance" in error awareness depends greatly on your purposes and intended use for the information.

Understanding that something outside our control caused an error may certainly alleviate a certain amount of guilt—and that's no small gain. Yet discovery of a cause that we had no power to prevent or correct, although perhaps briefly enlightening, does not add to our understanding—and therefore to the power we have to avoid such errors in the future. For our purposes then, *relevance means the causes of error must be (or have been) preventable or correctable.* Only the causes that we truly have the power to impact are relevant to error awareness.

Remember the case of the heart-transplant patient in Portland, Oregon, who received a donor heart of the wrong blood type (see Chapter 9)? Applying our definition of relevance to this case, you might come up with a number of significant causal factors. Haste was most probably a cause of this tragic mixup. Yet since a donor heart only retains its usefulness for a short time after the death of the donor, this urgency is real and unavoidable. Since the time pressure on the entire staff cannot be substantially reduced in this unique situation, this consideration is not truly "relevant" to our analysis, because we can do nothing to change it.

Another causal factor, however, cries out for attention. The timing of the tissue sample check played a significant part in compounding the error. Lab technicians tested a sample several hours into surgery, at a time when it was far too late to stop the operation. And since this poor timing might have been prevented, it has enormous relevance for our purposes. If the lab technicians planned to test a tissue sample anyway, why wait until after the operation has begun when the results would be worthless? In avoiding the recurrence of this kind of error, technicians should therefore test tissue samples *before* the operation reaches the point of no return. Because something could have been done about it, the tissue typing error was relevant to error awareness.

## THE FOLLY OF CASTING BLAME

You might be able to trace the cause of an airline crash all the way back to a malfunctioning bolt that cost less than two dollars. And the bolt manufacturer, at the very beginning of a long chain of contributors to the plane's construction, might indeed be the ultimate cause. In our blame-casting society, fingers would invariably point at this manufacturer. But should all blame really be fixed on the bolt manufacturer? Might not others have *prevented* or *corrected* the error before it led to disaster?

Certainly, attention to details and the physical condition of equipment are important measures that can help prevent errors. And this preventability makes it a relevant consideration for our purposes. But other issues have equal relevance: Should not a bolt in such a critical position in the plane have undergone rigorous testing? Should not a plane design incorporate safety measures that guard against the dependence on a single, cheaply made bolt?

In general, those who attribute errors to a single cause are interested solely in fixing blame, rather than in preventing future errors. Error awareness does not aim to point fingers of blame and shame. The key to increasing our awareness is not to find out *who* made the error, but *what* caused it. As Dianna Booher writes in, *Cutting Paperwork in the Corporate Culture,* "When things go wrong, the first question should be, 'What (not who) is the cause?' and the answer to that question will lead you to answer the next, 'How should we fix it?'"[1]

Fatigue, boredom, haste, and distraction—because they erode concentration—are the most common immediate causes of error in routine activities. Yet these error-causing agents, though they can become self-perpetuating, are not self-generating. They do not arise independently, but rather result from the action of other, earlier causes. Tracing the causes of haste, fatigue, boredom, or distraction (and therefore lapses of concentration that lead to error) back to their original sources will provide you with important insight into what actions or changes you must adopt to reduce the errors they generate.

## THE FOUR CLASSES OF CAUSATION

To make the picture of causation clearer, it may be helpful to classify errors according to their origin.

### MICROCAUSES VERSUS MACROCAUSES

The ultimate causes of error can be separated into two major classes according to where they originate.

*Microcauses* involve any source within the system itself. Workers, operators, or other individuals play a part in microcausation, bringing into the system their unique talents, education, training, and experience, as well as their individual propensities for lapses in concentration. Microcauses also include elements other than personnel, yet still part of the system— the immediate environment (the office, factory floor, kitchen, cockpit, laboratory) in which individuals perform the task.

The errors that keyboard operators make errors must be considered microcauses. However, we must also take into account all source materials, the keyboard itself, the terminal, and all other materials and equipment required to perform the task. We also should assess the possible error-causing influence of the design or layout of the source or of the forms to which the data should be transferred as well as the basic methods of copying. All components of the workspace (lights, furniture, traffic, decor) can also serve as microcauses. A sticky key, dust in the mainframe, a flickering overhead light, a noisy or distracting office, and errors contained *within* the source material can all serve as microcauses. They all lie within the immediate work environment.

Microcauses that lead to airplane crashes, for example, would go beyond the training, experience, and personality of the flight crew, although these must certainly be considered. NTSB and FAA investigators would also examine the plane's instruments, the control panel and all its elements, the traffic in and around the cockpit, and all other components of the workspace. The elements of standard in-flight operating procedure— including the protocol of transmitting and receiving information (and its accuracy) from air-traffic controllers and other sources—or deviations from these procedures can also function as microcauses of error.

*Macrocauses* exist outside the system, yet they can still exert a detrimental, and often powerful, influence on performance. Upstream sources of materials (customers, clients, suppliers of raw production materials, originators of data or processing software, equipment vendors) often function as macrocauses. These sources may not be subject to the same kinds of controls that can be introduced within the system. They may, therefore, provide faulty products, cheap materials, or inaccurate information that can lead directly to errors.

More often, however, macrocauses engender errors in more subtle and indirect ways. Anything outside the immediate work environment that affects concentration, and therefore performance, can be considered a macrocause. These include distractions such as threatened layoffs, takeover rumors, a local flood or other natural disaster, and domestic concerns such as a sick child or an impending divorce. All of these have the power to draw attention away from the primary activity. As long as a force outside the system exerts an influence powerful enough to interfere with concentration, it must be considered as a possible macrocause of errors— no matter how distant it might be.

The most obvious and most often cited macrocause of plane crashes is, for example, bad weather. Yet other forces outside the system also have the power to influence concentration and the performance of flight duties. These include such distracting personal concerns as the pilot's terminally ill father, the recently ended love affair between the copilot and one of the flight attendants, or the pilot's upcoming retirement. Work-related distractions that nonetheless exist outside the system such as negotiations between the pilot's union and airline management can also function as macrocauses of pilot error. Even more remote possibilities such as tainted food consumed by the flight crew just before boarding the plane can hinder accurate performance.

Why care whether an error is due to a micro- or a macrocause? This difference between causes inside and outside the system will help determine how you approach the problem. *You should aim at minimizing the negative impact of macrocauses; with microcauses, however, you can usually mount a direct attack.*

In some cases, as when a meter provides a faulty reading, it seems easy to determine whether a causal agent arises within the system or outside it. However, the line between micro- and macrocauses sometimes blurs. How do you determine what plays a part in the overall system and what lies completely outside it? Because micro- and macrocauses may interweave in complicated ways, the answer is often more grey than black-and-white.

To illustrate some of the difficulties that can arise in determining micro- and macrocauses, let's look at the following causal agents:

1. *An Inaccurate Reading Provided by One of the System's Monitoring Instruments.* Any monitoring instrument—whether a cockpit's altimeter or a car's speedometer, an electrocardiogram or internal fetal monitor, a Geiger counter or water pressure meter—functions as part of the system in which it operates. An inaccurate reading that leads to a performance error easily falls into the class of microcauses.

2. *Congressional Debate over a New Federal Policy That Will Have a Significant Impact on Corporate Operations.* Though government action can have a powerful impact on a company's policy and performance, the government functions outside the operating system. Even in the case of government agencies, Congress acts on the intraagency system from the outside. Therefore, debate over any federal policy, even when it distracts workers from the performance of their duties, must be considered a macrocause.

3. *The Relationship between Workers and Management.* The line between micro- and macrocauses blurs when considering the impact of management-worker relations. A case could easily be made that supervisors remain outside the system and only act on it. However, logic seems to dictate that the relationship between management and workers should be considered part of the system. Any errors that arise as a result of this relationship stem from microcauses.

4. *Credit Card Receipts.* Upstream sources of supplies, equipment, data, and raw materials, are macrocauses because they lie outside of the system. However, the forms through which these materials are often solicited—such as credit card receipts, order forms, and

insurance, license, or loan applications—fall into the class of microcauses. Since these forms function as an integral part of the overall system, the person performing the task (or management charged with supervising this performance) has a great deal of control over them (see Chapter 6).

5. *Faulty Materials Provided by Outside Suppliers.* Even when they come from external sources, faulty products, inaccurate information, or cheap materials quickly become incorporated into the system. Thereafter they function as microcauses, especially of future errors that result from a corrupted database or malfunctioning machinery. Ultimately, this microcause can be traced back to a macrocause (the upstream source), another illustration of the complicated ways in which microcauses and macrocauses can intermingle.

Analyzing a chain of causation often demands that you set priorities. In the preceding case, for example, the most pressing concern—the one that demands primary attention—is not pinpointing the ultimate source of the error (the macrocause), but rather locating and correcting the microcause before it does further damage. In identifying the microcause(s) in such cases, you will have a powerful clue that may point toward possible macrocauses. And this will allow you not only to correct the microcause, but to eliminate the macrocause (or at least its influence on your operations).

In certain cases, however, you can directly attack a macrocause. By bringing the faulty materials to the attention of the outside supplier—or by changing suppliers—you can sometimes eliminate the macrocause altogether. In general, however, you have much more power to influence microcauses.

## PROXIMATE VERSUS CONTRIBUTORY CAUSES

Both micro- and macrocauses can be further separated into two subclasses: proximate and contributory causes.

*Proximate* causes have a direct, one-to-one, cause-and-effect relationship with a specific, immediate, and clearly identifiable error. Proximate causes generally produce only limited adverse effects. Yet because they have a direct relationship to errors, they are usually easier to trace and identify than contributory causes.

A jostled elbow, for example, since it can lead to a specific, identifiable error, fits the criteria for a proximate microcause. A power failure, which can lead immediately and directly to readily identifiable errors such as the loss of computer data, qualifies as a proximate macrocause.

*Contributory* causes, by contrast, generally lead to errors indirectly by inducing one or more of the four great enemies of concentration: haste, fatigue, boredom, and distraction. For example, George went out drinking with his old college buddies on Thursday night. By two in the morning, he had lost count of how many Jack Daniels he had downed. Yet George kept drinking, staying out with his friends until the bars closed at 4 A.M. It was all he could do to drag himself to work on Friday morning, showing up 20 minutes late—and, needless to say, in less than peak condition. From the minute he arrived, George couldn't wait until the day was over. He felt fatigued and was unable to maintain interest in his work. Plagued with a headache, George found himself welcoming distractions from his duties. As a result, his output suffered and he made many more errors than he normally would have committed.

George's hangover must be regarded as a contributory macrocause of any errors he made on that fateful Friday. We may feel quite confident that the hangover—in creating fatigue, disinterest, and distraction—has caused or contributed to errors. Yet despite the strength of circumstantial evidence, we must recognize that George would have, or at least might have, made some of these errors anyway. We may believe that the increase in errors, if substantial, plainly indicates that the hangover caused them. Despite our strong belief, however, we cannot clearly and certainly differentiate between the errors due to the hangover and those that would have occurred without it.

If you can't say with certainty that a particular factor caused a specific error, that factor should be considered a contributory cause rather than a proximate one.

Contributory causes do not produce predictable results as proximate causes would. George's hangover undoubtedly increased the probability of error. Yet the hangover still did not have an identifiable and direct one-to-one relationship to a particular error. Unless George processes *every* item incorrectly throughout the day, no direct, cause-and-effect relationship can possibly exist in this case. Since the hangover had an indirect effect that increased the likelihood of errors in general, however, it must be considered a contributory cause.

Contributory causes include any events or conditions that influence the motivation, emotions, psychology, or abilities of one or more individuals powerfully enough to affect their task performance. Whether joyful or painful, such preoccupations have the power to claim a significant share of our thoughts and attention. By inducing haste, fatigue, boredom, or distraction, these events disrupt concentration, affect associative mechanisms, or otherwise impair the mental processing required for correct performance.

A 1991 survey conducted for the Northwestern National Life Insurance Company found that tens of millions of American workers suffer from job-related stress. This leads to fatigue and distraction, a subsequent loss of concentration, and therefore errors. According to those surveyed, the contributory causes of this stress include takeover or relocation rumors; a merger, acquisition, or other transfer of company ownership; layoffs or other reductions of the workforce; and a substantial reduction in employee benefits. In view of the relationship between stress and error, all of these should be considered as contributory causes of error as well.

Contributory macrocauses often involve the interference of emotional concerns with physical and mental performance. Certain personal situations, particularly those that powerfully affect an individual's emotions, sharply increase the likelihood of making errors. Strong emotions tend to disrupt our ability to concentrate on anything else besides them. And our work naturally suffers from such distractions.

Contributory causes can pop up almost anywhere as either microcauses or macrocauses. Contributory microcauses in the workplace, such as poor lighting or uncomfortable chairs, are often relatively easy to detect and identify. Yet they might also arise outside an individual's or group's specific work area, yet still within the overall working environment, as in the case of takeover rumors. In addition, contributory macrocauses occur to a significant degree outside the workplace. Contributory macrocauses, as we have already seen, may arise in the domestic environment in an individual's home or family life, or even a natural disaster.

It is generally easier to distinguish proximate from contributory causes than to differentiate between micro- and macrocauses. A proximate cause only exists if you can establish a direct link between the cause and specific individual errors. A computer glitch, which you can link directly to particular errors, obviously serves as a proximate cause. Concerns such as taxes or the corporate benefits package, which can impose burdens or distractions that increase the likelihood of errors but do not lead to specific, identifiable errors, function as contributory causes. Finally, if errors exist in the material received from upstream sources, the accurate transcription of this material yields direct links between source errors and output errors. For this reason, errors in source material must also be regarded as proximate causes of errors in production.

Unlike contributory causes, which can just as easily be either macro-causes or microcauses, virtually all proximate causes occur within the work environment. For this reason, very few macrocauses act as proximate causes of error. Upstream sources of error or massive power failures, as indicated earlier, might function as proximate *macrocauses*, as would lightning that strikes an airplane's wing; these, however, are the rare exceptions. In general, proximate causes are almost always microcauses. By contrast, both macro- and microcauses can contribute indirectly, and thus serve as contributory causes of error.

You may be surprised to learn that, though proximate causes lead more directly and clearly to errors, management will find it much more profitable to attack contributory causes whenever possible. Though contributory causes lead more indirectly to error, they lead to many more errors on a more widespread scale than proximate causes. In general, proximate causes are isolated occurrences. And though the errors that result from them are largely predictable, the causes themselves are difficult to predict and therefore to prevent. Management will yield significantly greater benefits by turning its attention to attacking or at least limiting the negative impact of contributory causes of error.

## CLASSIFYING YOUR ERRORS

Combining the two major classes of causation and the two subclasses yields four general classes of causation. The following matrix illustrates how to classify errors according to these four general classes.

| GENERAL CAUSATION OF ERRORS | Micro | Macro |
|---|---|---|
| Proximate | *Proximate* <br> *Microcauses* | *Proximate* <br> *Macrocauses* |
| Contributory | *Contributory* <br> *Microcauses* | *Contributory* <br> *Macrocauses* |

These are the four general types of causation for errors. Let's review each in greater detail:

1. *Proximate Microcauses.* Arise within the system, acting directly to produce errors. Examples include a bumped elbow, a mechanical failure, a computer glitch, or a jammed conveyor belt. Direct intervention and correction are sometimes possible, but preventive measures are often not worthwhile.

2. *Contributory Microcauses.* Arise within the system, causing haste, fatigue, boredom, or distraction, thereby producing errors indirectly. Examples include pressure from the boss, poor lighting, work quotas, or a poor benefits package. Direct intervention and correction are often possible, and efforts aimed at prevention are almost always worthwhile.

3. *Proximate Macrocauses.* Influence performance from outside the system, causing errors directly. Examples include upstream sources that provide faulty raw materials or inaccurate information, a temporary power failure, a lightning bolt or other natural disaster. Direct intervention, correction, and preventive policies are occasionally possible, and worthwhile if accomplished.

4. *Contributory Macrocauses.* Influence performance from outside the system, causing haste, fatigue, boredom, or distraction, thereby producing errors indirectly. Examples include a baby at home suffering from colic, a local crime wave, or a difficult commute. Direct intervention and correction are seldom possible, yet preventive measures to reduce their impact on performance and accuracy can prove worthwhile.

## A PLAN OF ATTACK

In most cases, errors result not from the action of one causal factor, but rather from the confluence of several. Attempts to single out just one "cause" are usually linked to efforts to cast blame on a single individual, company, or circumstance, and seldom represent a sincere effort to unearth the true causes of error.

Whatever types of errors you (or those who work for you) make, you can understand and then eliminate or minimize them more thoroughly by analyzing their causes. First, pinpoint whether they are micro- or macro-causes; then, hone in on whether the cause(s) are proximate or contributory. Assess their relevance at each step by applying the key question: "Could this have been prevented?" If you had eliminated that causal factor, might you have prevented the error or mitigated its negative consequences? If you answer affirmatively, then that factor deserves further examination—and often correction as well.

In classifying the causes of your errors in this way, you will gain considerable insight into the errors and their origins. You can then use this new awareness to determine the relative value of intervening to correct and prevent these causes of error. If you decide it will be worthwhile, your heightened awareness will help you develop the best way to address those specific causes.

# HEIGHTENING YOUR ERROR AWARENESS

### RELEVANCE

Single out the most important criterion to help you determine whether a particular piece of information about possible causes or causal factors is relevant to the purposes of error awareness. Is the ultimate cause of error the only relevant cause?

### MICROCAUSES OF ERROR

Consider data processors or other keyboard operators. What possible factors might serve as their microcauses of errors?

Consider the flight crew of a DC-10. What possible factors might serve as microcauses of errors made by pilots and other members of the flight crew?

Consider a hospital's surgical team. What possible factors might serve as microcauses of errors made by surgeons, anesthetists, nurses, and other members of the surgical team?

### MACROCAUSES OF ERROR

How can something outside the system produce errors within the system?

Why you should care whether a cause is a microcause or a macrocause? What difference could it possibly make?

*(continued)*

(*continued*)

Consider again the flight crew of the DC-10. What are some of the possible macrocauses of errors made by pilots and other members of the flight crew?

## MICRO- AND MACROCAUSES? YOU DECIDE

In which class would you place the following causal factors of error?

1. An inaccurate reading provided by one of the system's monitoring instruments.
2. Congressional debate over a new federal policy that will have a significant impact on corporate operations.
3. The relationship between workers or operators and supervisors or other management.
4. Credit card receipts.
5. Faulty materials provided by outside suppliers.

## PRIORITIES

When malfunctioning machinery or a corrupted database serves as a microcause of errors but itself springs from a macrocause, which aspect demands more attention first?

Which do you think management has the greatest power to influence: macrocauses or microcauses of error?

## PROXIMATE AND CONTRIBUTORY CAUSES

Think of incidents, events, and situations in your own life that have demanded significant attention and emotional energy. These might include the birth of a child, death in the family, amorous affairs, financial worries, and so on. Might any of these have contributed to causing certain errors that you made during that period?

In which subclass (proximate causes or contributory causes) would you place the following causal factors of error?

1. A computer glitch that destroys over a dozen documents.
2. A substantial rise in federal or state taxes.

(*continued*)

3. A hefty cut in medical or pension benefits.

4. Accurate transcription of inaccurate written material received from upstream sources.

Which would management find most beneficial to attack: proximate or contributory causes of error?

## THE MATRIX

Look at the matrix titled "General Causation of Errors." Think of several examples that belong in each class. Which classes would prove most open to corrective measures, and which would respond to preventive strategies?

Apply what you have learned from the matrix to errors you have listed previously. Where do the causes of most of your errors lie? Check your responses against what you wrote earlier. Do these earlier responses fit appropriately into the classes of causation you identified now?

# NOTE

1. Dianna Daniels Booher, *Cutting Paperwork in the Corporate Culture* (New York: Facts on File Publications, 1986).

# *14*

---

# A CHECKLIST TO INCREASE YOUR ERROR AWARENESS

**LIFE IS ONE LONG STRUGGLE BETWEEN CONCLUSIONS BASED ON ABSTRACT WAYS OF CONCEIVING CASES AND OPPOSITE CONCLUSIONS PROMPTED BY OUR INSTINCTIVE PERCEPTION OF THEM AS INDIVIDUAL FACTS.**

**—WILLIAM JAMES**

S ince they have a direct, one-to-one relationship with the errors they cause, single proximate causes—whether micro- or macrocauses—generally lead to single errors, or at worst a small group of errors (unless they go uncaught for a very, very long time). Attacking and avoiding them, whenever they can be predicted or discovered, will undeniably eliminate this handful of errors. But in many cases, this will not prove to be a substantial gain.

Single contributory causes, although they produce more indirect effects, lead to several or even many errors—and do even greater damage when combined with one another. Management would find it more beneficial, therefore, to tackle contributory causes of error rather than proximate ones.

Having eliminated proximate causes, we must next turn our attention to the choice between contributory microcauses and contributory macrocauses. Since microcauses lie within the system, they usually (though not always) exercise a greater influence on performance than macrocauses—and can therefore produce even more errors. More importantly, you also have the power to influence microcauses. Since they arise within or around the system itself, microcauses are more subject to individual (or management) intervention.

In this chapter, we will focus on contributory microcauses of errors. These can include everything from physical conditions (lighting, ventilation, and traffic) in the workspace through production quotas and other sources of pressure to the appropriateness and adequacy of prescribed methods and procedures.

Once you know exactly which contributory microcauses apply to your errors (and to those made by people who work for you), you can immediately begin formulating an appropriate strategy to eliminate them or at least minimize their impact. As Keki R. Bhote, writing in an AMA Management Briefing entitled *World Class Quality: Design of Experiments Made Easier and More Cost Effective Than SPC* concludes, "When these roadblocks to quality work are removed, workers—99% of whom are well-motivated to begin with—will almost always come through with sterling performance."[1]

## PINPOINTING THE CONTRIBUTORY CAUSES OF YOUR ERRORS

The checklists on the upcoming pages will serve as useful diagnostic tool in determining the factors that contribute to errors in many areas of your life, but especially in your work environment. These checklists will first help you identify the major factors that lead to the errors you (or your department, division, or employees) make. Then, they will help you zero in on the specific factors within those general areas that most contribute to *your* errors.

Most contributory microcauses of error fall into one of the following general areas:

- Human Resources.
- Physical Environment.
- Performance/Timing Requirements.
- Industrial Engineering.
- Human Engineering.

- Technical Elements.
- Operational Elements.
- Compensation.
- Organizational Elements.
- Supervision.
- Social Environment.
- Subjective Elements.

As you read through this chapter, give serious consideration to each listed factor. *Make a note next to each item that you feel might have contributed (or even led directly) to your errors.* The items you mark throughout this exercise will dramatically increase your error awareness. By identifying the critical areas that demand your attention and effort, this exercise will provide you with the focus you need to begin reducing or eliminating errors.

## HUMAN RESOURCES

Although records were closely guarded, the Soviet state airline, Aeroflot, earned an awful reputation for both safety and reliability over the course of the past few decades. In December 1987, *Pravda* asserted that half of Aeroflot's safety incidents resulted from "low professional levels among staff." Much of this lack of professionalism could be traced to poor training.

On April 4, 1991, a Piper Aerostar collided with a helicopter in midair, killing Senator John Heinz of Pennsylvania and six others. NTSB investigators later discovered that the captain of the plane had less than three hours of experience as pilot-in-command of the twin-engine plane—and that figure includes the 48 minutes of the final flight.

These are instances of weaknesses in human resources. Your background, qualifications, training, and personal characteristics (or those of your employees or staff), if unsuitable or inadequate for performing the work, can foster errors. You (and those who work for you) must be competent and both mentally and physically ready to cope with the performance demands placed on you. Consider the following elements carefully. Do you or your workers fall short in any of the following areas in a way that might contribute to the incidence of errors?

☐ *Numbers* (of personnel, if more than one). One of the leading causes of job-related stress[2] (and also error) is a recent reduction in the size of the workforce through layoffs or firings. Overstaffing, however, can also lead to errors by breeding idleness and boredom. Do you have enough people to do the job right? Not enough? Too many?

☐ *Qualifications.* Overqualified personnel, can grow bored and impatient with their job. Underqualified personnel, on the other hand, can become overwhelmed with job responsibilities. Are you (or your personnel) qualified for the job? Underqualified? Overqualified?

☐ *Background.* Do you (or your personnel) have a background commensurate with the responsibilities entailed by the job?

☐ *Education.* Have you (or your personnel) achieved the level of education required to complete the tasks accurately?

☐ *Training.* Many errors result from an incomplete understanding of the responsibilities, procedures, or appropriate behavior associated with the job. How well do you train those whom you then trust with critical tasks? How well were you trained?

☐ *Experience.* People get better at a task as they become more familiar with it. Conversely, inexperience can often lead to errors that a more experienced person might not make. Are you (or those who work for you) experienced at the tasks at hand? If not, are you (or they) being adequately supervised?

☐ *Home Situation.* The lifestyle and home situation of any worker has an influence on overall job performance. Just as many of us are guilty of bringing our work problems home, so do many of us do the reverse. Does your home situation (or that of your personnel) detract from accurate job performance?

☐ *Socioeconomic Status.* Differences in socioeconomic backgrounds can create pressures, such as discrimination, for some employees. Do such practices inhibit your performance?

☐ *Evaluation of Potential.* Did management accurately assess your potential (or the potential of those who work for you) in the light of all of the factors detailed above? Was your potential overestimated or underestimated?

☐ *Assignment(s) and Reason(s) for Assignment(s).* Were job assignments meted out in accordance with each individual's unique background, qualifications, and abilities? Do their individual strengths and weaknesses match the performance demands of the assignment?

☐ *Performance Record(s)*. Do you (or your personnel) have a track record of accurate performance? Or do you (or your workers) have a history of making many errors?

## PHYSICAL ENVIRONMENT

A work environment can be designed that tolerates individual differences and human fallibility, thereby resisting error. In addition to the workspace itself, the elements considered here also incorporate broader aspects of the physical environment such as geographic considerations associated with getting to or being at work. Do any of these distract you or otherwise interfere with your concentration or performance?

☐ *Workspace*. Does the overall workspace facilitate accurate performance of the task(s)? Is the space both adequate and suitable for the task? Does it promote concentration and enhance the physical and mental processes required to complete the task accurately?

☐ *Lighting*. The absence or scarcity of windows or natural lighting has been identified as a secondary cause of job-related stress. Do you have natural lighting in your workspace? If not, does your lighting closely approximate sunlight? Are fixtures well maintained and bulbs changed regularly?

☐ *Ventilation*. Ventilation that allows for the free flow of oxygen through the workspace enhances job performance. An inadequate supply of fresh air creates fatigue that can hamper concentration and lead to errors. Is your workspace too close and stuffy? Does air flow freely through the space?

☐ *Temperature*. A work environment in which the temperature keeps changing is a significant cause of job-related stress. Does your workspace maintain comfortable levels of temperature and humidity?

☐ *Furniture*. Does the height, comfort, and function of the furniture facilitate or detract from the task(s)?

☐ *Position and Comfort of Body*. Does the workspace encourage proper posture? Does it facilitate physical movements required to complete the task without error?

☐ *Physical Arrangements*. Do the overall physical arrangements (decor and backgrounds, positioning of furniture and other equipment, location of the door, and so on) contribute to errors? Or do they help promote accuracy?

☐ *Noise Levels.* High noise or vibration levels are a significant cause of job-related stress and error. Does the noise level in your workspace interfere with your ability to concentrate?

☐ *Location of the Workspace within the Overall Work Environment.* Is your workspace located in the spot that best facilitates both the receipt of the incoming materials you need and the transmission of the end products of your work? Are similar, cooperative, or connected activities grouped together physically? Are incompatible activities physically separated?

☐ *Traffic through or around the Workspace.* Little or no privacy is a secondary cause of job-related stress. How much traffic passes by or through your workspace? Does it distract you from your job? Can coworkers circulate through the workspace without intruding on your concentration? Do you (or your personnel) have so much traffic that privacy seems impossible?

☐ *Corridors, Elevators, and/or Stairs.* The presence of any of these near the workspace can increase the traffic in the area. This can provide a high level of distraction for those trying to concentrate on their work. Are you distracted by everyone who enters, leaves, or moves through the general workspace?

☐ *Restrooms.* Are restrooms spaced regularly throughout the overall work environment, so that you (or those who work for you) don't have to waste a lot of time and energy just to get to the restroom and back?

☐ *Locker Rooms.* Locker rooms are notorious as places where workers can vent their personal antagonisms. Does the environment of the locker room allow any difficulties that arise to become readily apparent to management?

☐ *Cafeteria.* Is the cafeteria close enough to the work environment so that workers don't spend half of their lunch hour getting to and from the cafeteria, yet still far enough away to give personnel a real sense of a break from the work environment?

☐ *Vicinity of the Work Environment within the Community.* The distance between your place of work and the community in which you (or your personnel) live can exercise a positive or negative influence on levels of fatigue and distraction. How close is home from your place of work?

☐ *Accessibility.* A difficult commute can increase the stress and fatigue associated with the job. How easy or difficult is it to get to the workplace from other areas of the surrounding community?

☐ *Transportation.* Does available public or private transportation provide a pleasant, hassle-free way to get to and from work?

## PERFORMANCE/TIMING REQUIREMENTS

The job of an international airline pilot is paradoxically both sedentary *and* physically exhausting. Although virtually all the work is done while sitting down, the work period extends over many, many hours and often crosses several time zones—a schedule that exhausts the human body (and mind). "A lot of the scheduling we work under," Captain David Linsley of the Air Line Pilots Association admits, "doesn't make sense in regard to proper rest, circadian rhythm, flying on the back side of the clock, extended schedule after an all-night schedule, a variety of different complications which have been proven to be less than efficient for the human body." This progressive wearing down of the body increases the likelihood of pilots making "silly mistakes"—errors that could prove fatal to their passengers.

Unrealistic performance or timing requirements can often increase stress and encourage haste, thereby leading to errors and inaccuracy. Could any of the following requirements of your operation (or that of your parent company) contribute to causing errors?

☐ *Tasks Involved.* Work that is either entirely sedentary or physically exhausting is a secondary cause of job-related stress. Does the work itself encourage errors in its completion?

☐ *Work Methods Used to Accomplish the Task(s).* When work methods are unclear, confusing, incomplete, or occasionally irrelevant, the omission of steps often causes errors. Are the work methods appropriate to the accurate completion of the tasks? Have new work methods recently been introduced? (The introduction of new ways of working is a significant cause of job-related stress.) Are all work methods well understood?

☐ *Designated Procedures.* Error-free performance often depends on the adequacy and appropriateness of prescribed methods and procedures. This encompasses the procedures themselves as well as the clarity of directions, the characteristics of supervision, the responsibility for detection and correction of error, and the nature of feedback on discovering an error. Are your procedures appropriate to the task? Do you need to carry out too many tasks at once or perform tasks in an illogical or impractical order? Have procedures been established to deal with unusual situations and nonstandard work? Is there a safe plan already in place to deal with contingencies, emergencies, or unusual circumstances? Are there designated procedures aimed specifically at the reduction of errors?

☐ *Informal Procedures.* Workers for whom formal procedures as cumbersome, obsolete, inappropriate, inadequate, or nonexistent tend to develop their own to accomplish work-related tasks. Although they sometimes work well, such shortcuts and jerry-built procedures may not conform to the overall objectives of the organization, and therefore often lead to errors. Are you aware of the informal procedures that you (or your staff) have substituted for designated procedures? Have you thoroughly evaluated their effectiveness, conformity to organizational goals, and vulnerability to error? Does the staff rely solely on informal procedures to cope with unusual situations or nonstandard work? Could procedures be designated more clearly in a way that eliminates the need for informal procedures?

☐ *Industry Practices.* Do standard industry practices facilitate error-free performance of the task? If so, do you deviate from them? If not, why not try to set a new standard?

☐ *Routines.* Are the routines associated with the job appropriate to accurate performance? Have work routines become outmoded?

☐ *Written Instructions, Manuals, Checklists, and Procedures.* To minimize the likelihood of errors, written procedures must be clear, easy to use, and accessible. Yet far too many equipment manuals focus on hardware and systems rather than situations that need attention and/or correction. Do your written instructions and procedures employ clear, specific language? Are they incomplete, failing to cover all possible contingencies? Is there a checklist that details any step-by-step procedures to make sure you (or your staff) don't omit any steps? Do you (or your employees) use the checklist properly, checking off each item as you complete it? Or do you do several items on the list and then check them off all at once—a method that can lead to errors of omission?

☐ *Forms Employed.* Do the forms used in connection with the work facilitate performance? Does the layout of forms employ a logical progression that corresponds as precisely as possible with the processes necessitated by the task(s)?

☐ *Workloads.* One of the leading causes of job-related stress is an inconsistent workload. It's not so much the amount of work, but its unpredictability that causes stress. Because it produces alternating periods of haste and tedium, this erratic pace also increases the likelihood of errors.

☐ *Quotas.* Quotas tend to place a premium on quantity at the expense of quality—encouraging haste and inducing fatigue. In addition, failure to meet quotas is a significant cause of job-related stress. Stretching people to (or beyond) their limits may increase output, but it also heightens the incidence of error. Do you (or your personnel) have to meet work quotas? If so, are they realistic and reasonable?

☐ *Time Study.* Taken alone, time studies, whether produced internally or externally, may lead to standards that contribute to errors. Has any time study applied to the work in your department been counterbalanced with a consideration of the adequacy and accuracy of the work? Has feedback been encouraged and acknowledged following the time study?

☐ *Production Standards.* Production standards, whether formally mandated or informally arrived at among fellow workers, reflect what workers expect (or management expects) to accomplish. Exceeding, meeting, or not meeting these standards can affect workers' morale and job satisfaction. Are the production standards applied to your job realistic, unrealistically high, or undemandingly low? Are standards clearly prescribed so that workers do not need to set their own standards?

## INDUSTRIAL ENGINEERING

In the localized power failure that crippled AT&T's long-distance telephone service in the New York area in September 1991, an entire switching station had been operating on batteries for almost six hours before any of the company's technicians noticed. Although most of the visual warning lights worked but went unnoticed, the audible alarms intended to warn of such an emergency had been clamped down so that they would ring softly. As the *New York Times* (September 21, 1991) described it, "On the 20th floor, a visual alarm, a blinking bulb, worked, but an audible alarm could be heard only lightly; on the 15th floor, another visual alarm also worked, but an audible alarm could not be heard at all, and on the 14th floor, both the visual and audible alarms did not work."

With such poor maintenance of essential equipment, it's no wonder that the power failure escalated to a full-scale blunder that blocked five million New York calls and paralyzed air traffic in the area for an evening. Such inappropriate or faulty industrial engineering can lead directly or indirectly to errors. Do the following allow you to perform at peak efficiency and with maximum accuracy?

☐ *Equipment.* Does the equipment used in the performance of the task(s) function efficiently, appropriately, and reliably? Has the equipment become outmoded? Is it well maintained?

☐ *Tools.* Do the tools fit the job? Do you have the best tools in the best possible condition to facilitate the work? Are they reliable, suitable, and easy to use? Are they regularly checked and cleaned?

☐ *Supplies.* Are the supplies you regularly work with the best suited for the task(s)? Could changes in the supplies you use improve job performance?

☐ *Layout.* In addition to being well designed, equipment must be well positioned and easy to use to minimize errors. Does the layout of equipment, tools, and supplies facilitate accurately completing the task? Would an alternate layout help cut down on errors?

☐ *Processes.* Are the processes involved in completing the task appropriate to the job? Do you regularly review processes to make sure they haven't become outmoded or otherwise inappropriate?

☐ *Work Flows.* Work should flow in a natural way that conforms to normal human behavior. Does the flow of work proceed in a direction and at a speed that conforms as precisely as possible to the order and timing of the processes that must be performed to complete the task accurately? Or does the flow of work proceed unpredictably or erratically in terms of both volume and pace?

☐ *Capacity.* Does the capacity of your equipment, tools, supplies, and other elements of industrial engineering meet your production needs?

☐ *Capability/Requirements Ratios.* Are the studies of industrial engineering used in connection with your work capable of meeting the requirements of the task(s)?

☐ *Capability/Performance Ratios.* Do you (or your personnel) perform at levels that meet, exceed, or fall short of the capabilities of industrial engineering used in connection with your work?

## HUMAN ENGINEERING

Whether or not you get the top-of-the-line equipment and other machines, errors may arise in the interplay between those machines and the people expected to operate them. Consider the following aspects of the relationships between people and machines. How well do you (or your personnel) get along with *your* machines?

☐ *Comfort with the Machine(s).* A significant cause of job-related stress is the introduction of new machines into the work environment. Do you (or your personnel) feel comfortable with the machines you need to operate? Have you been adequately trained in or at least familiarized with their use? Do you have any doubts or unanswered questions about the machines?

☐ *Ease of Use.* Do you need a doctorate in physics or mechanical engineering to operate the machine? Or can a reasonably intelligent person learn how to use it within a few days? Is the machine difficult to operate?

☐ *Facilitation of Tasks by the Machine(s).* Do the machines you operate actually make it easier for you to accomplish essential job-related tasks? Or do they end up further complicating the tasks?

☐ *Minimization of Fatigue by the Machine(s).* Does operation of the machine require any physical or mental strains that increase fatigue — and the incidence of errors? Consider not only physical exertion, but also posture, eyestrain, and so on.

☐ *Adaptation to the Sensory Requirements of the Machine(s).* How well have you (or your personnel) adapted to the demands the machine(s) place on your eyesight, hearing, and sense of touch?

☐ *Adaptation to the Activity Requirements of the Machine(s).* How well have you (or your personnel) adjusted to the reactions, responses, and other movements you must make to operate the machine(s) properly? Are you and the machine(s) in sync?

☐ *Your Perception of the Controls.* Do you feel that the machine's operating controls are best suited to the activities required of you to complete the task(s) accurately?

☐ *Best Use of those Controls.* Have you become familiar and adept enough with the machine(s) and the controls to make the best possible use of them?

## TECHNICAL ELEMENTS

When the technology does not suit the demands of the task, errors invariably follow. Are the following suitable for the purposes of your task(s)?

☐ *Operating Controls.* Do the operating controls (like the keyboard of a computer) facilitate accurate performance of the critical operations? Or do they hinder performance, contributing to errors?

☐ *Quality Control Methods.* Do the quality control methods you use apply to on the job tasks and methods of operation? Can quality control methods facilitate error-free performance in your human operations?

☐ *Separation of Digits.* If working with any kind of keyboard, are the digits (and/or letters) far enough apart so that they minimize the likelihood of hitting the wrong key (or more than one key at a time), yet still close enough so that they don't strain hand muscles?

☐ *Computer Edits.* Are your computer edit programs up-to-date, complete, accurate, and reliable? How effectively do they catch errors before they have any real consequences?

☐ *Individual Identification with Work and End Products of Work.* How much do you (or your personnel) identify with your work and the end products of work? Do you derive satisfaction from doing the job well? Do you appreciate the significance of your work in terms of the overall aims and products of the organization?

☐ *Availability of Feedback from the Technology Itself.* Does the technology provide any feedback regarding the accuracy of performance? Does it recognize errors or provide any warnings of operator error?

☐ *Measures of Productivity.* How does the technology measure productivity? Solely in terms of quantity? Or is quality considered in conjunction with quantity?

## OPERATIONAL ELEMENTS

On a space shuttle mission prior to the Challenger disaster, a console operator inadvertently activated the wrong switch. As a result 18,000 pounds of liquid oxygen were dumped onto the launchpad. Investigation of the error revealed that the worker was in the eleventh hour of the third straight night of 12-hour shifts. Under these conditions, according to experts on shift work, management should expect and guard against a low level of on-the-job performance.

Do any of the following factors imposed by management provoke fatigue, boredom, distractions, or especially haste, and thereby eat away at concentration?

☐ *Pressure.* Pressure, which results from a combination of workload, difficulty, working conditions, and subjective personal factors, does not always detract from performance. Indeed, too little pressure (by inducing boredom) can lead to almost as many errors as too much. Stress, however, defined as an uncomfortably high degree of pressure, undeniably heightens the risk of error. One of the leading causes of job-related stress is an atmosphere in which constantly changing conditions demand that employees react quickly and accurately. Do conditions of the job create unnecessary pressure that management has some power to curb? Does management add to this stress by placing undue pressure on personnel to get the job done quickly?

☐ *Pace.* Another leading cause of job-related stress—and errors—is work that, for the most part, is either fast paced or machine paced. Do you (or your personnel) always feel rushed on the job? Do machines determine the pace of your work? Does this pace detract from accurate performance?

☐ *Schedules.* Inflexible work schedules are another leading cause of job-related stress; a secondary cause is the unpredictability of meal breaks. Does your work schedule have some consistency, while at the same time allowing for flexibility? Do you have regularly scheduled breaks during the day?

☐ *Shift.* The rotation of employees between shifts, a working condition experienced by 27 percent of American workers, is a significant cause of job-related stress. For most people, working the night shift doubles the incidence of errors (and increases dissatisfaction with the job). Fatigue causes people to lower their standards regarding acceptable performance. According to recent studies by shift-work researchers, found long shifts also exact a heavy toll on performance: In the last 4 hours of a 12-hour shifts, the incidence of errors is three to four times higher than in the first 8 hours. Finally, many shift-work researchers feel that employers in the United States shift their workers too often — and in the wrong direction. Do you (or your personnel) work the shift best suited to your lifestyle and personality? Do you work long shifts with very little break between shifts? Do you regularly have to reorder every other aspect of your life to accommodate changes in work shifts?

☐ *Overtime Work.* The frequent imposition of mandatory overtime is another leading cause of job-related stress. Studies suggest that after 60 hours of work a week, alertness and attention to detail decrease significantly. How often are you (or your personnel) forced to work overtime? Do you receive sufficient warning before the overtime is required?

☐ *Delays.* Unforeseen delays cause haste, frustration, and other distractions that can cause errors. Does your job tend to proceed fairly smoothly? Do you usually get the information and/or materials you need when you need them?

☐ *Supply Shortages.* Supply shortages can cause severe delays, which can lead to haste, distractions, and ultimately errors. Do you regularly run out of essential supplies? Are supplies ordered well before they run out?

☐ *Discipline.* Do the reins of discipline decrease creativity and increase stress on the job?

☐ *Penalties.* One of the leading causes of job-related stress is the infliction of severe consequences on those who make a mistake. An inordinate fear of making errors can not only breed timidity, but actually increase the likelihood of errors. Do you (or your personnel) get severely penalized for making human errors? Mistakes (errors in judgment)?

## COMPENSATION

An article in *The Wall Street Journal* (August 29, 1991) compared the productivity and defect rates at two GM auto plants: one in Orion Township, Michigan, with a miserable record (as many as 88 cars with defects per 100 produced); the other in Oklahoma City, Oklahoma, with a sterling record (producing the Pontiac 6000, one of the 10 most trouble-free cars according to J.D. Power & Associates).

Although many factors contributed to the differences in quality between the two plants, two of those mentioned by the article were that the Oklahoma City employees "get substantially higher wages than do most such workers in the state" and that they have a generous benefits package. As a result of their relatively error-free performance, demand for their car increased sharply, leading to an increase in well-compensated overtime for the workers. This, no doubt, heightened the workers' job satisfaction and motivation, thereby maintaining or even further improving the quality of their performance.

Could disgruntlement regarding any of the following, by eroding motivation and attitude, be a contributory cause of errors?

☐ *Pay.* Pay that compares unfavorably with the "going rate" is a significant cause of job-related stress. How does your pay (or that of your personnel) compare with that of others who do similar work? Are you paying (or being paid) a fair wage for the work done?

☐ *Overtime Pay.* Do you (or your personnel) receive adequate compensation for mandatory or optional overtime?

☐ *Bonuses.* Do you receive bonuses based on job performance? Are bonuses earned primarily through error-free performance or by meeting rigid timetables?

☐ *Incentives.* Are incentives offered for error-free performance? Are they monetary (salary raises, bonuses, higher commissions), promotional (better job, more authority), or both? Are the incentives valued highly enough to motivate better performance?

☐ *Benefits.* Benefits have become increasingly important to American workers. One recent survey showed that about 25 percent of American workers would change their jobs, but stay solely because of their benefit packages. Accordingly, one of the leading causes of job-related stress is a recent, significant cut in employee benefits. How do your benefits stack up against the competition? Do you (or your personnel) feel adequately protected so that worries about health costs, life insurance, or retirement do not become a preoccupation or distraction?

☐ *Vacations.* Vacation and sick benefits that fall below the norm are significant causes of job-related stress. Do you get regular vacation time? Is it difficult to get the time period you want for your vacation? Does your allotted vacation time compare favorably with that received by others in similar positions?

☐ *Holidays.* Do you have to work on holidays that most other people take off? Do you receive extra compensation for working on holidays?

☐ *Privileges.* Do the privileges that come with the job compare favorably with those received by others in similar positions with other companies?

☐ *Parking Spaces.* Are there enough parking spaces to go around? Are parking spaces assigned according to job prestige? Has this become a source of resentment among either colleagues or subordinates?

☐ *Other "fringes."* Are the fringe benefits and perks (e.g., the use of expense accounts) that come with the job comparable to those provided by other companies? Do fringes set up echelons within the company that help breed resentment?

## ORGANIZATIONAL ELEMENTS

Do the following elements of your relationship to the organizational unit, other units, and to the organization as a whole enhance or detract from your performance (or the performance of your department)? Does the organization as a whole create systems, policies, and practices that make error more likely or less likely? Does internal organizational negotiating go on?

☐ *Organizational Source of Input for Your Work.* Do those who provide you with the input or other material that you (or your department) need to complete the task accurately understand and appreciate your requirements and aims? Do they supply you with what you need? Do you have all the information and materials you need when you need it? Or are information and/or materials often incomplete, inadequate, confusing, or late?

☐ *Organizational Recipient of Output of Your Work.* If you don't clearly understand what those who will receive your work want and need, you will continually disappoint them and necessitate endless revisions of your work. Do you (and/or your staff) understand and appreciate the needs and goals of the organizational recipient of the output of your work (or your customers, if you deliver the finished product)? Do you regard the next person to receive your work as if he or she were your customer? Do you serve this person efficiently, courteously, thoughtfully, and in a timely manner?

☐ *Staff Departments That Affect Your Work.* Red tape is a significant cause of job-related stress. Do other departments create bureaucratic hindrances to your job performance? Is communication and the exchange of information among departments clear, timely, and relevant?

☐ *Staff Departments That Affect Overall Employment.* Do other departments (personnel, payroll, benefits, custodial), though unrelated to the specific nature of your work, create conditions that distract you (or your staff)? Could changes or improvements in these departments affect your performance for the better?

☐ *Organizational Elements at Levels above Immediate Supervision.* If not at the executive level yourself, does the organization of the executive level have an impact on your performance (or that of your department)? Is the management stable or constantly in flux? Is there a formal means by which anyone in the company can voice concerns at the highest level? How many executive-level meetings need to be held before improvements can be instituted in your department?

☐ *Individual Personalities Identified as Representative of Management.* How do the majority of workers regard management? Do workers identify with management, regarding them as allies or even partners? Or do they have a largely antagonistic perspective of company management? Do they regard management as indifferent to their needs and concerns?

☐ *Corporate Management Style of the Organization (and overall culture).* Do managers take a hands-on approach to their duties? Or do they delegate responsibilities and trust that they will be completed? Do managers support and reward members of their staff who uncover, acknowledge, and/or tackle errors? Do managers spend an inordinate amount of time catching or correcting the errors made by those who work for them?

☐ *Developments, News, or Rumors about Planned, Prospective, or Possible Changes.* Two of the *leading* causes of job-related stress are a recent transfer in the ownership of the company and employee fears or expectations that the company will be sold or relocated. Are such rumors flying? If untrue, what can management do to dispel them? If true, what can management do to ease the concerns of employees?

☐ *Other Factors That Affect the Interests of Members of the Organization, Especially Members of Your Group.* A major reorganization of an employee's department or employer is a major cause of job-related stress. In addition, a significant cause of stress is the limited availability of opportunities for advancement. Do conditions like these affect you (or your staff)?

## SUPERVISION

Relationships with supervisors can exercise a powerful influence on attitudes and motivation. How does your supervisor—or how do you as a supervisor—rate in the following areas?

☐ *Relevant Knowledge and Ability.* Does the manager have the experience and expertise needed to perform supervisory tasks adequately? Was she or he promoted from within the department or brought in from outside the organization? Does the manager relate the lessons learned from his or her own mistakes to the employees?

☐ *Reputation.* What do employees know about the manager? Do they respect him or her? Does the manager have a reputation for knowledgeability, fairness, and hard work?

☐ *Values.* Do the values of the manager correspond to those of the workers? Does the supervisor appreciate the value of accuracy? Does the manager place a premium on quantity over quality? What values will the manager instill in employees?

☐ *Attitudes.* What attitudes most characterize the manager? How does the supervisor regard those who work under her or him? What attitudes does he or she express regarding upper management?

☐ *Personal Appearance.* How does the manager dress and appear? Is she or he generally neat and clean? Does the manager have an air of authority?

☐ *Style.* Does the manager tend to work with employees or tower over them? How well does he or she delegate responsibilities? Does the manager encourage, support, and reward the detection and reduction of errors? Or does he or she quickly find a target for blame or recrimination?

☐ *Patience.* Does the manager demonstrate patience with mistakes or errors made by those she or he supervises? Does he or she acknowledge that errors are unintentional? Or does the manager regard mistakes as if they were deliberate acts? Does the manager allow and encourage employees to take the time to master essential job skills?

☐ *Consistency.* Do employees consider the manager consistent and dependable? Are reactions and responses to employee performance even, measured, and fair? Does the manager expect the same quality of work and maintain the same standards even during difficult times? Does the manager acknowledge his or her own mistakes as freely as he or she expects others to admit theirs?

☐ *Clarity or Ambivalence.* Does the manager provide clearly understood instructions and requirements? As Michele Schermerhorn wrote in *Quality Digest* (May 1991), "In some cases employees' efforts are handicapped because they don't have clear, specific requirements for their work activities. They have to guess what is meant . . . and when their guess is wrong, they suffer the consequences of management's wrath." Does the manager make sure she or he is understood?

☐ *Impartiality or Partiality.* Do employees believe the manager has favorites? Do they believe that everyone in the department gets fair and equal treatment?

☐ *Effectiveness as a Leader.* How well does the manager set a course, establish operating procedures, and motivate employees to meet the goals he or she has prescribed? Does the manager know how to get the best out of each employee?

☐ *Effectiveness as an Administrator.* How well does the manager handle the various administrative responsibilities that come with the job? Does he or she oversee every aspect of the operation?

☐ *Effectiveness as a Communicator.* How well does the manager communicate with employees? Are goals, procedures, intentions, and needs expressed in clear and unambiguous language that all employees understand? When the manager is dissatisfied with an individual's performance, does he or she speak directly to that person or communicate indirectly through other employees, public notices, or other means?

☐ *Willingness to Listen.* "If people feel they are valued," Judy Rosener, coauthor of *Workforce America! Managing Employee Diversity as a Vital Resource,* told *Quality Digest* magazine, "they are more committed and highly motivated. They tend to work harder." Listening can demonstrate that a manager values an employee as a person. How well does the manager listen to those who work under her or him? Does he or she provide formal ways for the staff to raise grievances or suggest improvements? Does the manager actually consider suggestions and then implement them or explain why she or he has chosen not to?

☐ *Sympathy and/or Empathy.* Does the manager understand the difficulties that an employee might have in completing jobs accurately? Does he or she exhibit empathy for employee concerns—whether work related or not?

☐ *Flexibility of Response to Individualized Interpretation of the Supervisor's Directives by Employees.* Does the manager exhibit rigidity of thought or procedures? Does everything have to be done one way— the manager's way? Does the manager keep an open mind to new ideas or methods that employees suggest?

## SOCIAL ENVIRONMENT

Group composition invariably affects performance. How do each of these factors affect the interrelationship of colleagues in your group? How do they mesh or work together? Do they cause any clashes?

☐ *Personalities.* One of the leading causes of job-related stress is personal conflicts on the job. Do the personalities of the people with whom you work mesh? Do any open or barely concealed hostilities interfere with error-free performance? Have friendships formed that extend beyond the workplace?

☐ *Company Customs.* The customs of the company can influence how people interact with one another. A significant cause of job-related stress, for instance, is the general isolation of employees from one another. Are employees allowed and encouraged to interact freely? Is a "No Talking" or "No Fraternizing" policy enforced on the job? Do any other company customs restrict the interaction among members of the group?

☐ *Individual Traditions.* Do certain employees have individual traditions that influence or determine how they relate to others in the group?

☐ *Personal Habits.* Do the personal habits of various employees complement one another? Are some personal habits so unique (or even offensive) that they create a distraction (or annoyance) for other employees?

☐ *Mores.* Do employees share the same general sense of right and wrong? Do they agree, for instance, on what to do when they discover they have made an error? Do they share standards regarding acceptable behavior?

☐ *Informal Leadership.* The absence of leadership, whether formal or informal, can lead to disunity and often to errors. Do any of the employees have the ability and inclination to take charge when a situation demands it? Do colleagues respect the informal leadership of this individual?

☐ *Uniformity or Diversity of Economic, Social, Cultural, Ethnic, Racial, or Religious Backgrounds and Characteristics.* The makeup of the group has an impact on productivity and accuracy. "In organizations we've studied that value diversity," insists Judy Rosener, coauthor of *Workforce America!*[3] "morale is up, absenteeism down. Productivity increases; turnover is down." Does your department or group exhibit demographic uniformity? Or does a diversity of backgrounds (and ideas) exist? Do any elements of your demographic backgrounds cause conflicts?

☐ *Uniformity or Diversity of Age, Education, Family and Social Status, Career Objectives, Aspirations, Needs.* Does your group share similar social and educational backgrounds? Do you share similar goals and aspirations? Do any goals or elements of your backgrounds conflict?

☐ *Uniformity or Diversity of Attitudes toward Authority Generally and Toward the Supervisor in Particular.* Do group members share a common respect or distrust of authority in general? Do most individuals share similar attitudes regarding the group supervisor? Is this a positive attitude or a negative one?

☐ *Group Attitudes toward the Work, the Compensation, and the Working Conditions.* The facts regarding the work, the equity of compensation, and other aspects of working conditions can differ quite significantly from subjective perspectives. Do the people in your department share similar views of the work in general, the workspace, the compensation, and so on? Would these attitudes be described most accurately as positive or negative?

☐ *Attitudes toward Working in General.* The general work ethic of group members naturally has an impact on job performance. Do members of your group have a positive work ethic? Do they care about the work and value a job well done?

☐ *Sensitivity to Status.* Sensitivity to relative status on the job can lead to conflicts between workers that detract from concentration and performance. Do individual members of your group value the job they do? Do they feel that their contributions are recognized and valued by others in the company?

☐ *Class Consciousness.* Sensitivity regarding class can also prompt hostilities among members of a group in close daily contact with one another. Are there class conflicts among members of your group?

☐ *Political Ideologies.* Contrasting political beliefs can also create conflicts on the job. Do heated political arguments ever carry over into on-the-job personality conflicts?

## SUBJECTIVE ELEMENTS

Your perception of work conditions can have just as powerful an influence on performance as the "objective" existence of those conditions. Do any of these "intangibles"—which may themselves be influenced by many of the factors listed in the previous checklists—interfere with your performance or accuracy?

☐ *Values.* Your values can have an impact on your performance. Do your values (or those held by individuals who work for you) ever provide an obstacle to error-free performance? Do they ever contribute to errors? Do you derive satisfaction simply from doing your job well?

☐ *Your Attitude.* Your attitudes can increase or diminish the likelihood that you will make errors. Do you (or your personnel) generally have a positive attitude about yourself and about the work that you do? Do you feel your job is worthwhile?

☐ *Motivation.* Strong motivation is one of the keys to error awareness, and its absence is a formidable contributing cause of errors. Have unrealistic objectives, lack of resources, and/or rewards that you regard as unfair or inadequate eroded your motivation to achieve error-free performance? Do you feel highly motivated to avoid, correct, and prevent errors?

☐ *Your Mood.* Your mood, which can change from day to day—not to mention from hour to hour—affects your performance. How often does your mood disrupt your concentration on the task at hand?

☐ *Your Perception of Group Morale.* The way you regard the overall morale of your group can influence your own performance. Do you perceive that your colleagues and coworkers feel good about their work? Do they (and you) recognize their own contribution toward achieving the goals of the department as well as the company as a whole?

☐ *Your Participation in Group Esprit.* Your sense of belonging and contributing to a group with common goals can have a powerful impact on your performance. Do you feel as if you're part of a successful team? Do you feel that your colleagues and coworkers are depending on you to do the best job possible? Do you feel you can contribute to achieving the goals of the group? Are they trying to do the best job they can, too?

☐ *Overall Atmosphere.* Do you feel comfortable with the general atmosphere of the work environment? Do you feel you can do your best work in this atmosphere?

☐ *Interpersonal Ambience.* Do you feel comfortable with your colleagues? Your supervisors? Your subordinates? Do you get along with most of the people with whom you work? Do they seem friendly, capable, accommodating, and dependable?

☐ *Reaction to Incentives.* How would you assess the incentives offered by your company? Do you feel motivated to do better work by the incentives offered? Would you like to earn those incentives?

☐ *Sense of Personal Control over Work.* Of the leading causes of job-related stress, the most common by far is that employees have little control over how they do their work. A feeling of powerlessness regarding the problems and frustrations that arise at work destroys the motivation and commitment to do a good job. Do you feel you have some control over your work? Do you have some flexibility to do certain aspects of the job your way (with the proviso that you do the job right)?

## USING YOUR CHECKLISTS

Review the items you've marked on the checklists. Rank each on a scale of 1 to 5, where 1 has the most damaging impact on your (or your department's) accuracy and error-free performance, and 5 has the least damaging influence. This ranking will help you concentrate on the most prevalent contributory causes of error first.

Now that you know the contributory microcauses of your errors, you can begin addressing the problems they present. Knowing the factors that make a task vulnerable to human error will point you in the right direction toward reducing that risk. In many cases, your new awareness and understanding of the causes of error can develop into recommendations for reducing the risk of recurrence.

The great variety of causal factors gives you a wealth of options to reduce your risk of error. You will need to evaluate the cost and ease of implementation to decide which options to choose first. While you may find it either impractical or cost-prohibitive to eliminate some of these causal factors, you may find that by tackling the factors that are accessible to your intervention, you can significantly reduce your risk of error. Initiating improvements that attack just one of these error-causing factors will have a number of beneficial effects. If you have used this exercise to pinpoint one or more contributing factors that exert a particularly strong influence, correcting it or suppressing its influence will probably reduce the errors you make and may even eliminate certain kinds of error altogether.

Will eliminating the most powerful contributory microcause of errors make you entirely error-free? Simply put, no. These factors seldom act independently of one another. So addressing problems involving just one factor (no matter how detrimental) in just one of these general areas cannot eliminate errors altogether. Correcting one factor at a time, however, can bring into much sharper relief the effects of other contributing factors.

No one can correct everything that causes errors in one fell swoop. So concentrate on dealing fully with just one factor at a time and observe the impact of its correction on the incidence of error. This will help you develop a better idea of what you should tackle next.

As you proceed in your efforts to control as best you can the contributory causes of error, you might find it helpful periodically to refer back to the checklists and also to ask yourself the questions detailed in the following progress check. Taken together, they will help ensure that you don't overlook anything in your attempts to increase your error awareness and decrease your errors.

## HAVE YOU DONE WHAT YOU CAN TO REDUCE THE MICROCAUSES OF ERROR?

☐ Have you evaluated the physical environment of the operation in terms of light and noise levels, crowding, movement and other distractions, facilities and accommodations, ventilation and temperature, comfort, and the general absence of unfavorable factors?

☐ Have you reviewed operations and tasks—procedures, methods, written instructions, and other activities required to perform the work—in terms of the demands that they make on the people involved in completing them?

☐ Have you reviewed the qualifications, training, and background of everyone involved in completing the work (including yourself) to determine their suitability for the task(s) involved?

☐ Have you evaluated the equipment used in these operations in terms of their suitability for and adaption to the requirements necessary to complete the process accurately?

☐ Have you carefully evaluated all forms, formats, and any other rigidities involved in the completion of the task, including programmed sequences and formats in computer software or on computer terminals, in terms of their optimal adaptation to their purpose and use in completing the task?

☐ Have you considered the nature, form, and other characteristics of the input received and other materials employed in this operation in terms of the effects they produce on the people and processes involved in the operation?

☐ Have you thought of any changes or corrections that might improve, modify, or simplify the system as a whole or any of its elements to render it less vulnerable to error?

☐ Have you done everything in your power to implement these ideas, or to pass them on effectively to others who have the power to implement them?

Once you can honestly answer "yes" to all the preceding questions, then you have done virtually everything in your power to eliminate contributory microcauses.

Contributory microcauses of error generally demand and deserve your primary corrective attention. Once you have dealt with their much more pervasive (and yet more readily reparable) negative influence, you can direct your efforts toward eliminating or at least minimizing the impact of the macrocauses of error. By combining aggressive efforts to attack microcauses of error with secondary measures aimed at discovering and guarding against macrocauses, you will invariably reduce the errors you—and those who work for you—make.

## HEIGHTENING YOUR ERROR AWARENESS

### MICRO, MACRO, PROXIMATE, CONTRIBUTORY?

Of the four general classes of error detailed in Chapter 13, (proximate microcauses, contributory microcauses, proximate macrocauses, and contributory macrocauses), which should management attack first? Why?

*(continued)*

## EVALUATE YOUR CHECKLIST

Review the notes you made next to each item you felt contributed to your errors. Now reconsider these causes in relation to the kinds of errors you have made and their effects. Which causes most often correspond to the kinds of errors that produce the worst effects? What actions can you take to eliminate these causes—or at least minimize their impact?

Would you say that the errors you—or those who work for you—most commonly make arise as a result of shortcomings in certain areas more than the others? Which areas plague you (or your department) most often?

# NOTES

1. Keki R. Bhote, writing in an AMA Management Briefing, *World Class Quality: Design of Experiments Made Easier and More Cost Effective Than SPC.*
2. Throughout this section, the material on the leading causes, significant causes, and secondary causes of job-related stress (in descending order of influence) has been drawn from the previously mentioned study of job-related stress sponsored by the Northwestern National Life Insurance Company.
3. Marilyn Loden and Judy B. Rosener, *Workforce America!: Managing Employee Diversity as a Vital Resource* (Homewood, IL: Dow Jones-Irwin, Inc., 1987).

PART V

# STRATEGIES TO REDUCE YOUR ERRORS

# *15*

---

# IMPROVING
# YOUR MEMORY

**THE TRUE ART OF MEMORY IS THE ART OF
ATTENTION.**

**—SAMUEL JOHNSON**

E ach of us has the capability to remember a great many things. You may recollect the name of the girl who sat next to you in seventh-grade algebra. You may recall the exact date you first bought stock in the Apple Corporation—and precisely what you paid per share. You may be able to recite the Nielsen or Arbitron ratings for every television program in last year's fall lineup. Or you may call to mind an obscure precedent that applies to a current legal case.

Yet despite your great capacity to remember, whether with ease or with a little effort, your memory may still fail you on occasion. We all suffer from memory lapses, and make errors or mistakes as a result. And some of us experience forgetfulness more often than others.

## THE CAUSES OF MEMORY LAPSES

Why do you forget certain things? Why do you sometimes find it difficult to recall where exactly you put your glasses or car keys? Why do you head for the grocery store, needing to buy only five things, and then stand in Aisle 3 for five minutes trying to remember two of them? Why do you forget the names of people you've met once, twice, or even half a dozen times? What makes you grope for bits of information that seem as if they should be easy to remember?

In Chapter 11, I compared the misreading of symbols to the act of passing someone you know on the street without recognition. Let's use a similar example here. Have you ever forgotten the name of someone with whom you were acquainted? This is a memory lapse rather than a recognition error. This tip-of-the-tongue phenomenon can be much more frustrating than failing to recognize the person altogether. You know that you should know, but you still don't!

What are some explanations for memory lapses? The answers could lie in one or more of the following possibilities:

- You did not consider the person important enough to commit his or her name to memory. Interest plays an important role in the functioning of memory. If you thought you would never meet the person again, perhaps you paid less heed than you otherwise might have.

- You did not focus your attention properly when first introduced to this person. Perhaps the setting was somewhat turbulent or you were distracted by other thoughts.

- In organizing your memories, you did not link the person's face with the memory of his or her name. It becomes much more difficult to form such a link after the fact—which you must do to remember the person's name (unless he or she provides other information that helps form other identifying links).

- The context was too dissimilar from the situations in which you had previously met. Just as context can help recognition, it can also form associative links that spark memory.

The preceding circumstances can have a negative impact on any attempt to remember—whether it involves a person's name, a fact, items on a list, or any other information you want to recall. The functioning of memory depends strongly on:

1. Interest.
2. Attention.
3. Mental organization.
4. Associations (placing the memory in context).

By learning how to focus interest and attention, how to forge associative links, and how to organize these links in your mind, you can improve your memory. "Method," as Thomas Fuller once wrote, "is the mother of memory." No matter how well your memory works now, you can do things to make it even better. And as a result, you can make fewer errors.

## THE INFLUENCE OF INTEREST

In the following rectangle, draw the flag of the United States of America (if you are a citizen of a different nation, draw your own country's flag). Don't copy it from another source; rely solely on your memory.

Now compare what you have drawn to the actual flag. You may be surprised to discover that you have made an error. In taking this test, most people have trouble replicating the image precisely.

If you made a mistake, consider why your memory might have failed you. Since you have, no doubt, seen the flag thousands of times before, your memory lapse cannot be due to a basic unfamiliarity with the image. In all likelihood, however, despite the many times you have "seen" the flag, you have probably seldom really looked at it. You may never have *focused attention* on the details—the order of the stripes, the arrangement of the stars. This is not a criticism. There's no particular reason that you *should* have focused attention on the flag. Perhaps you had *no interest* in its details. Interest or desire can motivate us to apply some effort to concentrate or focus attention. And lack of interest can therefore lead to faulty memory.

## FOCUSING ATTENTION

Now, create a mental picture of the face of a current United States penny. (Don't actually take one out of your pocket and examine it. That would be cheating.) Then answer the following questions about the coin:

- Who is depicted on the penny? (That's the easy one.)
- Does he face to the right or to the left?
- Which of the following phrases appear on the *face* of the penny?
  1995 (or some other date of minting).
  DEPARTMENT OF THE TREASURY.
  E PLURIBUS UNUM.
  FEDERAL RESERVE BANK.
  IN GOD WE TRUST.
  LIBERTY.
  ONE CENT.
  UNITED STATES OF AMERICA.
- Where do each of the phrases you've chosen appear on the penny? (For example, if you've chosen the date, where is it stamped? Above the image's head? In front of his nose? Below his chin? Behind his head? Behind his back? Across his chest? Behind his neck?)
- In the following circle, draw the penny you've described through your answers.
  (Don't worry about artistic talent.)

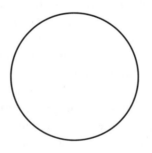

EXTRA CREDIT: Which of the preceding phrases appear on the *back* of the penny?

Now, take out a real penny and compare your answers with the coin in your hand. How did you do? More than half the people in the United

States are unable to answer all six questions correctly. Although we may use pennies every day, few of us pay attention to its details, except those that distinguish it from a nickel, dime, quarter, or half dollar: its color, size, and the absence of ridges around the edge. For this reason, though we can recognize it instantly, we may find ourselves unable to recall it in detail.

The exercises in this section and the previous one provide clues about how to commit the information that we want or need to remember to memory. Since our focus of attention plays such a critical part in forming lasting memories, we need to improve our concentration to enhance our memories. So when confronting something that you wish to remember, observe the following tips:

- Avoid distraction. Do not become overloaded.
- Pay attention. Listen, watch, read, and observe carefully and thoroughly.
- When taking in information, consciously use two or more senses or aspects of senses. Apply sight and hearing, color and touch, figure and word, all to the same experience.
- Concentrate on the important points.
- Form a specific intention to remember.

## ORGANIZING MEMORIES

Now that we've looked briefly at the role of interest and attention in the functioning of memory, let's look at mental organization. Organizing experiences and information is a distinctly human way of attempting to make sense of events, data, and the world in general. When confronted with new material or occurrences, we try to place them within a framework of already known concepts. In general, we find it easier to retrieve information when we want it if—at the time of memory storage—we can make sense of it and organize it within a context of other memories or acquired knowledge. If the material makes little or no sense to us therefore, we should try to rework it, structure it, and interpret it in a way that will ultimately assist retention.

Many people find that immediately organizing their thoughts or experiences can help them recall this information later. You may, for example, take notes to help you remember the most important points you want to recall. Many people employ this strategy in schoolroom situations. Yet the strategy has enormous value outside the classroom, too.

Don't underestimate the power of a memory aid as simple as note-taking. Whether attending a lecture, listening to a business proposal or presentation, sitting in on a negotiating session, or evaluating a recently completed business meeting, note-taking can exercise a dramatic and positive influence on memory.

Conventional note-taking, however—virtually a word-for-word transcription—is inefficient and often irrelevant. You will almost certainly miss some information. To make matters worse, any later attempt to review the material will be time-consuming. And, if you focus your attention on words instead of key points, you will probably cheat yourself out of a certain degree of meaning as well as the formation of memories (knowledge).

When taking notes, you can actually begin organizing your memories. Instead of trying to make sense of every word you have written, just jot down and remember key words that signal the most important ideas. Remain flexible, adapting yourself to the subject matter. Later, when you recall these key words, you will draw up all the information you wanted to remember by recalling associations, inferences, and interpretations.

To help establish these associations, you may find it helpful while taking notes (or shortly thereafter) to develop a chart of key ideas. You can use circles, arrows, underlines, and colors to connect these key ideas or distinguish them from one another. This technique produces a memorably graphic presentation—a mind map of the experience.

## RETRIEVING MEMORIES THROUGH ASSOCIATIONS

The mind map brings us to the fourth essential ingredient in the foundation or improvement of memory: associations. Most memory-enhancing techniques concentrate on the formation of associative links that will help spark memories. These techniques build on the realization that no memory is an isolated bit of information. Each fits into a pattern of relationships.

What's the first thing you do when you realize you have misplaced an important memo, your wallet, or your keys? Most people try to retrace their steps. They may attempt to reconstruct the exact context of movements and thoughts that prevailed at the time they last held the missing object. If you employ this strategy, you are implicitly acknowledging that your memory is not isolated, but rather part of a larger pattern.

Memory-enhancing techniques allow you to construct your own relationships, to create your own associative patterns. In this way, you can enhance the memorableness of the information and events.

## MEMORY SYSTEMS

Each of the following methods offers cues that will help you recall those items that you need to remember. You will no doubt find it helpful to apply one or more to your own situation. Keep in mind, though, that each of us has unique ways of thinking. For this reason, you may find some of these systems more useful than others.

*Spatial Associations*   This system, like the six that follow it, dates back to Aristotle. In your mind, you create a floor plan of your home or apartment, or some other spatial structure. By then creating associative links, you relate the pieces of data you want to remember to different rooms in the home. Then, whenever you need to recall the data, just think of the floor plan.

For example, if you wanted to remember a list of groceries, you might set up a floor plan as follows: milk in the hallway; bread in the living room; eggs in the dining room; orange juice in the kitchen, and so on.

*Temporal Associations*   This system calls for you to set up an imaginary schedule following an hourly, monthly, or yearly progression. Many people use a rudimentary form of this temporal memory system without even recognizing it—in setting alarms on their clocks or watches to remind them to take a pill, make a phone call, or perform some other specific act.

If you needed to remember the names of customers to visit, you might try this method: At 9 A.M., I visit Jones. 10 A.M.: Go to see Smith. 11 A.M.: I see Williams. Noon: I visit Morrison. As you think of each hour, you will recall each name. If you do not remember a name associated with a particular hour, you know what you have missed and can concentrate your thinking on recalling that name.

*Class Associations*   This system establishes a relationship among objects you want to remember. Relationships can be found—or created. Or you can relate the objects you want to remember to a single class of more memorable objects—animals, for example.

Imagine that you wanted to call to mind the names of a dozen colleagues you met at an important business meeting. Until you get a chance to actually write them down, you might find class associations helpful. Using the class of animals, you could associate each person with an animal—either the first one that strikes you when meeting the person (resemblance) or perhaps using initials or words to cement the connection. In this way, you could remember: bear: Wendy Brown; bull: John

Blorkum; cat: Kate Cherkisov; dog: Rex Douglas; and so on. When you think of the animals at the meeting, it will aid your recall.

***Creating Contrasts***   Statements of contrast can be used to help you remember individual items. In trying to remember one thing, think of its opposite. You can always establish contrasts, even comparing something with itself, as in whiter than white. Contrasts generally work best when you make them as extreme as possible.

***Establishing Causal Links***   This method depends on establishing a true or whimsical cause-and-effect relationship among items you want to remember. A causal link forming a concrete image that you can see with your mind's eye works best.

For example, in remembering a grocery list, you might come up with a causal chain like this one: When the peaches fell from the tree, the milk-fed chicken eating rice and beans stopped and turned but slipped in oil. This will help you remember the peaches, milk, chicken, rice, beans, and oil.

***Relating Parts to the Whole***   Establish operational relations among things you want to remember. Consider the individual bits of information as ingredients that come together to form a whole. Then fix the relationship between the parts and the whole in your mind.

This technique works best when you are working with something that's an organic whole. For instance, if you wanted to remember a speech or a musical piece, you might find it helpful to note how the whole relates to each of its parts and vice versa.

***Numerical Associations***   The last of Aristotle's seven systems of memory classification calls for applying numbers to the data you want to remember. The numerical alphabet readily allows you to recall information in sequence. The Periodic Table is organized in this way: 1. hydrogen; 2. helium; 3. lithium; 4. beryllium; 5. boron; and so on. But it can also help you recall data out of sequence—that Abraham Lincoln was the 16th president; Jimmy Carter the 39th; Andrew Jackson the 7th. Our culture has already assigned numbers to many different lists.

***Rhymes***   Rhymes and verse can be used to stimulate memory. It's often used to good effect to help youngsters remember the alphabet and their phone numbers and addresses.

*Alphabetizing* Ordering names alphabetically can often encourage recall. For example, the alphabetical progression of Alabama, Alaska, Arizona, Arkansas, California, Colorado, Connecticut, Delaware, Florida, is much easier to remember for many people than the west-to-east, north-to-south sequence of Hawaii, Alaska, Washington, Oregon, California, Nevada, Idaho, Utah, Arizona, and so on.

*Acronyms* These are a single word or set of words using the initial letters of the key words that you need to remember. Acronyms can sometimes be used to remember items in a sequence like ROY G. BIV for the colors of the spectrum in order: Red, Orange, Yellow, Green, Blue, Indigo, Violet. But more often, they provide a useful way to remember a list that need not be placed in any special order For instance, you can use HOMES for the Great Lakes: Huron, Ontario, Michigan, Erie, and Superior.

If you had the 15 initial letters R, U, U, K, B, A, G, M, T, K, L, A, T, L, and E, you could rearrange them to form the words: BARK TALK MUTE LUG. This, in turn, could help you remember Byelorussia, Azerbaijan, Russia, Kazakhstan, Tadzhikistan, Armenia, Latvia, Kirghiziya, Moldavia, Ukraine, Turkmenistan, Estonia, Lithuania, Uzbekistan, and Georgia—the 15 republics formerly in the Soviet Union. Eliminating the 3 Baltic republics who declared their independence from the Soviet Union, you could use the acronymic GRAB KUMKUATT to remember the remaining 12 republics.

*Initials in Sentences* If initials of key words do not readily form acronyms, you might want to use words with these same initials to form a memorable sentence. "Every Good Boy Deserves Fudge," for example, helps one remember musical scales.

*Free Association* Relate names or items of information that you want to remember with other things that you know well. This may involve associating people or things that you want to recall with members of your family, career leaders in home runs, famous actors and actresses, pieces of fruit—anything that you know very well and can already recall easily.

*Diversification* Use different skills to perceive and then store an item or idea in different areas of the brain. Listen, write, read, recite. By using more than one of these skills you will establish different neural pathways, thereby committing the information to memory in several different ways. For example, when first introduced to someone (Listen), it can be helpful to repeat his or her name several times in conversation (Recite), so as to imprint in on the brain.

*Use Words to Remember Numbers* This method, adapted from Bruno Furst's memory courses, associates numerals with letters. You can then remember long sequences—or sequences of pairs—of numbers by forming words out of the letters associated with the digits in each number. Although somewhat complicated to learn at first, this system becomes easy once the original associations are mastered. The technique proceeds in two phases. The first involves associating numerals with sounds, while the second incorporates these sounds with vowels to make words associated with multidigit numbers. The accompanying charts show how it works. The letters W, H, and Y (WHY) as well as the letters Q and X and the five vowels are not assigned any numerical value under this system.

---

### PHASE I: ASSOCIATING NUMERALS WITH SOUNDS

| Digits | Sounds | Hints to Help You Remember the Link |
|--------|--------|-------------------------------------|
| 1 | T,D | T has *1* downstroke. |
| 2 | N | N has 2 downstrokes. |
| 3 | M | M has 3 downstrokes. |
| 4 | R | R is the *4th* letter of "four." |
| 5 | L | L is 50 in Roman numerals. |
| 6 | J, soft G SH,CH | J looks like 6 when reversed. |
| 7 | K, hard G hard C | K can be printed with two 7's on their sides. |
| 8 | F,V,PH | F, in lower-case script, has two loops, like the figure 8. |
| 9 | P,B | P looks like 9 when reversed. |
| 0 | Z,S soft C | Z is the first letter of *zero*. |

By combining these "null" letters with the "numerical" letters, you can create descriptive words that many people find much easier to remember than the numbers themselves. Although you can continue this list up to any number you find necessary or desirable, here's a list of sample words that can be used to remember the first twenty numbers:

---

**PHASE II: ASSOCIATING NUMBERS WITH WORDS**

| | | | |
|---|---|---|---|
| 1 = Hat | 6 = Shoe | 11 = Tide | 16 = Dish |
| 2 = Hen | 7 = Cow | 12 = Tin | 17 = Dog |
| 3 = Ham | 8 = Hive | 13 = Team | 18 = Tub |
| 4 = Hair | 9 = Ape | 14 = Tire | 19 = Tape |
| 5 = Hill | 10 = Woods | 15 = Hotel | 20 = Nose |

---

The key to using Furst's memory system successfully is simply memorizing the list of words so that you can recall them as quickly and easily as you do the alphabet.

### COMBINING METHODS

In general, the more associative connections you can make to what you want to memorize, the better your chances of remembering exactly what you need to recall. For this reason, it may help to combine two or more of the preceding methods.

For example, combining Temporal Association and Free Association, you could render your list of customers to visit even easier to remember. At 9 A.M. (at the start of the day), I visit Jones. At 10 A.M. (for a coffee break), I go to see Smith. At 11 A.M. (as the mail arrives), I see Williams. At 12 noon (lunchtime already!), I visit Morrison.

If you find any of the systems covered briefly in these pages useful, you may want to consult some of the many excellent books available on memory systems. If you want to improve your performance and reduce errors due to forgetfulness, you would do well to improve your memory.

## MEMORY AND AGING

Does memory inevitably decline with age? Certain types of memory do deteriorate as we get older. Yet studies have shown that not all types degenerate. In examining this question, psychologists distinguish among at least three (and maybe more) kinds of memory:

1. *Episodic (short-term) memory* is used to recall specific events.
2. *Semantic (long-term) memory* recalls information and experience, facts and knowledge.
3. *Implicit memory* is exercised in such automatic skills as driving, typing, or hitting a golf ball.

Of these three, only episodic memory worsens significantly with age. Semantic memory, far from deteriorating, actually seems to improve as we get older. And though the skills in which implicit memory is exercised might degenerate, the faculty itself does not decline.

Also, you can compensate for the decline in episodic memory. Developing strategies such as writing notes to yourself can help fix ideas in your mind. You can talk or think about events after they happen, a tactic that seems to transfer episodic memories into the semantic memory, making it part of our accumulated experience.

An exercise was suggested to me that might help overcome problems with episodic memory by connecting them to semantic memories. Suppose that you constantly misplace your address book. (For the purposes of this activity, the psychological reasons for misplacing the address book should be considered irrelevant.) The following steps might make it easier for you to avoid this habitual forgetfulness.

- Write yourself a short note saying, "Hand, I will not misplace this book again. I will remember what I do with it!" Place the note on the book.
- Read the note aloud two times.
- Link your commitment to remember with your long-term memories associated with the address book, particularly those with strong emotional content, such as important recollections triggered by the names it contains.

This strategy should help create an association between the short- and long-term memories. And since long-term memories are often fixed in the mind, this association may help you remember where you left the book.

In addition to transforming episodic memories into the semantic memory (or linking short- and long-term memories), Dr. David Mitchell, a psychologist at Southern Methodist University who has studied the effects of aging on memory, suggests, ". . . if older people are able to focus on what is happening without distractions, their memory may be just as good as ever." Dr. Mitchell's assessment indicates that concentration—focused attention—plays a key role in the formation and retention of memories. This applies to younger people as well. If you can improve your ability to concentrate, then you should be able to improve your memory. If you are already suffering from some episodic memory loss, you may find the compensation of memory-enhancing techniques even more useful than younger readers will.

If you dedicate yourself to learning one or more of these methods and use them to remember all the important items you need to cover in the course of a day, you (and those around you) will be amazed at how well you remember everything. With your improved memory, you will find that you make significantly fewer errors. You will find that your performance improves in many day-to-day tasks that you may never have associated with the exercise of memory before.

## HEIGHTENING YOUR ERROR AWARENESS

### MEMORY LAPSES

Analyze some of your memory lapses. Determine where they most often occur. For example, do you always misplace your sunglasses? Where do you ultimately find the lost article?

### MEMORY AIDS

What type of mental system works best for you? Mathematical, verbal, pictorial, logical, other? Make a list of the memory aids described in this chapter or others with which you are familiar. Use a different one every several days to see which prove most effective for you. Keep using those that work.

### NOTE-TAKING

How do you take notes? Do you try to jot down every word? Do you proceed down the page in an orderly fashion, listing chronologically each idea as it is presented? Or are you all over the page (or even several pages), establishing a different location for each new key idea and then centering other notes around these key ideas?

# 16

## RECOGNIZING PATTERNS IN ERRORS

I magine that you're a detective conducting a murder investigation. You will need to examine every bit of evidence to make sure you haven't overlooked clues to the murderer's identity. Certainly, if you find the butler standing over the corpse with a smoking gun in his hand, you can cut short the scope of your investigation. However, most murderers don't remain at their victim's side, waiting to be caught.

Now consider that you've been assigned to the case of a serial killer. How would this investigation compare with the first? The high and grisly cost exacted by a serial killer heightens the urgency; you must solve this case before the killer strikes again. On the other hand, because the serial killer has murdered more than once, the larger pool of evidence works to your benefit, increasing the chances of finding telling clues. When investigating an isolated murder, you might overlook a relevant clue. However, when probing a series of murders, patterns and commonalities that can indicate the killer's identity may become easier to spot.

So it is with the causes of errors. When you (or those who work for you) make a *single* error, with some labor, you can often discover the major causes with a thorough examination and analysis of the circumstances that led up to it. In many cases, applying the insights you achieve as a result of this analysis will allow you to correct the error appropriately and efficiently, and perhaps even prevent future errors of a similar nature.

But, when you analyze *several* errors at once, you may discover patterns of error-making with promising clues to help you identify overlooked yet potent causes. And this insight will prove even more helpful in preventing future errors. By attacking the contributory causes of past errors, you significantly enhance your efforts to eliminate similar errors in the future.

## A POOL OF ERRORS

Why scrutinize a pool of errors rather than dissect them individually? Analyzing single errors (especially major ones), can increase your understanding of how you make them. Yet studying a significant pool of errors can yield even more insight:

- You will assemble concrete evidence that demonstrates the *kinds* of errors you (or those around you) most often make.
- You will know *when* errors most often occur.
- You will recognize the *forms*, *material*, or *processes* most subject to error.

Identifying patterns of error can help you determine not merely how to correct them, but also how to prevent or reduce their recurrence.

Only after building an awareness of patterns can you most profitably analyze individual errors as they arise. Moreover, your awareness of error patterns in your employees will lead to a greater understanding of how common causal factors can affect more than one person.

Your recognition of patterns will heighten your appreciation of how the errors you once regarded as isolated, individual, and perhaps random can all result from the same causes. This will allow you to subject individual errors to analysis soon after they have occurred. However, you will no longer see these errors as separate events, but as components of a larger pool. Consequently, you will recognize the kinds of error you have made more easily, while becoming aware of general patterns.

## WHAT YOU SHOULD LOOK FOR

Pinpointing the causes of your errors calls for detective work. A cause that leads to more than one error commands a certain sense of urgency. Yet more often than not, certain characteristics of errors (or groups of errors) provide important clues. The reappearance of certain types of errors—or an identifiable pattern of occurrence—generally suggests the presence of a persistently repetitive problem.

Uncovering the patterns of occurrence of your errors will determine the areas in which you or your staff are most vulnerable. By identifying where, when, and under what conditions you have made the most errors in the past, you will alert yourself to the places, times, and conditions to watch in the future. Then, even if you can't change the prevailing conditions under which you must perform, you will know whether those conditions are problematic.

In analyzing your pool of errors, identify as many potential contributory causes as you can—even macrocauses, which may seem to lie well outside your control. You may have more influence over these factors than you first realize. The more thorough your analysis, the more you consider every possible causal factor, the better your chance of eliminating (or at least minimizing the impact of) the causes that have the greatest error-inducing influence.

## THE STEPS IN ANALYZING PATTERNS

In searching for patterns among a pool of errors, you might use the following steps for a logical sequence of analysis:

1. *Kind.* Roughly categorize the entire pool of errors according to type, nature, or characteristics.

2. *Patterns of Kind.* Examine the categories of errors you have established in Step 1 to see whether they offer hints about their causes.

3. *Effect.* Consider the possible immediate and long-term effects of any recurrent errors.

4. *Distribution.* Check the distribution (who, where, and when) of the entire pool of errors.

5. *Patterns of Correlation.* Correlate your answers to Steps 1 and 4 to see if any patterns reveal themselves.

6. *Upstream Sources*. Determine the origins of the raw materials involved in erroneous outputs to see whether a pattern exists. If working on an assembly line, for example, test samples of raw materials or manufacturing output. You may discover that many recurring errors spring from the same upstream originator of source materials.

7. *Computers*. If working with a computer, evaluate it and its programs to make sure they function properly. Since they can corrupt all data entered into a system, flaws in the database or programming need to be caught as soon as possible. If not, they will continue to generate errors in processing otherwise correct input. Database and programming errors not caused by tampering often result from acquired obsolescence.

8. *System Elements*. Evaluate all other elements of the system that the recurring errors of a particular category have in common.

In reviewing these steps, you no doubt recognized that the first three focus on the kinds of errors and their effects. They thus conform to the elements of the error-awareness explored earlier in this book. Steps 4 through 8 probe for possible patterns that might point toward proximate or contributory causes. Since we have looked at Step 6 in Chapter 7 and 7 in Chapter 6, and will examine Step 8 in Chapter 16, let's focus now on Steps 4 and 5.

## THE DISTRIBUTION OF ERRORS

In conducting your analysis of the distribution of errors, you should look for patterns in relation to:

- Time.
- Location (in conjunction with time).
- Context.
- Singularity.

Let's look at each of these elements in greater detail.

### TIME

The time when a number of errors occurs often provides important clues regarding contributory and proximate causes of error. The timing of errors can also alert you to moments at which you (or your staff) are particular vulnerable.

In NASA's Magellan spacecraft, for example, one of the memory units in a critical control system started to generate garbled data readouts recently, causing the entire system to shut down. NASA engineers noted that the garbled signals had begun immediately after Magellan jettisoned the rocket that had carried it into Venus's orbit. This suggested that the rocket separation had caused an electrical short or some similar malfunction. Knowing when the mishap had occurred helped engineers identify what went wrong where. As a result, NASA was able to correct the error from 155 million miles away!

Even the most complex machines are simple compared with people. NASA engineers were able to determine *precisely* when the errors had begun on the Magellan, and also to pinpoint everything else that was occurring within the system at the same time. This made it relatively easy (although no less astonishing) for them to narrow down a list of causal factors.

It is far more difficult to pinpoint precise times and concurrent events with people (unless they were interfacing with a machine that recorded the time of every action). Yet even if you can't determine the timing of an error to the second, if you establish the minute, or quarter of an hour in which it occurred, you may derive important clues about its origins.

An analysis of errors made by members of the accounting department over the course of several weeks, for example, demonstrates a pattern of errors occurring more frequently from 3:30 until 5:00 in the afternoon. Although this pattern does not provide a definitive answer regarding causes, it suggests fatigue as an influence. The department manager might find it effective to enforce a 3 P.M. "coffee break" or other respite to reinvigorate the staff for the rest of the afternoon.

Alertness and performance tend to vary with the time of day, reflecting workers' circadian rhythms (see Chapter 12). Different individuals may work more accurately in the afternoon than in the morning—or vice versa.

Certain times of the day or week are more conducive to errors for almost everyone. Analysis often shows that mistakes occur more frequently on Monday mornings or during the tail end of the night shift (from 6 A.M. on). Holidays, anniversaries, and special dates can also impact errors. Anticipation and/or remembrance can render concentration much more difficult. Looking for patterns in the incidence of errors on certain dates can thus provide you with clues to their origins which might otherwise go unnoticed.

The recognition of short-term (hour-to-hour, day-to-day ) or long-term (time of year) patterns of errors generally demands a long-term study extending over several months—or even years. The capacity to recognize such patterns therefore lies outside the abilities of most individuals. Corporations, on the other hand, have more practical and immediate means of measuring and charting the incidence of errors over years and decades.

Time should always be an important consideration in any investigation and analysis of errors. This can do more than change your approach to a particular task; knowledge of your own times of vulnerability can also influence the way you design future tasks.

## LOCATION (IN CONJUNCTION WITH TIME)

"Nothing puzzles me more than time and space," the essayist Charles Lamb once wrote. "And yet nothing troubles me less, as I never think about them." In looking for patterns in the incidence of errors, however, we must think about them. Albert Einstein noted that we can never consider time without also considering place. So in scrutinizing the timing of your errors, consider also any patterns of place.

The more specifically you can identify the place and time when a number of errors occurred, the greater your error awareness will be. The discovery, for example, that a single person (or a specific group of people) in a particular place made a great number of errors can provide important insights about their source. If you then couple these insights with the general time frame in which the errors occurred, contributory causes such as domestic difficulties, deadline pressure, collective bargaining, or other distractions often become more readily identifiable.

Although proximate causes that affect just one individual can often be difficult to recognize, those that affect several people are more readily identified using clues regarding place and time. If two people in the same vicinity (or different yet related locations) both make errors simultaneously (or at approximately the same time), this "coincidence" almost always points to a single, proximate, error-causing event such as a power surge or poor source materials used by both people. Knowing where and when the errors occurred can therefore facilitate identification of this event or material cause.

## CONTEXT

When a large number of errors repeatedly occur in relation to certain output (e.g., the same final products, or in the case of symbolic information, the same numbers, words, or other symbolic elements), this pattern often provides an important clue that these errors might result from a persistent microcause.

If your analysis uncovers this sort of pattern in a data-processing context, first focus on the upstream sources of raw materials. Examine not just the raw materials themselves, but also their antecedents—forms, instructions for filling out forms, tabulations, original reference materials, codes, and so on. Study all these carefully with an eye toward identifying any elements or characteristics that have caused or might have caused the observed errors (see Chapters 6 and 13).

## SINGULARITY

Singular events, or conditions often serve as proximate causes of error, accounting or helping to account for their incidence. In *The Turbulent Mirror*,[1] John Briggs and F. David Peat describe such a singular event in pinpointing the cause of a plane crash. A DC-9 taking off in a snowstorm in Denver stalled and flipped over only a few feet above the ground, killing 28 people. Investigators narrowed down the possible explanations to two that involved chaotic air currents or turbulence. "In one scenario, an unruly vortex of air, spun up in the wake of a jet landing on a nearby runway, failed to dissipate; it lingered for several minutes while other air currents nudged it into the path of the DC-9 and formed a fatal clot in the plane's compressors. In the alternative scenario—which investigators finally decided is the correct one—the culprit is a few grains of ice that passengers reported seeing on their plane's wings after the final deicing. These small seeds built up a turbulence powerful enough to bring the giant jet down."

Analysis of the distribution of errors, when correlated with categorization may yield significant insight. Regularity of distribution often suggests regularity of cause. Your discovery of a pattern in the occurrence may therefore provide important clues that point toward the origin(s).

# WHEN ERRORS SEEM TO OCCUR AT RANDOM

In some cases, your search for patterns will yield definite and conclusive results. In others, however, you may have difficulty recognizing orderly, detectable arrangements in the distribution of errors (time, place, or context) . Patterns are not always identifiable, or at least not immediately evident. In these situations, you will probably conclude that the errors occurred randomly. You should always regard apparent randomness with some suspicion, however. Many events only seem random until explained through analysis—precisely the kind of exploration demanded by the error-awareness system.

In discussing "random errors," an important distinction must be made between apparent haphazardness and truly random cause-and-effect relationships. A series of errors may occur with no apparent regularity or pattern. Yet they may still result from a consistent and regular cause-and-effect relationship.

In analyzing a large pool of errors, you may discover a few occasional fluctuations and regard these as being consistent with chance. Yet a closer look might reveal that errors increased on the days that less skilled temporary personnel were introduced into the system. Since these people are needed only sporadically, the errors that may have resulted *directly* from their presence may seem random, but only until you discover the actual explanation.

Before ascribing the bulk of errors to "chance," "randomness," or "fate," recognize that this assertion (whether accurate or not) means giving up the search for more meaningful, *controllable* causes. Appearances can be deceiving. Often in such cases, the error seems to occur irregularly only because the cause occurs irregularly. Once the cause is in place, however, the resulting error can be inevitable. This observable "pattern" means that these errors are not truly random. They have resulted from a regular, direct, one-to-one, cause-and-effect relationship with a proximate microcause—generally occurring within or very close to the process. The *appearance* of randomness is due only to the haphazard occurrence of the cause.

Although uncovering such a direct cause-and-effect relationship generally suggests increasing your alertness to the presence of that proximate cause, it may not suggest how to handle the problem. In comparing the costs of error with those of prevention, you may discover that some proximate microcauses just aren't worth fixing. The employment of temporary personnel, for instance, may occur so infrequently that it may cost more to avoid them than to correct the errors they make. You might weigh the relative damage of temporary personnel against the lessened productivity that would result from leaving vital positions vacant. Or you may compare the cost of increasing supervision of temporary workers' performance against the costs incurred from their errors.

After discovering a proximate cause of "random" errors, you should take the time to examine carefully their source and potential effects. Assess the likelihood that this proximate cause will occur often enough to constitute a significant and unaffordable cause of errors. And evaluate whether the errors from this proximate cause produce significantly adverse and costly effects themselves.

Apparently random errors may also spring from contributory causes of all kinds. Since these generally produce indirect effects, however, they can be difficult to identify. The effects of contributory causes may appear so random as to raise doubt about their influence altogether. Just because we find it troublesome to make the connection, however, does not mean that none exists.

Instead of automatically attributing undiscovered patterns to randomness, view them as consequences of the infinitely complex workings of the human organism. Continue your search for causation in contributory conditions or events that might have affected task performance, recognizing that the causal factors you at first considered random would more properly be called "unassignable causes." Your difficulty in trying to assign patterns may simply result from your own inability to isolate and identify one or more actual and significant contributory causes from among the infinitude of possibilities.

## EXAMINING THE ORIGINS AND EFFECTS OF CONTRIBUTORY CAUSES

Uncovering contributory causes is especially important because they often affect the task performance not merely of one individual, but of several, most, or even all members of a particular work group. Managers must do everything they can to identify the adverse conditions contributing to the production of errors, and then try to reduce their effects. Identification of relevant contributory causes is half the battle. If you can identify them, then you can probably take action either to eliminate them altogether or minimize their influence.

Yet if you plan to attack contributory causes, you will first need to analyze where they originate and the impact they have. Taken by themselves or correlated with additional information, these determinations can yield the best approach to eliminate or mitigate the damage. According to the Pareto-Lorenz maldistribution law, originally developed by Italian economist Vilfredo Pareto, 80 percent or more of all effects can be traced to 20 percent or less of all causes. That is, a few causes produce most of a given effect. By identifying and isolating these few causes, we can take the most efficient action against them.

## MATRIX OF CONTRIBUTORY CAUSES

|  | A. Affecting Individuals | B. Affecting Groups |
|---|---|---|
| C. Origins Within Workplace | AC. Originates within workplace and affects individual. | BC. Originates within workplace and affects group. |
| D. Origins Outside Workplace | AD. Originates outside workplace and affects individual. | BD. Originates outside workplace and affects group. |

Although the line that separates contributory causes of errors that act on just one or more individuals and those that affect a large group is often readily apparent, the dividing line between contributory causes that arise inside the workplace and those that arise in the "rest of the world" is not always so clear. However, since preventive and corrective measures differ depending on the source of the error, this distinction is important.

If you determine that factors quite remote from the workplace are generating contributory causes of error, you probably have little power to attack them directly. Though not subject to management control, however, contributory causes that arise outside workplace may nonetheless be affected by the influence of management action. Management can often use economic clout to influence contributory macrocauses of error that arise in business contexts outside the immediate sphere of management control. For example, many businesses today are looking for a way to reduce their responsibility and investments in employees' pension plans by having the federal government recalculate the value of assets and the contribution required by federal law.

Contributory causes may also arise in areas where management may have some voice—union organizing, for example—yet significantly less influence. They also arise in areas truly outside management's sphere of influence: the homes, families, neighborhoods, and friends of employees. When dealing with causes that arise outside the workplace, it's necessary to adopt measures that will *minimize the adverse effects* of this cause rather than eliminate the cause itself.

If the contributory causes seem to originate within the workplace, you can do much more to attack them directly. These, whether micro- or macrocauses, are subject to at least some degree of modification (or even elimination). Optimizing the physical conditions of the workspace, for example, can produce a surge of satisfaction and subsequently improve general performance among all the employees who work there.

If, after analyzing errors at your workplace, you determine that one or more contributory causes fall under the BC heading, take immediate and decisive action to eliminate, defuse, or correct them. These contributory causes demand the most attention from management for two reasons:

1. Because they affect most or all of the group, attacking these causes will improve the *everyone's* overall performance.

2. Because they arise within the workplace, management has more power to institute feasible changes that will affect and often eliminate them.

Contributory causes that fall under the BC heading include most of the same factors singled out as major causes of job-related stress. (This correlation should not really surprise anyone, since job-related stress often leads to physical ailments such as exhaustion, headaches, and muscle pain—all of which can reduce productivity and accuracy. In addition, job-related stress causes many workers to quit or stay home sick.)

A recent study commissioned by the Northwestern National Life Insurance Company (see Chapter 14) identified the following, all of which fall under the BC heading, as some of the most common causes of job-related stress:

- Employees have little control over how they do their work.
- Employees believe that the company will be sold or relocated.
- Making a mistake on the job leads to severe consequences.
- Employees almost always work quickly—often at a pace dictated by a machine.
- Constantly changing conditions require employees to react quickly and accurately.
- Personal conflicts on the job are common.
- Employees need to deal with lots of red tape to get anything done.
- The company rotates shifts among employees.

- The company has recently introduced new machines or methods of working.

- Adverse physical conditions, such as high noise or vibration levels or changing temperatures, exist.

- Employees generally have little contact with one another.

- The workspace has few windows, no windows, or little natural lighting.

- Employees have little or no privacy.

- Work is either sedentary or physically exhausting.

Tackle head-on causes that arise within the workplace. In many cases, you might find it most effective to adopt the hypothesis that you can *eliminate the cause completely.* Then set out to prove your hypothesis. But be prepared to be stymied from time to time. You may not be able to eliminate some contributory causes of error (such as a lack of privacy) completely. You may not be able change others such as the sedentary nature of a job. Or occasionally, you may eliminate the contributory cause—a substandard benefits package or some other subject of general complaint among employees—and discover that even after "solving" the problem overall task performance still does not improve.

If this were to occur, what would you conclude? That you had originally overestimated the influence of the dissatisfaction with benefits as a contributory cause of error? Would you therefore revoke or reverse the "corrective" action (if possible) and try something else?

This problem further illustrates the importance of a thorough analysis of the causes of error. Mistakes made in corrective efforts, like the original errors themselves, often cannot be recalled. To cancel an upgraded benefits package shortly after introducing it breeds greater resentment and dissatisfaction than having done nothing at all. In such a situation, management should not rescind its previous improvements (which may in fact have had a positive—albeit unnoticed—impact on performance). Rather, you should look for additional conditions that might contribute to causing errors.

Perhaps some elements of dissatisfaction have not yet been fully articulated. Unexpressed yet smoldering resentment, apprehension, anger, or condemnation can impair motivation, create distractions, and otherwise interfere with concentration on contributing to a proliferation of apparently random errors. What's worse, this kind of antagonism can foster defensiveness or hostility in the face of management's constructive criticism.

In all likelihood, this increase in negative attitudes will in turn contribute to more errors. Bad feelings feed on themselves.

Unearthing and defeating contributory causes of "random" errors demand a long-term plan of action. If such errors abound and no sources of contributory causation become immediately evident, an employee survey or a series of exploratory interviews may help you uncover some of these causes. In general, the identification of remote contributory causes of error requires gathering as much information as you can about the values and priorities of the workers in your group. Examining their attitudes, motivations, and overall values—as well as the factors that influence these attitudes—can increase your awareness of the contributory micro- and macrocauses of their errors. Yet you will still need to exercise considerable powers of deduction, associative connection, and rapport in your role as manager.

Personal dialogue with all workers open to such an approach frequently improves performance. Nothing guarantees the proliferation of error as certainly as a system that fails to provide for the psychological needs of its people. Conversely, nothing minimizes error more effectively than a sincere effort to optimize the mutual adaptation and adjustment of all workers to the system where they must function together.

One of the most effective strategies in improving worker satisfaction, morale, and motivation centers on providing employees increased opportunities to articulate not only their resentments and gripes, but also their ideas and suggestions. Group discussion often makes it easier find the source of problems. When a contributory cause such as a general reprimand or the improper firing of a colleague exercises a similar effect on the more-or-less shared attitudes and motivations of a group, its members often feel more inclined to discuss the problem in a group setting.

The concept of "quality circles," introduced to Japanese corporations by Dr. W. Edwards Deming in 1950, rests on this foundation. Quality circles, which helped build the reputation of Japanese manufacturers for efficiency, productivity, and quality, encourage everyone involved or affected by a particular problem to come together to brainstorm, discussing possible alternatives and solutions, regardless of their level in the corporation. The value of quality circles, originally applied only to manufacturing, extends far beyond this original aim. Quality circles can also be used to help deal with contributory causes of error.

Although most valuable at first simply to uncover contributory causes of error, quality circles or "team meetings" should not stop there. As D. S. Fletcher describes the process in "The Team Meeting" (*Quality Digest,* May 1991):

The question that needs to be asked [after discovering a costly error] is, "What needs to be done so this problem never happens again?" The group needs to probe for the root cause. Why did the "O" rings fail during the launch of the Challenger? Why didn't management know? Improving processes and the concept of continuous improvement are tackled here. . . .

[Before the meeting ends,] the team member briefly proposes action steps he or she believes must be taken to eliminate the root causes, to achieve the results and eliminate the symptoms.

Error awareness does not aim solely to increase our knowledge and awareness, but to put that awareness into action. Quality circles, team meetings, and gripe sessions devoted to error awareness must therefore not be satisfied merely with uncovering contributory causes of error. We must also develop concrete strategies to eliminate these causes or soften their impact.

Getting everyone at every level involved in defining and attacking contributory causes of error will in itself improve performance. Increasing everyone's sense of involvement heightens team morale, thereby eliminating one of the most common contributory causes of error. Even more significant, it can set in motion a mechanism for making gradual improvements in quality and accuracy that, like a good investment, increase in value over time.

Soliciting opinions and suggestions from everyone affected by a problem or its solution does not necessarily mean that everyone plays a part in making the decision. Ultimately, one person—or a small group of people—must exercise the authority to make a final decision.

Honda, to name just one corporation, believes that the use of quality circles may have gone too far in certain Japanese corporations. As Nobuhiko Kawamoto, president of Honda Motor Company told *The Wall Street Journal* (April 11, 1991): "We do too many things in groups. We've lost a sense of responsibility, the feeling that every individual has his [or her] own specific duties. . . . We'd get the people from research, sales, and production together and . . . we'd talk, but there would be no agreement. . . . We'd have another discussion, and another study and then more preparation. And finally, the decision would come months later."

With these considerations in mind, Kawamoto has instituted a new management approach at Honda that emphasizes more individual responsibility for decisions. At the same time, however, Honda does not plan to abandon the practice of seeking input from people in all its divisions and departments.

It's important to get everyone involved in the teamwork required to set and achieve goals. However, corporations—even Japanese ones—cannot be run as democracies. Someone needs to take authority and assume responsibility for making decisions.

The effort to discover contributory microcauses and macrocauses of error often reveals causes that management can influence to a significant degree, especially if they tackle them head on. These include issues that affect employer-employee relations, news or rumors about the company's safety or environmental problems, or plans for moving the business, closing shop, acquiring or being acquired. Yet even the best managers must resign themselves to their inability to correct—or even pinpoint—many remote yet potent contributory macrocauses of error. Inevitably, despite all efforts to track them down, some contributory causes remain so remote from the workplace that they are essentially undiscoverable to management. Yet these inevitable shortfalls should not discourage managers from making the effort. For attacking the contributory causes of error, no matter how remote, will almost invariably minimize their distracting impact.

# HEIGHTENING YOUR ERROR AWARENESS

## THE POOL OF ERRORS

Identify specifically the causes of some of the errors you (or those around you) make most often. Don't simply look for easily identifiable proximate causes, but for more subtle contributory causes—both microcauses and macrocauses—as well. You will have greater success if you collect and analyze a pool of errors rather than single, isolated errors. Attempt to trace these errors back to their sources.

## THE TIMING OF ERRORS

Is searching for the timing patterns practical for individuals? For corporations?

*(continued)*

## PATTERNS OF DISTRIBUTION

Do you recognize any patterns or regularity of distribution in any of the errors that you listed in response to previous chapters of this book? Or do they all appear random? Does this give you any clues about possible contributory causes of these errors?

## RANDOM OCCURRENCES

Do you agree that errors with no identifiable patterns of distribution must have occurred as a result of random causes? What would you do if faced with a situation such as sporadic errors correlating with temporary help? Could you still find any clues to causality in such cases? Given the circumstances (and your awareness of them), what action would you take?

## USING THE MATRIX OF CONTRIBUTING CAUSES

Where do the contributory causes of error in your situation most often arise? How many people do these contributory causes affect? Use the matrix to determine the origin and influence of contributory causes in your department, office, or business. Does this yield any additional insight into contributory causation?

Of the four groups described in the matrix, which demands the most management attention? Why?

## WORKER DISSATISFACTION AND ERROR

If you know or come to recognize that vague complaints, unexpressed resentments, and unarticulated sources of dissatisfaction are having a negative impact on the performance of the people you supervise, what should you do?

# NOTE

1. John Briggs, *Turbulent Mirror: An Illustrated Guide to Chaos Theory and the Science of Wholeness* (New York: Harper & Row, 1990).

# *17*

## MANAGING AND SUPERVISING TO REDUCE ERRORS

**THE MAN WHO ESCAPES WITH CLEAN HANDS FROM THE MANAGEMENT OF "BUSINESS" AFFAIRS ESCAPES BY A MIRACLE.**

**—PLATO (PARAPHRASED)**

Whether or not they cause errors, managers must take more responsibility for reducing them. Some management experts place much of the onus for reducing errors in business and manufacturing on the shoulders of managers and supervisors. Dr. W. Edwards Deming, for one, goes even further, attributing the origins of 85 percent of quality errors to poor management practices, rather than workers.

Most traditional managers would disagree with Deming's numbers. A few years ago, for example, California business managers were surveyed about whom they regarded as accountable for quality. Fifty-five percent fingered the worker; 25 percent identified the supervisor; 12 percent pointed to engineers and other specialists; and only 8 percent named management. Despite management's apparent reluctance to hold themselves accountable, according to Deming's view, improving quality and cutting down on errors center on modifying managerial practices.

Some error reduction options available to management can be relatively easy to introduce, while others may be more difficult. No universal cure exists that will fit every situation. The effectiveness of any error-reducing strategy applied to a particular set of circumstances depends on the following seven error-reducing criteria:

1. The kinds of error(s) to be minimized.
2. Who makes the errors.
3. Why the errors are made.
4. The plan chosen to remedy the errors.
5. How good the remedy is in general.
6. How well the remedy fits the situation.
7. How effectively the remedy is applied.

The principles of error awareness play a critical part in determining and implementing the best possible strategy to combat the prevalence of error. Two of the fundamental benefits of error awareness—knowledge about the kinds and causes of errors—play a critical role in determining the most appropriate remedies. For no matter how good they may be in general and how well they might be applied, remedial strategies inappropriate to the unique circumstances of a particular situation—those that don't take into account the specific kinds, sources, and causes of error—won't work!

## HOW HIGHLY DO WE VALUE QUALITY?

Countless manufacturing and service companies have taken up the term "quality" as their buzzword in advertising campaigns over the past few years. But really, how committed are American businesses to the goal of quality?

I believe that until recently, our practices have given short shrift to the concept of *quality: providing the best product or service attainable, as free of errors (or defects) as possible.* In North America, numbers were all that mattered to most business executives: production quotas, products sold, costs per unit, profit margins. At the same time, other significant numbers, such as products recalled and the costs of error, were ignored.

The rule of numbers has prevailed in the United States and Canada since the end of World War II. The scarcity of consumer goods available during wartime helped propel a boom in demand in the subsequent decades. People would buy almost anything—as quickly as a manufacturer could produce it. In such an atmosphere, the quality of goods mattered little as long as the volume of production, and sales, remained high.

The enormous demand for consumer goods after the war thus gave rise to the misconception (still prevalent in many management circles) that the production of mediocre goods was more profitable than that of top-quality products. (This misconception would later be applied to the provision of services too.) Planned obsolescence had begun. Each novel product was hailed as "new and improved," only to be replaced within a year by a newer, more improved model.

Under these conditions, businesses placed little emphasis on building quality into products. If considered at all, quality was merely an afterthought. In mass production, quality control methods would try to catch the *really* defective products before they reached the customer, but only after they had already been assembled. Manufacturers operated under the implicit—and often explicit—assumption that quality costs too much. Although 25 percent of the typical manufacturer's budget went toward repairing and reworking poorly built products, most managers regarded this as proof that quality is too expensive to maintain. Very few recognized that repair and rework are costs incurred through *lack of quality*, rather than through the pursuit of quality. No one seemed even to consider that manufacturing so many defective products—and then trying to catch them afterward—might cost more than building quality products in the first place.

Even more damaging than the financial costs of error were the psychological costs incurred through a widespread, systematic, cultural acceptance of shoddy workmanship. The elevation of volume over quality has had a profound impact on American workers and consumers. We began to expect less from and to accept greater mediocrity of our products—and ourselves.

Good managers can reverse this shortsighted and economically dangerous trend. Managers need to commit themselves to—and instill in their workers—the notion that good quality saves money and poor quality costs money in the long run. Instead of concentrating shortsightedly on the bottom line, we need to shift our focus to continual improvement, the true key to lasting profitability.

Many Japanese companies, tutored and encouraged by quality pioneer W. Edwards Deming, trumpet the ideal of total quality: a philosophy and way of life that permeates an entire company. The concept of total quality, which more and more American companies are also adopting, stresses that corporations design quality into their products, not inspect for it (through quality control) after the fact. Total quality links everyone in the company, from top management to the assembly-line worker, in a commitment to excellence. All employees are expected to perform with minimal errors. Secretaries are anticipated to avoid typos; clerks, shipping errors; accountants, billing errors; and executives, strategic errors. According to this concept, the individual accepts responsibility not only for his or her own work, but for that of the entire group.

Federal Express made quality its watchword in the 1980s. The company instituted a massive training program that taught its 17,000 couriers how to use hand-held computers called SUPERTRACKERs. The corporation encouraged trainees to provide feedback on the system and to solicit comments and requests from customers to provide just the services wanted. As *Quality Digest* noted (May 1991), "The blend of employees listening to customers, managers listening to employees, and managers working with employees to make things work, has helped Federal Express weave quality improvement into its entire corporate system."

Everyone in the corporation became dedicated to providing the best, most error-free service possible. As a result, Federal Express became the first large service corporation to win the Malcolm Baldrige National Quality Award.

In Japanese industry, improvement means higher performance throughout the development and delivery of the product or service from the company to the customer. With this goal in mind, the Japanese are not satisfied with mere enhancements, such as making a TV with a larger screen or stereo sound. Instead, they aim at delivering a product that performs better, has less defects, elicits fewer customer complaints, and requires a smaller repair team. Quality is expected to permeate every aspect of the company. And the results are impressive: Many Japanese manufacturers now measure their error rates in parts per million!

Japanese engineer Genichi Taguchi, whose quality methods have been adopted in this country by Xerox, AT&T, and Ford, among many others, is one of the pioneers of total quality. *The New York Times* described Taguchi's philosophy as follows:

> While Americans set specification limits, Dr. Taguchi preaches *that all variations from ideal values [defects] cause a loss of quality and impose a cost. . . .* Anything short of ideal dimensions results in some economic loss, he argues, whether it is in greater warranty costs, consumer dissatisfaction, or a loss of reputation for the company. . . . This economic justification . . . demonstrates that *improving quality is not just a worthy goal but good business* [emphasis added].

Quality in products and service is the by-product of error-free performance. For this reason, becoming more error-free too is not merely a worthy goal, but good business.

## CAN QUALITY CONTROL HELP MINIMIZE HUMAN ERROR?

Lacking the advantage of error awareness, many managers in the past confined their attempts to identify and correct errors to "quality control" methods. Quality control prescribes standards for work done on physical materials and then provides quantitative information about the incidence and cost of specific types of deviation from these standards. Quality control often depends on statistical techniques, a useful tool in determining problems related to mechanical operations. And these methods have proven their effectiveness in identifying errors in mass production.

The most important applications of quality control are found in the promotion of the uniformity of physical characteristics in the mass production of nearly identical units. Quality control methods ensure, for example, that Jeep Cherokees all conform to prescribed standards for size, engine specs, and interior.

Many operations involved in the processing of information or data can reasonably be regarded as similar to certain manufacturing operations. Clerical operations such as copying are primarily physical in nature and are not intended to affect the value or meaning of the symbols in any way. An error occurs, therefore, when the clerical operations alter the intended significance of the symbols. The deviation of a transcript from the source material can thus be likened to the deviation of a Cherokee from company standards.

Jobs that are primarily routine and repetitive lend themselves to certain quantitative measures of performance. Such productivity indicators as trucking miles driven per week or number of rooms mopped and cleaned per night provide useful and informative measures of performance. Despite the implication of the words "quality control," however, jobs that involve *qualitative* performance are much harder to measure by quantitative means.

In principle then, *some* quality control methods have *some* usefulness in evaluating the incidence of errors in *some* human tasks. Quality control methods might be applied to errors that occur in quasi-mechanical human operations like transcription. But since human behavior (and the nature and manifestations of human error) involves an infinite number of variables, quality control applies only in the most limited of contexts.

There are fundamental differences between symbolic units of data and physical units of manufacture. Data-processing and information systems, unlike mass production, almost never aspire to the manufacture of identical units. Each unit of symbolic material is unique, identifiably distinct from the units that surround it. In addition, the cause of machine-made errors is generally far simpler and more obvious than the multifarious combination of factors that can cause or help cause the errors that people make. These basic discrepancies affect the validity and applicability of conventional quality control measures to human errors.

Even when quality control methods can be applied to human errors, its techniques are somewhat limited. Quality control focuses primarily on the result of an error: the flawed product. It catches errors after the fact, recognizing their effects rather than their origins.

But although its methods can confirm the existence of a problem, quality control does nothing to *solve* that problem. It evaluates errors solely in terms of their effects: Is the product flawed enough to warrant rejection? In many cases, quality control does not even recognize errors unless the answer to this question is yes. But rejection does not solve the problem that led to the defective product; it does not point to the cause(s) of error. So although quality control can be helpful in identifying errors through their effects, it provides little or no insight into the causes of errors that people make.

## THE WRONG PATH FOR MANAGERS

Suppose that the probability you will get the 100th item wrong after building 99 items (or even 999 items) correctly is 1 in 100. Although very few people would insist that the 100th item *must* be incorrect, most wrongly assume that the odds start to work against you the more items you correctly process. For any individual item, however, the odds remain the same: 1 in 100.

Although errors may be inevitable when considered on a probabilistic basis, this generalized statement does not apply to any *particular* error. Statistical statements that apply to the whole, often have no validity out of context and no relevance to individual items. Particular errors are *not* inevitable and need not be accepted as such.

Conventional managerial wisdom, however, often regards errors as an inescapable part of the cost and trouble of doing business. And most managers therefore assume that they can't do anything about it. Far too many people in management accept the following simplistic syllogism:

1. Errors are inevitable.
2. This is an error.
3. Therefore, this error is (or was) inevitable.

And this managerial attitude can damage the entire organization. For when managers believe errors to be inevitable, the same attitude becomes deeply rooted in those who work under them. Mistakes become commonplace because the organizational culture succumbs to learned helplessness. The organization as a whole begins to tolerate and even expect error.

If, as W. Edwards Deming maintains, 85 percent of quality problems are caused by management, attitudes such as these prevent managers from solving their problems. It's no wonder, then, that we've made little progress in reducing the incidence of error over the past few decades.

The factors that prevent most managers from effectively reducing the incidence of errors under their supervision include:

- No leadership or coherent policy in error reduction.
- No resources or time allocated to error prevention, but unlimited quantities of both expended on containing the damage that results from error.
- Ignorance about the impact of error on overall quality and cost.
- No error awareness and/or no follow-up of awareness with action.

The attitude that errors are inevitable justifies these shortcomings, rationalizing inaction by arguing that any steps to prevent them would be futile.

Learned helplessness prevents managers and employees from growing. The organization, failing to collect and analyze information about errors and causal factors, cannot use this awareness to identify situations that increase the risk of errors. The organization ignores and accepts minor errors, regarding them as an unavoidable annoyance, and springs into desperate action only when a crisis occurs. The panic of the moment prevents any thorough analysis, and therefore any error awareness (see Chapter 18).

Whether serious or minor, the organization neglects to identify roots of the error or attributes them to a particular set of circumstances, thereby slighting broader implications. And lacking error awareness, the organization neither solicits nor accepts suggestions on changes that might reduce the risk of errors. Since the false premise that individual errors are inevitable renders organizations impotent in the face of them, it must be discarded for managers to make headway in attacking the problem.

## THE RIGHT PATH FOR MANAGERS

Instead, it's best to adopt the assumption that errors do not occur without a cause. Building on this assumption, you could establish the following line of reasoning:

1. Every error results from some cause(s).
2. Analysis of errors can uncover these causes.
3. The causes of errors can be eliminated or their effects minimized or reduced.
4. Accomplishing this, will reduce the number of errors.

This syllogism, in a compressed form, presents the basic argument that underlies all the material in this book.

Since we have examined other generalized statements regarding errors, probing them to uncover any hidden assumptions that might invalidate them, we need to apply the same sort of analysis to error awareness itself.

Error awareness begins with three postulates. The first declares that we will benefit from analyzing human error in terms of functional and qualitative classification as well as quantitative measurement. The error-awareness program classifies different kinds of error according to their significant characteristics, effects, and importance.

The second asserts that any individual who can perform a simple, repetitive task correctly much of the time can satisfactorily perform that task even more often. The individual has actually demonstrated possession of sufficient knowledge and skill to perform the specific task correctly on typical units of work. Any unsatisfactory performance on one or more specific units must therefore be due not to incompetence, but rather to other causes.

The third insists that whenever an individual has the capability to correctly perform a repetitive task more often than he or she does, then something can be done to improve performance. In short, anyone can achieve their potential if they take the right actions.

An obvious conclusion based on these postulates is that many—probably most—individual errors are *not* inevitable. Managers and individuals therefore can reduce the incidence of error. We must first, however, find out what gives rise to them and then adopt an effective strategy to overcome those sources. Making errors is a function of human behavior, of human imperfection or indifference. By applying the techniques of error awareness, we can identify the wide range of influences on human behavior that might cause error.

## MOUNTING AN ATTACK ON ERROR: COMBINING AWARENESS AND ACTION

The path toward improvement combines AWARENESS and ACTION. You need to know everything you can about your (or your department's or organization's) errors, and then apply that knowledge productively.

Begin by building AWARENESS. The following strategies may prove helpful:

- *Document the Errors.* Establish a section of your diary, Filofax, or scheduling program in which you itemize, collect, and later analyze your errors. In addition to accumulating knowledge by setting up a systematic approach to increasing error awareness, you can instill the habit of examining your errors and discipline your attempts to add to your awareness.

- *Analyze the Errors.* List some errors that you or those who work under you have made which have damaged the overall quality of your performance. Now ask yourself: What kinds of errors occur most frequently? Which errors produced the most damaging *effects*? Write down all the factors—micro-, macro-, proximate, and contributory causes—that *might* have contributed to *causing* these errors. Which of these factors have exercised the strongest influence?

- *Create a Flowchart.* If you have difficulty zeroing in on where errors arise (and therefore on their causes), you might find it helpful to prepare a detailed flowchart of the process or sequence of activities through which the error came to your attention. For each individual or department involved in the process, analyze the:

—Receipt of information or materials from the previous individual or department.

—Main processing activities.

—Decisions taken and criteria used.

—Transmission of processed information or materials to the next individual or department.

Errors can occur in any of these stages. Work backward from the final activity on your flowchart until you reach the source. Communicate directly with each person involved in the process. Make sure that the individuals or departments who interact with each other agree about what should happen or what actually did happen. Disagreements about the essential processes might very well be how the error(s) originated. Make notes on your flowchart whenever anyone gives you any indication where the error might have arisen.

In preparing a customer's bill, for example, the clerk's section of the work-sequence flowchart might include the following activities: receiving a completed product order form or work order from a service technician; entering data into the computer, printing the billing statement and verifying entries, then forwarding the bills to shipping for postage and mailing.

Flowcharts that detail work sequences can help you shift your orientation from the results (in this case an error) to the essential elements involved in the process. While traditional quality control methods focus on results (defective or acceptable products), the Japanese concept of total quality embraces this kind of process orientation. If you concentrate on getting the details right, the results will take care of themselves.

Acquiring individualized knowledge regarding your own errors or those errors of your employees and colleagues calls for analysis that only you can do. But you might find it helpful to invite everyone involved to participate by gathering and/or offering information regarding the error and its cause(s). Actively solicit information about errors from your employees. This strategy will help promote group error awareness while simultaneously increasing the breadth of your investigation. For just as individuals acquire more experience and (hopefully) greater awareness as they mature, a group can gain access to more extensive experience—and hence increased awareness—by sharing their individual experiences with one another.

*One caveat!* The introduction of a policy aimed toward group error awareness may result in an *apparent* upsurge in the incidence of errors. Though the number of errors *reported* may initially increase, however, this may not indicate an increase in the incidence of errors. In all likelihood, the rise in reported errors simply demonstrates that prior to the institution of the new policy, employees had brought attention to errors only grudgingly.

To contribute toward organizationwide error awareness, you might find it helpful to establish a database containing your information and analysis of errors. By sharing error awareness through a system accessible to everyone within the organization, you can simultaneously demonstrate management's commitment to reducing errors and heighten the error awareness—and performance—of all your employees. An accessible database should allow anyone to search for errors according to the kind of error, the context or activity in which the error occurred, and the factor(s) that contributed to causing it.

After building AWARENESS, the right path then demands a competently planned program of ACTION. Awareness without action accomplishes little. If you were driving on a mountain road, no matter how aware you were of the turns, if you took no action based on your awareness, you'd still plummet over a cliff. The same reasoning applies to error awareness. If you are aware of the kinds, effects, and causes of error and do nothing, you might as well be entirely unaware.

After increasing your error awareness in reference to a specific error or group of errors, you will need to take action to minimize or eliminate a significant number of the causal factors. The primary responsibility for accomplishing these ends fall on management—although naturally in cooperation with all other employees. Managers must develop and communicate a guiding philosophy of continual improvement, integrating policies of error reduction as a matter of routine into every level of work and every job task. Every employee should be encouraged to increase his or her error awareness and take action to reduce error in the performance of his or her job.

- Managers must demonstrate—through both their words and their actions—their commitment to error awareness and error reduction to every person in the organization.
- Managers should instill a policy that holds all workers accountable for their actions.

- Managers should avoid blaming or punishing workers for their errors, instead helping them avoid repetition of any errors. All workers need to understand their responsibility to identify the factors contributing to errors in their department.

- Managers must empower workers to decrease the risks that affect their own work.

- All obstacles that prevent workers from reducing error (or offering suggestions to reduce error) must be removed.

- Managers should actively solicit suggestions from workers on how to reduce errors and improve performance.

Discussing alternatives to decrease the risk of errors with those affected by your decisions and actions will help you arrive at a consensus—a group commitment to cut down on error. As Jane Brody noted in an article for the *New York Times* (July 10, 1991) on reducing job-related stress (an accomplishment which would also cut down on errors):

> As many people have realized in rearing children, there are often situations in which parents, instead of dictating a course of action, could offer children a choice and an opportunity to decide for themselves. This gives children an emerging sense of power and control over the course of their lives. Similar circumstances often prevail in the workplace, even for highly stereotyped jobs like assembly-line work. Workers can at least be permitted to participate in decisions that affect the quality of their work lives. They should know that management listens to them and takes them seriously.

In general, you will find that solutions are accepted more readily when developed through teamwork rather than imposed from above.

Empowering workers is an essential part of group error awareness. Employees need to know that managers trust them, and depend on them, to complete their jobs with as few errors as possible. A climate of trust diminishes workers' self-doubt and insecurity, thereby removing two powerful contributory causes of error. Whenever possible, therefore, employees should be expected to inspect their own work; in general, a strategy that proves more cost-effective for the organization and more psychologically fulfilling for the worker than the use of inspectors, who often breed resentment in overseeing the work of others. Self-inspection helps foster a commitment to quality from every individual. And overall quality comes through instilling an organizationwide commitment to achieving it.

## EXPLORING MANAGEMENT OPTIONS

The most appropriate and effective remedial program will depend on the circumstances and causal factors that you identify. Armed with this specific knowledge, however, you can then plan and implement programs that will provide greater reliability and more accurate and error-free performance.

Managers cannot survive, however, by adopting the same knee-jerk programs regardless of the specific circumstances and causes that have led to error. Instead, you must remain flexible and creative enough to formulate individualized plans to eliminate and/or correct the particular kinds of error that afflict your operations.

Though appropriate and effective solutions must be tailored to individual circumstances, the general procedure applies in all cases. If, for example, you discover that certain operations produce more errors than others, you will need to take remedial action directed specifically at that operation, or the personnel involved. Your exploration of possible remedial actions should include the following:

Possible Remedial Actions

- Provide encouraging and supportive feedback so that employees become more aware of their errors.

- Offer incentives for accuracy.

- Give rewards or provide incentives for error admission, detection, and correction.

- Provide, increase, or improve training and instructions.

- Improve staffing, acquiring more and better qualified employees.

- Use redundancy: Have several systems or people repeating the operation at the same time.

- Improve error detection and correction procedures within that operation.

- Change methods, procedures, documentation, forms, or other elements in the process.

- Provide more elaborate equipment: Where warranted, automate, computerize, or increase the degree of automation or computerization.

- Change the entire system where errors occur.

- Oversee, better train, or change supervisors.

- Apply disciplinary measures.
- Delegate the operation or function to an outside service.
- Give up the operation.

Before making wholesale changes in processes or the entire system, be sure to proof the new process. Run the changes on a small scale at first, verifying through your test runs that the new or improved process or system actually does improve performance.

When confronted with an inaccurate and unreliable data-processing or information system, management cannot simply pull up stakes and abandon the operation. When an assembly line is plagued with errors, an auto manufacturer doesn't just choose to close up shop. For this reason, the final option of closing down is the alternative of last resort in almost any organization. However, most managers will do everything they can to avoid firing their supervisors or delegating the work to an outside service—each of which threatens the security of their own jobs.

## CHOOSING THE RIGHT OPTION

When confronted with a persistent problem of error, many baffled managers randomly try one or more of the preceding solutions. Remedial action lacking error awareness is usually as fruitless as awareness without action. Instead of first analyzing the nature and source of the errors and then determining which of the alternatives best suits the *particular* problem(s), these managers just try one action after another, hoping they'll be lucky enough to choose the right one before upper management turns to one of the last three options.

But unless management makes an informed choice from among these strategies, their remedial efforts amount to little more than a shot in the dark. With so many available options, management has poor odds of choosing the adequate alternative first. And even if the strategy management chooses has a positive impact on error, it may still not be the *most effective* one.

Pinpointing the kinds, costs, and causes of error *before* attempting to minimize or eliminate them is the hallmark of efficient, effective management. This doesn't mean avoiding action altogether until you've developed complete error awareness. Yet having as much error awareness as you can will invariably lead to better, more informed actions than random stopgap solutions, as in the following cases of GM and AT&T. The checklists of contributory microcauses detailed in Chapter 16 can be of enormous help in determining the most effective managerial strategy from among these alternatives.

## The Problem of the Revolving Door

All too often, upper management assigns the handling of the problem to a succession of hopefully chosen managers over a period of many, many years. And in time, because each of these managers fails to apply the systematic approach of error awareness, he or she gives way to another.

This revolving-door style of management damages the organization and cripples its ability to reduce errors. It eats away at the morale of everyone in the company. Employees begin to find it pointless to establish ties to a manager they believe they will outlast. And as a result, one of the cornerstones of commitment to quality and error-free performance—the good working relationship between managers and workers—slowly disappears.

*The Wall Street Journal* (August 29, 1991) compared the quality and performance records of two GM plants: one much better than average in terms of quality; and one much worse. Although not singled out as the cause of the Michigan plant's troubles, the newspaper strongly suggested that management practices influenced worker performance and has had a deleterious effect on the Orion plant: "Trying to get [its Orion Township, Michigan plant] up to speed, GM keeps changing the management; the plant has had four plant managers in its seven years, compared with only one at Oklahoma City during the same period. But all the switching seems to have backfired: It has reduced union officials' confidence in the management's stability. Why try to develop a working relationship with a manager, they wonder, when he will soon head out the revolving door?"

## For Want of Redundancy

On January 4, 1991, an AT&T technician accidentally severed the wrong cable. This single snip disrupted the vast majority of AT&T's long-distance telephone service out of New York. It was the second time that such a severed cable had had such a catastrophic effect on AT&T's customers.

After the first severed-cable incident, management certainly might have benefited from changing methods, procedures, forms, or other elements in the operation. They might have found it helpful, for example, to introduce new labeling or color-coding methods to differentiate cables from one another—and especially to distinguish this one critical cable from the rest.

The most shocking revelation, however, was that though this kind of disastrous error had occurred once before, no one at AT&T had fought to use redundancy; that is, to have several systems or people repeating the operation at the same time. As William F. Squadron, New York City's telecommunications commissioner, told the *New York Times,* January 5, 1991, "It's amazing that someone didn't say that if we're going to concentrate all this traffic in a single sheath of fiber, we should have a redundant path."

In this instance, as well as many others involving human or technological systems, redundant systems can cut down on errors (or at least minimize their damaging effects). Nevertheless, AT&T has seemed particularly obstinate in refusing to recognize their value. In the space of just two years, in addition to two severed cable incidents, AT&T suffered two other significant disruptions of long-distance service, all of which could have been avoided through the use of redundant systems. As the *New York Times* (September 18, 1991) noted in its coverage of a later breakdown, "The disruption once again illustrated how dependent telephone networks have become on a few pieces of equipment."

Of course, just because an alternative might be the most appropriate or effective does not necessarily mean you should implement it. You must undertake a cost benefit analysis to estimate whether the cost of implementation will be offset by the savings incurred as a result of the reduction in error. In examining the alternatives available to you, concentrate on identifying the factors that can be controlled at a reasonable cost in an organized manner, and for now, ignore those too expensive to control. In some cases, for instance, you may find that the most cost-effective strategy temporarily postpones dealing with root causes of error and instead focuses on short-term strategies designed to contain their impact.

## WHEN AN INDIVIDUAL IS AT FAULT

With certain adaptations, many of the same remedial options listed for errors in operations could also prove effective with certain individuals who most frequently make errors. You might choose to:

- Provide encouraging and supportive personal feedback so that these individuals become more aware of their errors.
- Provide, increase, or improve training and instructions.
- Offer incentives for accuracy.
- Transfer these individuals to less sensitive work.
- Remove them from positions for which they are unsuitable.

Imagine that you're in charge of a word-processing department. You discover that two people from your staff of 14 account for 43 percent of all errors. In reviewing the preceding five alternatives above, which would you most want to avoid? Which seem inappropriate? Which will best promote error awareness?

Certain contributory causes of error are certainly wreaking havoc on the performance of these two processors. On a head-to-head basis, they are making 4½ times as many errors as their colleagues average.

Without knowing much about the specifics of the case, however, you can still reach certain conclusions. Offering incentives seems inappropriate in this case, because if you give them to these two employees, you would need to do likewise with the rest of your staff, who already perform much better. Disciplinary measures might prove effective in motivating the two processors to improve their performance. Yet in general, "negative incentives" should only be attempted after other alternatives have already failed: Punishment tends to make people defensive or secretive about error, which *drives error awareness underground.* Just as closing down shop was the alternative of last resort when errors centered in specific operations, transfer and removal of employees are generally the options managers most want to avoid. Although sometimes necessary, firings and transfers also entail finding replacements who may or may not perform any better than those removed.

In most cases then, the first two options are usually preferable. Depending on the specifics of the case involved, additional instruction can prove effective because training programs often attack the causes of error directly. In general, however, *always* the first option you should attempt—is the providing of feedback. With the exception of additional training, all the other remedial methods, though effective in certain cases, reward error awareness that already exists or punish the lack of error awareness. But providing personal feedback actually *promotes* the development of error awareness.

Offering encouraging feedback to employees who frequently make errors can accomplish two goals simultaneously. It can increase the error awareness of the individuals who receive the management feedback. But these same employees, in response to this encouraging feedback, can often bring to your attention sources of distraction or contributory causes of error that you either did not know about or had overlooked. In this way, *personal feedback can also increase your error awareness as a manager.* And this can help you develop even more appropriate strategies to overcome these causes of error.

When the management of Oklahoma City's GM plant announced its commitment to work together with its employees toward improvement, many of the workers were initially skeptical. But management won them over simply by listening to the workers, and responding to them. As *The Wall Street Journal* (August 29, 1991) described it:

"For Ed McCracken, an assembly-line worker and former union official at the plant, the effort to improve boiled down to a table. When he started his current job of attaching passenger-side mirrors not long ago, he told his bosses the table where the mirrors are stacked was too low, and he had to bend over, with some physical strain, 600 times a day. He asked for a higher table and got one within days."

One result of this encouraging feedback—in which management communicated the company's desire to improve performance and quality, and then listened to workers' suggestions on how best to achieve those results—has been the high quality of Oklahoma City's products. The Pontiac 6000, manufactured at the plant, broke into the top 10 in J.D. Power & Associates 1991 rankings of troublefree cars, the highest rated car produced by the Big Three automakers.

## HOW TO PROVIDE FEEDBACK THAT WILL HELP MINIMIZE ERRORS

Only comments offering encouraging feedback can lead to improved accuracy, performance, and productivity. Since comments offering merely discouraging feedback often create resentment and bad feeling, they can in themselves become contributory causes of further errors. Because individuals are unique, you cannot rely inflexibly on the same sort of relationship and the same methods of correction with every employee. Some general rules apply, however. Here are some tips on how an encouraging feedback session might proceed:

- *Plan.* Organize the details of your feedback and error instruction in advance. Be as specific as you can regarding the aspects of the individual's performance that could stand improvement. Say what you don't like and why you don't like it.
- *Choose the Setting.* Select a proper time and place. Although you may want to deliver the message as soon as possible after discovering the error, show some discretion. Private conferences in which the individual can give you his or her full attention are preferable to public

humiliations. No matter how tactful and positive you are, pointing out a person's errors in front of his or her colleagues can often embarrass the person—and sometimes further damage performance.

■ *Communicate.* Create a situation that provides for *mutual* conversation, give-and-take. Don't simply call your employee into your office for a "talk." Make it easy for the person to talk to *you* as well. Let your subordinate know he or she can be direct with you. Listen and remain open to the employee's questions or concerns.

■ *Reward.* Praise or otherwise reward the employee's disclosure of his or her errors.

■ *Start with Positive Reinforcement.* Use supportive statements that affirm the individual's value to the operation. For example, you might say, "You have been very conscientious."

■ *Stay Calm.* State the error without resorting to accusation, blame, scolding, or threats. Try a matter-of-fact statement like, "Many of the words in this letter have been misspelled." It is a much more effective approach than, "You idiot, you misspelled half the words in the letter."

■ *Don't Jump to Conclusions.* Check your assumptions with the individual to make sure they're correct. For instance, rather than assuming he or she knew certain information or a particular instruction, you might say, "I believe you already know that. . . ."

■ *Continue to Provide Positive Reinforcement.* Throughout the discussion, use comments that reflect your confidence in the individual's good intentions, abilities, and skill. People often feel stung by criticism. You may need to remind your employee repeatedly that you don't believe he or she is bad or stupid or incompetent simply because of some errors.

■ *Get Feedback.* Check the individual's understanding of the error, and his or her ability to learn what might be done to correct it and/or prevent similar errors in the future.

■ *Clarify.* Encourage the employee to learn and improve while clarifying and explaining his or her job responsibilities. Make sure the person understands all your assumptions about the work, so that he or she might better meet your expectations.

■ *Encourage Independence.* Whenever possible, let the person find his or her own solution to correct the error and/or avoid its recurrence.

Make it clear that you welcome suggestions. Perhaps ask, "How can we simplify this for next time?" or "What can we do to avoid having this happen again?"

- *Suggest Alternatives.* Whenever you suggest a remedy, do so firmly but courteously and respectfully. For example, "Here's a new spelling dictionary (or a new spelling program for your computer). Would you please check your spelling against it from now on?"

- *Demonstrate Mutual Understanding.* You might say, "I know you will find it as useful as I do."

- *Summarize the Discussion Positively.* Leave the person with positive feelings and encouragement at the end of your conversation.

- *Take Stock.* After the discussion, review the conversation thoroughly in your mind. Did you avoid piling blame or shame on the person making errors?

- *Apologize.* If you decide, on review, that you handled the conversation poorly or destructively, apologize. Admit your own mistakes as freely as you want those working for you to acknowledge theirs.

- *Don't Reserve Feedback for Errors.* In addition to bringing mistakes to your employees' attention and holding them accountable for their errors, remember to applaud them when they do good work. Celebrate your workers' successes with them.

In dealing with errors, your aim is to expose the *errors*, not to humiliate the people who made them. Everyone makes mistakes, and everyone can cut down on the errors they make. The job of management is to help employees accomplish this goal.

Always remember that dealing with people—communicating with them and eliciting their best possible performance—is perhaps the most important function of management. Encouraging feedback gets people to change in precisely the way you want them to. If you can increase the error awareness of those who work for you or under you, you can minimize future errors. Exposing the people you manage to the principles in this book will make them much more sensitive to errors. If you can accomplish this modest goal, you will substantially decrease your group's problems with errors. And this will make your job as a manager much, much easier.

# HEIGHTENING YOUR ERROR AWARENESS

## APPLYING WHAT YOU KNOW

If you hold a managerial or supervisory position, you are now much better equipped to reduce the errors of those you supervise. Your new and still growing error awareness has probably yielded insights into the errors you make and those made by the people who work under you. Do you have any ideas on how to cut down on some of these errors, now that you better understand them?

## ERROR-REDUCING CRITERIA

Reevaluate your responses to the preceding question. Applying your error awareness, which of them most completely addresses the first three elements of the Error-Reducing Criteria listed at the beginning of Chapter 17? Compare them to see which best:

1.  Attacks the specific kinds of error(s) you want to minimize?
2.  Applies to the personnel who most often make these errors?
3.  Eliminates the cause(s) of these errors or reduces the impact of these causes?

Now that you've chosen a remedial plan and established that it addresses the unique circumstances of your situation, ask yourself how good the remedy is in general? Finally, do you have the authority and ability to apply the remedy effectively? If you feel confident that your plan(s) meets the seven Error-Reducing Criteria, then you're on your way to managing for less errors.

## QUALITY CONTROL AND THE HUMAN FACTOR

Can quality control methods be applied to nonmechanical operations like clerical work? How adequate do you think these methods and techniques are in evaluating the incidence and impact of human error, as opposed to machine error?

(*continued*)

## THE ODDS ARE WITH YOU

Assume that, on the average, you make errors in one percent of the products you manufacture or the data you process. If you build or process 99 items in a row correctly, what are the odds that you will get the next item wrong?

## MOUNTING AN ATTACK ON ERROR

Review the errors analyzed in the section "Mounting an Attack on Error" in Chapter 17. Does your analysis suggest any remedial course(s) of action? Which causal factors deserve the most immediate attention? What might you do to eliminate them or minimize their influence?

## REMEDIAL OPTIONS

Imagine that you're in charge of a word-processing department that suffers from an inordinately high rate of error throughout the operation. In general, which of the possible remedial alternatives would you most want to avoid?

## CHOOSING THE RIGHT SOLUTION

Which of the 14 management alternatives presented in the section "Exploring Management Options, in Chapter 17, if implemented after AT&T's first error, might best have prevented the disastrous impact of the later recurrences?

## BECOMING AN ERROR-AWARE MANAGER

List all the error-awareness methods or insights that you can apply while supervising your staff and perfecting your own work routine.

# 18

## HOW ACCURACY IMPACTS CRITICAL THINKING AND JUDGMENT

'TIS WITH OUR JUDGMENT AS OUR WATCHES, NONE
GO JUST ALIKE, YET EACH BELIEVES HIS OWN.
—ALEXANDER POPE, *ESSAY ON CRITICISM*

As computers become ever more sophisticated, many of us are increasingly turning over to them some of the responsibility for making simple decisions. Yet no matter how much authority we yield to them nor how much assistance they provide in organizing and evaluating more complex decisions, each of us must ultimately reach our own judgments and take responsibility for our actions based on those judgments.

In business, actions could include the allocation of R & D funds, forecasting sales of a new product, selecting new equipment and predicting its impact on workers and productivity, diagnosing causes of errors or a systems failure, hiring (or firing) personnel, interpreting market trends, and evaluating the quality of a product. And if we want to make as few mistakes as possible in reaching these judgments, we need to work on improving our ability to think critically.

For this reason, although the previous chapters have concentrated exclusively on errors and error awareness, in this chapter we will analyze mistakes—errors in judgment. As the National Transportation Safety Board's Barrie Strauch once urged, ". . . we know and keep saying that in most accidents there is poor decision-making somewhere down the line, and decision techniques ought to be improved."

The newspapers are filled with mistakes in judgment that have nearly ruined large corporations:

- Peter F. Drucker in the article "Five Deadly Business Sins" (*The Wall Street Journal,* October 21, 1993) cites the example of the near collapse of the Xerox Corporation in the 1970s due to its insistence on high profit margins for its invention—the copier: ". . . Xerox soon began to add feature after feature to the machine, each priced to yield the maximum profit margin and each driving up the machine's price." Xerox's profits did soar, as did its stock. But consumers wanting a simple, inexpensive machine had nowhere to go, until the Japanese company, Canon, developed just such a copier. "It immediately took over the market, and Xerox barely survived."

- On March 29, 1993, the *New York Times* reported on the loss of tens of millions of dollars by Empire Blue Cross and Blue Shield, the nation's largest nonprofit health insurer due to management problems. One glitch involved overreliance on a computer system that "could not understand bills of $100,000 or more. A $103,000 premium, for example, would be interpreted as only $3,000." That same failure occurred 29 times!

Recently, *The Wall Street Journal* reported on the cancellation of the launch of Elizabeth Taylor's fourth fragrance, "Black Pearls," after a change in management at Elizabeth Arden caused the company to abruptly cut the contribution to help cover salaries of department store counter salespeople to 3 percent from the usual 5 percent. As a result, the stores refused to stock the perfume. Meanwhile, Arden had already begun its publicity for the product: a $12 million ad campaign that included a "blitz of 42 million fragrance strips" and print ads showing Ms. Taylor immersed in a tropical lagoon that had already run in several magazines. Arden's president resigned and its parent company stands to lose $15 million after the fiasco.

To avoid similar costly mistakes, we all need to focus on improving the process of decision making. We must learn from our failures as well as our successes, from our mistakes as well as our correct decisions. We need to improve our good judgment continually—building progressively on each improvement.

## MISTAKES AND ERRORS

Although an error and a mistake may lead to similar consequences, each encompasses a different process:

- *Errors* involve doing something other than what you intended—regardless of whether that intention would have proved right or wrong.
- *Mistakes*, by contrast, involve choosing the wrong action due to poor planning (overlooking some fact or factor in deciding what to do), poor timing, and/or inadequate, incorrect, or out-of-date information.

"Mistakes," as Donald A. Norman defines them in his fascinating book, *The Design of Everyday Things*,[1] "result from the choice of inappropriate goals. A person makes a poor decision, misclassifies a situation, or fails to take all the relevant factors into account."

For example, in the aftermath of an earthquake that rocked Guatemala in February 1976, killing 23,000 and injuring 75,000 more, the world's many relief agencies rallied to the aid of the disaster victims. Within weeks, CARE and the Catholic Relief Service had shipped 25,000 tons of food to Guatemala. These two disaster relief agencies, having failed to take into account all relevant factors, made a big *mistake*. They came up with an intention (feeding the victims of this disaster) that proved entirely inappropriate to the circumstances. What relevant factors had they overlooked? The most critical was that the earthquake, although it had created widespread destruction, had not led to any food shortages in Guatemala. As a result, the shipments from the relief agencies caused the demand for, and the price of, native corn to plummet. The "disaster relief" ended up ruining Guatemalan farmers. The relief agencies were misguided in their intentions; they, therefore, made a mistake, not an error.

Despite the difference between errors and mistakes, the methods, objectives, and benefits of error awareness can play a significant role in improving our judgment, too. For one thing, improving and maintaining standards of accuracy in data, one of the fundamental aims and chief benefits of error awareness, will improve the quality of information used in making decisions.

In addition, as Donald A. Norman rightly points out, "Many mistakes arise from the vagaries of human thought, often because people tend to rely upon remembered experiences rather than on more systematic analysis." The methods and techniques of error awareness are based upon precisely the kind of systematic analysis that Norman advocates.

Finally, good judgment also demands that you learn from your mistakes—the first and foremost principle of error awareness. This will train you to think more critically and improve your ability to handle new challenges.

## CRITICAL THINKING

Critical thinking is the application of reasonable skepticism in the examination of so-called "facts" or opinions offered up as if they were facts. The critical thinker uses the analysis of all pertinent "facts" not only to test their accuracy, but also their factuality. The objective is to distinguish between those statements that truly reflect facts and those that are merely assumptions or inferences. Without this kind of critical thinking, good judgment is impossible. And without forming judgments, action is impossible.

Donald A. Norman identifies seven stages of action that humans must perform to do anything. These stages are:

1. Forming a goal.
2. Forming an intention.
3. Specifying an action.
4. Executing the action.
5. Perceiving the state of the world.
6. Interpreting the state of the world.
7. Evaluating the outcome.

With the exception of actually executing the action, all these stages involve the exercise of judgment. In forming goals and intentions as well as in specifying an appropriate action, a decision maker needs to choose from several alternatives. And each of these choices demands the application of critical thinking. Likewise, perceiving and interpreting the state of the world—judgments that help determine the appropriateness of a chosen action—also call for critical thinking. Finally, evaluating the outcome of the action demands the exercise of judgment and critical thinking.

## INFORMATION AND UNCERTAINTY

In attempting to exercise good judgment when making a critical choice, you must acquire as much *accurate* and *relevant* information as possible. Only after consideration of all the salient facts available at the time should you arrive at a sound judgment.

Gathering enough information to make an informed decision may sound like simple common sense, yet research has shown that stockbrokers, doctors, and other professionals seldom follow it. In reaching their decisions, most of these professionals use very little information at all, even in cases where they have specifically requested a great deal of data. Yet research has also shown that decision makers tend to exercise their judgment with more confidence as the amount of available information increases.

Although you should gather all the *available* facts before exercising your critical judgment, you must also recognize that you can never have *all* the facts. Why not? Well, for one thing, people seldom have enough time to fully inform themselves. Since you can't put it off forever, time pressures often impose certain constraints on your fact-finding ability. But even more importantly, no one has the capability to assemble all the facts that might affect or influence the outcome of a decision. As Sir Hubert Shirley Smith, a member of a Royal Commission investigating the 1970 collapse of a bridge over the River Yarra near Melbourne, Australia, put it to a witness about to testify before the commission: "Engineers do not know everything. They cannot pretend they know everything and the sooner they admit they do not know everything, the better. We must make adequate allowance for the factor of ignorance. Do you agree?"

None of us, engineers or otherwise, can know everything relevant to the decisions we must make. Perhaps the most fundamental fact can never be known at the time we exercise judgment. For no one can ever know with absolute certainty what the future will bring.

## THE CHANGE FACTOR

Perhaps the most common cause of poor judgment is the failure to remember that things change all the time. Interest rates go up and down; real estate markets fluctuate, not always predictably; friendships and alliances form and dissolve; government regulations come and go; public opinion suddenly shifts; consumer demand changes; markets become

weaker or stronger; new people come on the scene; new inventions introduce new capabilities and competition. Time changes everything. And
each of these changes can influence the outcome of decisions.

In the latter half of the 1980s, for example, Honda's domestic sales
sagged dramatically because the company failed to anticipate, or even
recognize, the changing demands of Japanese consumers. When the yen
surged in value in 1985, the Japanese began to covet more distinctive and
sporty cars. Over the next few years, however, Honda heedlessly continued to crank out four-door family sedans that closely resembled models
from previous years. This strategy severely damaged the company's standing in its domestic market.

Instead of ignoring change or downplaying the likelihood of future
change, the best critical thinkers anticipate—and even count on it—in
reaching judgments. Good judgment calls for an educated guess, based on
all the facts available as well as an understanding of probabilities, about the
direction of change. Judgment thus involves making certain predictions
and hoping the future will conform. Honda, for example, should have recognized the likelihood that increased affluence would change the demands of Japanese consumers.

While guessing at the direction of change, however, you should also
prepare yourself to change your mind in light of any new facts that arise.
Have an alternative plan ready just in case change proceeds differently
than anticipated and a list of warning signs that will call this shift to your
attention.

The importance of contingency plans cannot be overstated. When
changes come rapidly or when a decision turns out to be wrong, you may
need to act quickly to correct the mistake. You may have little time to
fully consider all the alternative courses of action if you need to take fast,
positive action. Situations that call for contingency plans include work
surges, worker absences, start-ups, and close-downs. Contingency plans
should also address the possibility of mistakes and errors. The failure to
plan for the occurrence of random errors or human fallibility will catch
your staff unprepared and perhaps unaware, thereby allowing mistakes to
wreak considerable damage. For this reason, you should have procedures
in place that can contain the costly effects of errors and mistakes before
they get out of hand, and can also give you sufficient warning to minimize the effects of errors.

Emergencies and unanticipated changes have a way of confusing our
thoughts, making it difficult, if not impossible, to think clearly. That's
why you need to plan for such situations when you have the time to
evaluate thoroughly the possible alternatives. This will increase the

likelihood that you will make the best possible decision under the most trying circumstances.

## THE UNCERTAINTY FACTOR

Planning for the inevitability of change is not the only challenge you face in exercising good judgment. The unavoidable presence of uncertainty can also make choices difficult. Uncertainty is the hallmark of decision making, since certainty—if it existed—would eliminate the need to make difficult choices. The presence of uncertainty is what forces a person to exercise judgment and make choices in the first place.

We can reduce uncertainty to a certain degree. We can follow certain guidelines regarding our decisions, for instance. Or we can take advantage of books or courses on successful decision-making techniques. And we can consult with experts who might guide our judgments. But no matter how hard we try, we can never eliminate uncertainty completely.

Exercising good judgment would be easy if there were no uncertainty, if you had a clear-cut choice between "good" decisions and "bad" ones. Unfortunately, absolutes—clearly defined blacks and whites—seldom exist in the real world. In almost all cases, critical judgment therefore centers on making a choice among many degrees. For this reason, a specific decision may look poor in retrospect, yet still result from the exercise of good judgment. All too often, these "bad" decisions involved nothing more than guessing wrong.

Professional sports offers countless examples of good judgments that led to bad results. Sports fans love to argue (after the fact) about whether a manager should have ordered an intentional walk to the other team's slugger rather than let him win the game with a home run. Or about the wisdom of their team failing in its attempt to gain a first down in a fourth-and-two situation (or the wisdom of *not* going for it if the opposing team scores on its next possession). Yet the popularity of second-guessing managers and coaches and Monday-morning quarterbacking usually demonstrates little more than the advantages of hindsight.

## PERFECT HINDSIGHT

Around the turn of the century, asbestos came into widespread use in construction and manufacturing, especially as a fire retardant in buildings. The resistance of asbestos to fire made it seem like the ideal substance for the manufacture of construction materials, thermal insulation, electrical equipment, brake linings, theatre curtains, and safety apparel. In 1938, the British went so far as to supply their entire population with gas masks containing asbestos filters! By the 1970s, however, the inhalation of asbestos fibers was found to damage lungs severely, often causing respiratory diseases and even a rapidly fatal form of lung cancer.

In hindsight, the decision to use asbestos proved to be dead wrong. But was it bad judgment at the time? Considering the information available to manufacturers earlier in the century, the choice to employ a material well known to resist fire in the construction of buildings, insulation, and other products cannot be regarded as a case of bad judgment despite its lethal results.

Does hindsight have any place in critical thinking? Of course it does. Hindsight—the recognition of what actually happened compared with what you had anticipated—provides essential feedback on the wisdom of your decisions. Evaluating the outcome is one of the seven stages of action; it calls for interpretation, judgment, and critical thinking.

In addition to depending on good judgment, however, hindsight regarding your errors and the mistakes made by others can also contribute to critical thinking by guiding future judgments. When it includes the analytical techniques of error awareness, hindsight can furnish you with priceless insight into your past mistakes, their consequences, and causes. The wisest judgments take into account all your errors, all the mistakes of the past, and everything you have learned from them. Yet how few of us use our past mistakes constructively in this way, to guide current and future judgments?

Hindsight can be a luxury denied to those on the cutting edge, whose decisions break new ground. Since the problems they face are always new, past experience may have little validity in present circumstances. That's where good judgment is especially important. It demands the analysis and identification of the similarities and the differences between past and present situations. This analysis can then be used to help guide current decisions.

## IS THAT A FACT?

As I suggested earlier, one of the primary objectives of critical thinking involves distinguishing between true facts and opinions, inferences, and assumptions that may or may not be true.

Good judgment does not require you to *discard* your assumptions or inferences. In fact, good judgment itself is little more than a reasoned *opinion* regarding the best course of action in a given set of circumstances. It does, however, demand that you recognize assumptions, inferences, and opinions for what they are. Confusing assumptions with facts can only lead to mistakes.

The following exercise by William Haney, PhD, will help you determine how well you presently distinguish fact from opinion.

"The Uncritical Inference Experiment"
Instructions

This test is designed to determine your ability to think *accurately* and *carefully*. Since it is very probable that you have never taken this type of test before, failure to read the instructions *extremely carefully* may lower your score.

1. You will read a brief story. Assume that all of the information presented in the story is definitely *accurate* and *true*. Read the story carefully. You may refer back to the story whenever you wish.

2. You will then read statements about the story. Answer them in numerical order. DO NOT GO BACK to fill in answers or to change answers. This will only distort your test score.

3. After you read carefully each statement, determine whether the statement is:

   "T"—meaning: On the basis of the *information presented in the story the statement is definitely true.*

   "F"—meaning: On the basis of the *information presented in the story the statement is definitely false.*

   "?"—meaning: The statement *may* be true (or false) but on the basis of the *information presented in the story you cannot be definitely certain.* (If any part of the statement is doubtful, mark the statement "?")

The following is a sample test, with answers.


**The Story**

The only car parked in front of 619 Oak Street is a black one. The words "James M. Curley, MD" are spelled in small gold letters across the door of the car.

## *The Statements about the Story*

1. The color of the car in front of 619 Oak Street is black.
2. There is no lettering on the door of the car parked in front of 619 Oak Street.
3. Someone is ill at 619 Oak Street.
4. The black car parked in front of 619 Oak Street belongs to James M. Curley.

## *Answers*

1. T          2. F          3. ?          4. ?

REMEMBER: Answer *only* on the basis of the information presented in the story. Refrain from answering as you think it *might* have happened. Answer each statement in numerical order. Do not go back to fill in or to change answers.

## The Story

Babe Smith has been killed. Police have rounded up six suspects, all of whom are known gangsters. All of them are known to have been near the scene of the killing at the approximate time that it occurred. All had substantial motives for wanting Smith killed. However, one of the suspected gangsters, Slinky Sam, has positively been cleared of guilt.

## *Statements about the Story*

1. Slinky Sam is known to have been near the scene of the killing of Babe Smith.
2. All six of the rounded-up gangsters were known to have been near the scene of the murder.
3. Only Slinky Sam has been cleared of guilt.
4. All six of the rounded-up suspects were near the scene of Smith's killing at the approximate time that it took place.
5. The police do not know who killed Smith.
6. All six suspects are known to have been near the scene of the foul deed.
7. Smith's murderer did not confess of his own free will.

8. Slinky Sam was not cleared of guilt.

9. It is known that the six suspects were in the vicinity of the cold-blooded assassination.

### The Answers

After taking the test, check your answers against the following explanations:

1. T  Slinky Sam has been identified in the story as "one of the suspected gangsters," all of whom "are known to have been near the scene of the killing."

2. ?  The story never classifies the killing as a "murder."

3. ?  Although the story does state that Slinky Sam has been cleared of guilt, it does not specify that he was the *only* one cleared.

4. T  This statement merely rephrases the third sentence of the story.

5. ?  Even though the police rounded up six different suspects, they may still know—or may not know—who killed Smith.

6. ?  The term "foul deed" conveys a matter of opinion. The story itself, however, never characterized the killing in this way.

7. ?  Perhaps the killer *did* confess. Indeed, this confession may have been what positively cleared Slinky Sam of guilt.

8. F  "Slinky Sam has positively been cleared of guilt."

9. ?  As in statements 2 and 6, the term "cold-blooded assassination" characterizes the killing in a way neither specified nor excluded by the story.

Have these correct answers caused you to reexamine your reasoning in any way? Did you make any assumptions about the story that you then regarded as indisputable facts?

## JUMPING TO CONCLUSIONS

All too often, we accept assumptions unquestioningly as facts. Such unwarranted assumptions, however, can cause us to make serious errors in judgment. They are not unlike errors of definition, which seventeenth-century philosopher Thomas Hobbes warned against over three hundred years ago. "The errors of definitions," Hobbes wrote, "multiply themselves according as the reckoning proceeds; and lead men [and women] into absurdities, which at last they see but cannot avoid, without reckoning anew from the beginning." People tend to build on their assumptions or inferences. If, however, these are unwarranted, the errors based on them can multiply and lead to absurd mistakes.

People act on the basis of their inferences. This circumstance in itself is neither bad nor necessarily an indication of bad judgment. Yet all too often, they don't recognize the possibility that their assumptions may be unwarranted, because they don't even realize that they may be assumptions. They believe their inferences to be the same as facts, and act accordingly.

Now, carefully examine Figure 18.1.

After examining the picture, make two lists. In the first, place the facts that you can determine through your observations. In the second, write down a number of inferences that the illustration leads you to believe may be true. Include inferences that at first may seem implausible as well as those that seem not only plausible, but highly likely.

What course of action would you take if you were the new plant manager and came upon this scene? You may have determined any number

Figure 18.1

Reprinted from *Handling Barriers in Communication* by Irving J. and Laura L. Lee. New York: Harper & Brothers, 1950. Used with permission.

of facts, such as that an open truck stands near the loading platform, that the man is sitting on a box, that wood shavings are on the floor, and so on. Your inferences may be considerably more far-flung, including any or all of the following:

- The truck is being unloaded.
- The man pictured should be loading the truck.
- The man works in the shipping department.
- The man is wasting company time.
- The man is on his coffee break.
- The man is carving a spear for his daughter to use as a prop in her school's Halloween pageant.

In their book, the Lees offer up the truth. A new plant manager on an inspection tour saw this young man carving on a stick. The manager, inferring that the man—whose job involved packing straw in and around castings to prevent them from breaking during shipping—was wasting time on the job, fired him on the spot. As it turned out, however, the young man had been sharpening the stick to use in tamping the straw down, a method that he had determined resulted in more effective and protective packing.

To improve your critical judgment and avoid falling into the same trap, test your assumptions *before* making critical decisions. This includes not only your own assumptions, but the assumptions of others that play an important part in your judgment.

Many mathematicians, for example, deplore the increasing reliance on computers to generate mathematical proofs. Rather than developing proofs through a chain of logic and deduction, computers test and discard countless assumptions to arrive at a proof through the process of elimination. Because few mathematicians can duplicate this computer process, proofs become accepted even though the reliability of the computer programs and the resulting proofs have not been independently tested and confirmed. This puts mathematicians in a position where they have to trust not only the computer, but the (unstated) assumptions made by its programmer.

None of us should blindly accept the assumptions of others without putting them under the same sort of scrutiny that we should apply to our own assumptions. You've already had some experience in testing assumptions (your own as well as some more general cultural ones) in Chapter 6.

Your exploration of the five half-truths and your assumptions regarding computers has already demonstrated your ability to improve your critical thinking. The best critical thinkers make this scrutiny of assumptions a regular element of their decision-making process. Like them, you not only need to test assumptions in reaching decisions, but also need to retest them regularly in evaluating and perhaps revising, amending, reversing, or otherwise correcting your decisions.

For example, what is $1 + 1$? Can you come up with more than one response that correctly answers this question? Many of us limit ourselves through hidden assumptions. The obvious answer is that $1 + 1 = 2$. But setting aside the assumptions that the question should only be considered in decimal terms within a base 10 system, we can come up with dozens of additional answers that are equally correct. Among these are: $1 + 1 = 10$ (binary system); $1 + 1 = 11$ (digits); $1 + 1 = X$ (matchsticks); and $1 + 1 = 50$ (the Roman Numeral "L" in matchsticks). The system that you use determines the answers.

## OBSERVATIONS VERSUS INFERENCES

One of the obstacles to the recognition and testing of hidden assumptions is that we often obscure the difference between observations and inferences. We present our inferences as if they were plain facts. We observe a man whittling a stick; we infer that he is wasting time. Yet we accept that inference as if it were a pure observation.

To observe something, we must see, hear, feel, smell, or taste it directly. Observations are thus direct products of our personal experience, received through our senses. Inferences, by contrast, consist of interpretive decisions in which we organize and understand our observations by investing them with meaning. The chart on page 286 distinguishes between observations and inferences.

The qualifications appended to items 1, 5, and 6 in the column regarding observations should not be overlooked. Statements about observations are *not* objective certainties; observations are *not* pure facts; human perception has its limits and faults. As Mason Haire astutely points out in *Psychology in Management:* "[M]an's behavior depends, not on what is actually out there [facts], but on what he sees [observations]; not on the way the world is actually organized, but on the way he organizes it [inferences]. This is at first a deceptively simple point, but it is possible that more misunderstanding in human relations arises from this than from any other single factor."

---

**OBSERVATION VERSUS INFERENCE**

| *Observations* | *Inferences* |
|---|---|
| 1. They solely reflect actual experience, the "facts" as closely as we can define them. | 1. They are not limited to experience or "facts." |
| 2. They are confined to what you can sense or observe. | 2. They go beyond what you can sense or observe. |
| 3. Statements regarding your observations can only be made after the experience itself. | 3. Statements reflecting your inferences can be made at any time—before, during, or after your observation. |
| 4. You can only make a limited number of statements of experience or observation. | 4. You can make an unlimited number of statements of inference. |
| 5. Observations come as close to certainty as any human statement does. | 5. Inferences tend to reflect our opinions regarding degrees of probability or likelihood. |
| 6. Statements that consist of observations *only*, statements of "fact," should not give rise to any disagreements (were it not for the limits and faults of human perception). | 6. Statements of inferences can often result in significant disagreement. |

---

Many of us assume that our senses cannot deceive us, that what we see, hear, and touch are the "facts," plain and simple. Yet this unwarranted assumption can lead to errors and mistakes, in addition to the misunderstandings that Haire singles out. In exercising critical judgment, we need to keep in mind that though the senses may provide us with an approximation of the facts, the senses can deceive and they can be manipulated to deceive.

Which of the following lines is longer?

A) ⟵——————————⟶    B) >————————————<

The revelation that both lines A and B are equal in length, even though most people would say that B "looks" longer, should make it clear that our senses can deceive us. Yet how many of us keep this fact in mind in evaluating our assumptions and inferences? How many of us overlook the shaky foundation of assumptions, fallible senses, and inferences on which we base our attempts at critical thinking? Recognizing the possibility of error—in our observations as well as our inferences—and planning for that possibility is one of the hallmarks of good judgment.

## RECOGNIZING OUR OWN BIASES

Another important aspect of critical thinking involves the recognition that each of us has our own biases which influence the way we receive information and make decisions. Our memories, the way our past experiences have shaped our perception, our expectations, and our personal preferences provides each of us with a unique slant on information presented to us and judgments we must make. As outlined by John Evans of HEB Partnership, some of the many factors that can bias our perception, critical thinking, and exercise of judgment include:

- *Memory.* Memory assigns different weights to different events. The memory of a single, vivid incident can make us think, "That happens to me all the time," even if a hundred other, less memorable incidents suggest the opposite conclusion.

- *Relationships with Other People.* Most of us give greater weight to information received from people we know well than to data supplied by "outsiders." We may value personal recommendations more highly, for example, than statistical evidence. Sheer accessibility thus provides a bias in the information we gather.

- *Past Experience.* We approach situations on the basis of our experience. This can influence perception of information and events. For this reason, two people can read the same material or view the same incident in entirely divergent ways.

- *Expectations.* Most of us see what we want to see and hear what we want to hear. This can cause us to perceive events or take in information based on our expectations rather than reality.

- *The Desire for Consistency.* Propelled by a desire for consistency, we may discount or ignore information that contradicts our existing beliefs and views. We avoid views that clash with our own.

- *Rationalization.* Our desire to hold on to existing views may also encourage us to try to explain away discrepancies or inconsistencies. Rationalization can prevent us from acknowledging what is directly before us.

- A *Shaky Understanding of Statistics.* Many people have a limited understanding of probability. The sheer weight of higher numbers, for example, can influence perception—32 out of 100 seems like *more* than 2 out of 5, even though the relative frequency is *less*. Similarly, a poor understanding of statistical probability may lead us to conclude that the results obtained through a small sample—such as 5 or 10 tests—would hold true for larger numbers as well.

- *Overgeneralization.* The urge to generalize specifics can cause us to ignore important distinctions between two or more scenarios. Believing that all errors stem from the incompetence of the workforce can cause us to ignore the role of management, training, and environment, among many others.

- *Confusing Conjunction with Causation.* Our eagerness for explanations often leads us to conclude that because two events occurred in close proximity, they must be related. Inferring causation—of an error, for example—from mere conjunction, however, can prevent us from reaching sounder, more reasoned, and systematic judgments.

- *Conservatism.* Many decision makers like to play it safe, relying on precedent and traditional approaches to avoid criticism. This may cause them to ignore signs of change or information that suggests a more "risky" approach even when it is appropriate.

- *Wishful Thinking.* Our desire to remove uncertainty may lead us to believe that by developing a plan, we will invariably control its outcome. As a result, we may ignore the need to develop contingency plans.

- *Pressure.* Time pressures or pressure from the group, superiors, or influential advisers to choose a particular course of action may cause us to take shortcuts or ignore relevant factors and appropriate alternatives. For example, the desire to stay ahead of the Soviet Union in space exploration may have clouded the judgment of NASA's engineers in the 1960s (and again in the 1980s). As a result of these political pressures, most of the agency's efforts focused on conquering the difficulties of space travel. As a consequence, it paid inadequate attention to issues of safety—a tragic misjudgment that cost the lives of astronauts Virgil Grissom, Edward White, and Roger Chaffee. The inquiry that followed the 1967 launchpad fire that killed these men found numerous deficiencies in design, engineering, manufacture, and quality control. Safety may also have been sacrificed to political concerns in the 1980s, when the *Challenger* space shuttle exploded, killing seven astronauts.

The influence of any of these factors, which often occur in conjunction, can prevent you from thoroughly exploring all the alternatives, facts, assumptions, and other information available to you. Ultimately, this can prevent you from reaching sound judgments regarding what course to take.

Paradoxically, you can suffer from similar shortsightedness in exercising hindsight. Rather than objectively evaluating and learning from your "good" and "bad" decisions, you may allow certain influences to cloud your judgment. You may summarily dismiss the opinions you rejected and rationalize your choices despite conflicting evidence. You may look only for evidence that supports your choice selectively (and therefore incompletely) recalling the circumstances that led up to the decision, and in this way justify your choice. Or you may excuse poor judgments by attributing adverse results to bad luck or someone else's shoddy performance.

The exercise and continual improvement of good judgment—both in making decisions and later evaluating them—demands the elimination of such biases. We need to open our minds to all reasonable alternatives and then leave behind the desire to avoid blame by justifying our decisions. Ultimately, we need to make the best possible judgments we can and then take responsibility for them: good and bad.

## THE DIRTY DOZEN

In addition to confusing the distinction between observations and inferences, or facts and assumptions, and allowing biases to rule our decision-making processes, errors in critical thinking can arise through many other sources. The following list of errors, some of which were covered earlier, briefly suggests some of the traps. Any of these can cloud your ability to analyze data, develop appropriate goals and intentions, identify the most effective course of action, or evaluate the outcome of your decision and actions. These failings, whether taken singly or in combination, can foil your attempts to exercise critical judgment. And this can lead you to make serious mistakes.

290 STRATEGIES TO REDUCE YOUR ERRORS

## The Dirty Dozen: Errors in Critical Thinking

1. Failure to examine the problem, define it, and locate crucial points.

2. Failure to formulate or recognize suitable hypotheses.

3. Failure to select or recall relevant data accurately:

    Failure to differentiate between reliable and less reliable sources of information.

    Failure to tell the difference between statements that give observations, draw conclusions, make definitions, or make no sense.

4. Failure to make or recognize careful experimental plans.

5. Inductive fallacies:

    Insufficient cases.

    Cases not typical.

    Contradicting cases ignored.

    *Post hoc, ergo propter hoc* (After this, therefore: the fallacy of arguing that a mere temporal sequence is, in fact, a cause-and-effect relationship).

    False analogies.

6. Deductive fallacies:

    Taking for granted—

        Exceptions ignored.

        Exceptions overvalued.

        Begging the question.

        Complex question.

    Off the point—

        Red herring.

        Name calling (*ad hominem*).

        Appeal to prejudice.

        Employment of threat.

        Appeal to reverence.

        Appeal to pity.

        Mercenary appeal.

Various negative types—
>   Objections (trivial).
>   Appeal to ignorance.
>   Non sequitur.

7. Failure to recognize assumptions.

8. Failure to come to a conclusion.

9. Failure to test conclusion.

10. Failure to apply conclusion to a new situation.

11. Interpretation:
>   Failure to define.
>   Quoting out of context.
>   Failure to penetrate emotive coloration.
>   Failure to note complexity of term.
>   False classification.
>   Failure to amplify abstract terms.
>   Failure to make terms of quantity specific.
>   Taking figures of speech literally.
>   Ambiguity.
>   Quibbling.
>   Jargon.
>   Mistranslation.
>   Failure to understand nonverbal communication.
>   Failure to understand tone.

12. Attitudinal errors:
>   Lack of curiosity.
>   Narrow-mindedness.
>   Intellectual dishonesty.
>   Gullibility.
>   Lack of objectivity.
>   Failure to demand explanations in terms of universal laws of cause and effect.

Lack of persistence.

Inflexibility.

Examine the list carefully. Do any of these strike a familiar chord? To which of these errors and fallacies do you most often fall prey? Circle the fallacies and errors in critical thinking that most often lead you to make mistakes. In making future judgments, recheck the items you have circled and review your decision-making process before acting on it. Have these same errors and fallacies tripped you up again?

## HOW TO IMPROVE YOUR CRITICAL JUDGMENT

Critical judgment tends to improve with time. Why? Because all your decisions and actions—the successful ones as well as the mistakes—have the power to augment the faculty of critical judgment, if you devote the time and effort to analyze them. No matter how much guidance you receive, you will invariably learn life lessons of your own that will allow you to exercise and improve your critical judgment. You can, however, learn from the wisdom gained through other people's triumphs and defeats as well as that acquired through your own successes and failures. The following dozen tips, though not necessarily products of your own experience, may therefore help you avoid some errors in critical judgment:

1. Know and understand your present state.
2. Prioritize your goals.
3. Conform your expectations to your reality.
4. Evaluate the situation. Are the values only black and white or shades of gray?
5. Consider the lifetime patterns, processes, and inclinations of those who might influence or be influenced by actions based on your judgment, including your own.
6. Understand how your actions affect all others.
7. Use fact-finding analysis to help distinguish between a fact and an inference.
8. Understand that your hidden assumptions lead to your known assumptions, and that these assumptions help make up the "facts" as you see them.

9. Recognize that you create the relationships between things through the inferences you make and the connections you draw. Relationships are not absolutes, but remain within your control.

10. Understand that you control your evaluations.

11. Remember that time changes everything.

12. Since you can never know everything, don't be upset by uncertainty.

You can surely apply some of these rules to your situation. However, you will inevitably learn additional lessons from your own mistakes. And you should incorporate these lessons of experience into your future critical judgments.

## WHAT'S A GOOD APPROACH TO A CRISIS SITUATION?

From time to time, each of us faces crises in our work and/or home lives. Such an emergency usually demands that a decision be reached, often under extreme time pressure, regarding the action that will most appropriately and effectively address the challenges. This calls for the application of critical thinking and good judgment under the most trying circumstances. In addition to the tips already provided, the following may prove useful in crisis situations:

- Stay in control. Panic will disrupt your ability to think critically and to exercise good judgment.
- Communicate fully and openly with anyone who might be affected by the crisis or have valuable input regarding its solution. In a business context, this means establishing good lines of communication with those above, below, and on the same level as you.
- Gather the best resources available and get the best possible advice from experts.
- Use these resources and experts in planning for the future.

Gathering experts and establishing good lines of communication with them, although especially important in crisis situations, is also valuable in less dramatic situations that nonetheless call for the exercise of good judgment. As Judy Rosener, coauthor of *Workforce America!* explained in *Quality Digest* (May 1991), "If we acknowledge that, as individuals, we selectively perceive based on our experiences and backgrounds, then the more variety of people trying to solve problems, the better our chances of coming up with a range of solutions."

Each of us has the ability to improve our critical judgment through our experiences. Yet since this is by definition limited, the application of the experiences and the concomitant critical judgment of others can only help eliminate our individual biases, expand our critical thinking ability, and improve our good judgment. Seeking and applying points of view from professionals such as attorneys, accountants, mathematicians, and engineers can assist you by providing the wisdom gained through their experience in their areas of expertise. And this informed awareness can eliminate some of the uncertainty inherent in any decision.

Although all of us can benefit from opening ourselves up to the perspectives of others when we face a critical decision, the ultimate responsibility for our own decisions nonetheless falls on us. Remember, as the Honda Motor Company recognized (see Chapter 16), the value of quality circles and the desirability of input from people in all divisions and departments does not absolve individuals from taking responsibility for their own decisions.

One final tip regarding crises: Whatever your current situation, don't be afraid to abandon conservatism and take a fresh approach. Base your decision not only on awareness of strategies that have worked—or didn't work—in similar situations in the past, but also on the recognition of the circumstances that distinguish your current problems. Find creative alternatives that offer a fresh approach.

## MISTAKES AND ERROR AWARENESS

You can apply the principles and techniques of error awareness to mistakes (errors in judgment) and the objective of improving critical judgment. Whenever you make a mistake, don't waste time and energy judging yourself too harshly. Instead, as soon after the mistake as possible, while the memory of the decision is still relatively fresh, reconstruct the situation in your mind. Or better yet, write down the relevant considerations that factored into your decision. You will probably find it helpful to have other involved parties complement your memories of the decision.

Begin your analysis of the mistake by asking yourself the following four questions:

1. Applying all your senses, what *could* you have seen, sensed, known, understood, or realized differently? If you can, identify the particular error in perception that caused you to "see" the situation as you did.

2. Applying all your thought processes, what *could* you have thought, evaluated, or comprehended differently? Did you pause for reflection at all? If so, ask yourself what specific considerations and values triggered the particular decision, action, speech, or writing that you now consider a mistake.

3. What consequences of your actions *could* you have expected, anticipated, or foreseen at the time you made the mistake? Did you anticipate them?

4. Applying your overall evaluative skills, how could you have known, thought, or anticipated more appropriately and adequately?

Complete and accurate answers to these questions will provide you with considerable insight into the mistake you made and will allow you to answer the following questions. They provide a real payoff—guidance on how to exercise good judgment and act in the future:

- Where and when did you go wrong (identify the kind of mistake you made)?

- What was the significance (cost, effect, extent of damage) of the mistake?

- Why did you go wrong?

- How can you best correct the mistake and its effects?

- How can you best avoid making such or similar mistakes in the future?

The answers to these questions, though not always simple, will restore value to the mistake. No decision, no matter how severe the consequences, is a 100 percent flop. Every bad decision has some good in it. Salvage the positive aspects of your judgment rather than discarding the entire decision. If you can use the preceding questions to isolate the flaw(s) in your critical thinking, you may not need to scrub the whole plan. You may be able to revise it, retaining the steps or phases unaffected by the lapse(s) in critical thinking and replacing those that you now judge as mistakes.

Since error awareness demands that you take responsibility for your mistakes and errors, you may suffer the consequences or losses that ensue from your errors of judgment. But your acceptance of responsibility will also allow you to derive some benefit from the mistake. Your new error awareness may help you avoid similar misjudgments in the future that might prove even costlier to you and those around you. You'll still make *some* mistakes; that's inevitable. But you won't make the *same* mistakes over and over again. And that's what error awareness is all about.

# HEIGHTENING YOUR ERROR AWARENESS

## THE ROLE OF ASSUMPTIONS AND INFERENCES

Do assumptions, inferences, and opinions have any place in the application of good judgment when making an important decision? Consider and discuss one or two decisions you have had to make in the past. Weigh the relevance and value of assumptions and opinions in your decision-making process.

## IT'S AS EASY AS . . .

Leaving behind hidden assumptions that limit your perception, how many creative solutions can you conjure to solve the problem of what 1 + 1 equals?

## YOUR BIASES

What biases prevent you from exercising your best judgment? Identify the ones that most often interfere with your judgment. Which most often prevent you from objectively reaching decisions? What strategies can you adopt to overcome their influence?

## FALLACIOUS ARGUMENTS

Look through your daily newspapers, in particular the editorial sections and the letters to the editor, trying to pinpoint fallacious arguments.

Read some advertisements in magazines and newspapers with a critical eye and/or listen to radio and television commercials with a critical ear. Do any of these advertisements include misleading statements or fallacious arguments? What are they?

(*continued*)

## Looking Toward the Future

What lessons regarding critical thinking and good judgment have you already learned from your mistakes? From your successes?

Consider an important decision you will be required to make in the near future. Reread the material in this section and apply the principles of error awareness and hints on how to improve your critical judgment to this decision.

## NOTE

1. Donald A. Norman, *Design of Everyday Things* (New York: Doubleday & Co., 1987).

# 19

---

# No Shame,
# No Blame,
# Revisited

LOVE TRUTH BUT PARDON ERROR.

—VOLTAIRE, *DISCOURS*

HE THAT IS WITHOUT SIN AMONG YOU, LET HIM CAST
THE FIRST STONE.

—JOHN 8:7

TO ERR IS HUMAN; TO FORGIVE DIVINE.

—ALEXANDER POPE, *ESSAY ON CRITICISM*

If, at the conclusion of this book, you come away having learned just two fundamental lessons, let them be the following:

1. All of us make errors.
2. Errors can be substantially or completely reduced.

I strongly believe that error awareness provides the most efficient and effective means of reducing errors. In and of itself, however, even error awareness can only go so far toward eliminating them. If society wants to minimize errors, the practices of many of our institutions must change, as well. To augment the advances of error awareness, we must alter our collective and cultural attitudes.

As an attorney, I know firsthand that the judicial system, to point a finger at one glaring example, generally serves only to place blame. This approach attempts to redress the *effects* of errors, but does little to correct error itself. The best treatment for slips, errors, mistakes, and blunders involves admitting them, analyzing them, doing what you can to correct them, and doing your best to avoid their recurrence. However, an approach designed strictly to place blame and exact punishment only encourages people to conceal the truth.

In our litigious society, malpractice awards add $21 billion to the nation's annual health costs (nearly $6 billion in insurance premiums and another $15 billion in redundant diagnostic tests taken as self-defensive measures). But what's worse, "Many doctors [admit] they avoid discussing mistakes with patients for fear of prompting a malpractice suit," according to the *New York Times* (May 9, 1991). Excessive malpractice awards offer a powerful disincentive to doctors who might otherwise be inclined to admit their mistakes to patients and colleagues. And without the admission of mistakes, error awareness is impossible.

Whether or not one is faced with a malpractice suit, few people are willing to acknowledge having failed or having been wrong. Yet as Dr. Ruedi Knusel of Swissair, describing the selection process for candidates of pilot training programs, explained to writer Stephen Barlay, "An urge to be right at all times leads to the loss of ability to see and assess reality." Our present system actually cultivates the reluctance to acknowledge mistakes. This common failing not only can blind people to past errors, but can lead to additional errors in the future.

Sadly then, in the present social climate, individuals can seldom learn from their errors. Fear of liability too often discourages acceptance of responsibility. The present atmosphere of blame and shame rewards people for *hiding* their mistakes rather than divulging them. But if, as a society, we discourage disclosure of mistakes, how will we ever learn from them?

If we truly want to learn, we need to become more sympathetic to *unintentional* errors. Unless we feel free to admit our mistakes without fear of reprisal, none of us will have the opportunity to learn from our mistakes, let alone from the errors of others. So let's begin with the simple recognition that all of us make errors. If you can keep this in mind, you will see the need for all of us to look on errors with more sympathy.

Errors offer us a tool to educate all of society, not merely the individuals who make them. So instead of punishing those who err, we should actually *commend* them (or at least the disclosure of errors).

As a society, we need to do everything we can to encourage each of us to admit our errors to ourselves. This is the first step toward transforming them into learning tools. Then, to allow others to learn from our mistakes, we must admit them publicly. This means leveling with everyone who has in any way been affected by them.

In a climate motivated by the lust for punishment rather than the desire for growth and learning, most of us would find it difficult to accomplish these relatively simple demands. But, if we want to grow, we must set aside any finger-pointing or thirst for revenge or retribution. Instead of arguing over who is responsible, we must devote our time and energy toward working together to reduce errors.

When you suffer from another's errors, respond with the understanding and forgiveness you would hope for if you had made a similar gaffe.

## ADOPTING A NO-SHAME/NO-BLAME POLICY

Pioneers in some segments of our society—certain individuals, companies, and institutions—have begun to recognize the benefits of a no-blame/no-shame policy regarding errors. A few examples should inspire all of us to push further toward error awareness.

In the practice of medicine, doctors have begun to recognize that the admission and discussion of errors helps interns and residents become less error prone. Researchers at the University of California Medical School at San Francisco have taken the lead in this area, with a study that suggests that doctors-in-training should be encouraged to discuss their mistakes with senior physicians, patients, and patients' families. According to the *New York Times* (May 9, 1991):

> The researchers . . . said such discussions *could help prevent errors, lessen their effects and help doctors learn from their mistakes.* . . .
>
> [T]he study's lead author, Dr. Albert Wu, . . . said, "Medical training needs to change to allow residents to *'fess up to their mistakes,* to *face their mistakes squarely and discuss them openly, and learn from them* [emphasis added]."

The same study found that only 54 percent of the young doctors surveyed actually *did* discuss mistakes with senior physicians, and even less (only 24 percent) discussed them with their patients.

On the other hand, the best malpractice attorneys advise doctors to be frank with their patients regarding errors. The *New York Times* (May 9, 1991) quoted medical malpractice attorney Dan J. Tennenhouse as saying,

"I tell doctors, your best bet is to speak frankly and openly with patients. I also encourage them to disclose when it was clearly negligence and to hope for forgiveness and do it with suitable humility."

In the telecommunications industry, some executives are recognizing that most errors are unintentional, and not worthy of blame. Following a typographical error that resulted in telephone network outages in four cities in the summer of 1991 (see Chapter 6), the DSC Communications Corporation, manufacturers of the defective software, refused to reveal the name of the programmer who made the error. In explaining his decision to withhold the name, James L. Donald, DSC chairman, described the programmer as follows. "He's conscientious, he works hard, he wants everything to be right."

In the airline industry, Boeing—with the support of the National Transportation Safety Board and the Air Line Pilots Association—has analyzed 850 plane crashes in an attempt to increase error awareness (see Chapter 8). As a result, plane manufacturers and airlines have already redesigned certain cockpit systems and introduced some changes in protocol to provide greater protection from common errors, catching them or preventing them before they lead to future disasters.

Swissair, one of the leading innovators in airline safety, is looking for a new brand of leadership in their cockpits. "We want people who can make decisions," Swissair's Ruedi Knusel explained to Stephen Barlay, "and even bend the rules if need be, but they must be secure enough to face up to errors and listen to critical advice."

Error awareness has even found its way into the politics of the defense industry. In the wake of a single failed radar trial (following 10 previously successful ones) that threatened to result in a cutoff of funding for the entire B-2 bomber program, Air Force Secretary Donald B. Rice defended the program and called for patience. "Frankly, I'd expect events of this sort [errors that resulted in operation failure] would occur several more times again before we complete the development and testing of a complex system like the B-2," Rice told the *New York Times* (September 22, 1991).

Although you may or may not support funding of the B-2 bomber, you cannot help but support the understanding that we should expect errors and other failures in any enterprise—especially in developmental stages. That's the value of errors: to help us develop error awareness and more error-free methods, systems, and machinery.

These examples demonstrate that as error awareness is practiced, errors decrease. Although we can never achieve perfection, that shouldn't stop us from aiming for this ideal. The process of improvement, ever-active and ever-growing, stretches into infinity. Since we cannot attain perfection, we will never cross the finish line in our attempts to achieve error awareness. Yet though we may never cross the finish line, we can still win the race.

As Neil Postman has so wisely written in *The End of Education:*

> . . . It is in our nature to make mistakes. We can scarcely let an hour go by without making one. . . . That we may be mistaken, and probably are, is the meaning of "fall" in the fallen angel. The meaning of "angel" is that we are capable of correcting our mistakes, provided we proceed without hubris, pride, or dogmatism; provided we accept our status as the error-prone species. . . . Though we may learn by doing, we learn far more by failing—by trial and error, by making mistakes, correcting them, making more mistakes, correcting them. . . . Everyone makes errors, including those who write about them.

And to that, I add my humble Amen.

GERARD I. NIERENBERG
e-mail: 73020.3544
negotiation.com

# INDEX